The Unity of Nature and History in Pannenberg's Theology

THE UNITY OF NATURE AND HISTORY IN PANNENBERG'S THEOLOGY

by
Cornelius A. Buller

LITTLEFIELD ADAMS BOOKS

LITTLEFIELD ADAMS BOOKS

Published in the United States of America
by Rowman & Littlefield Publishers, Inc.
4720 Boston Way, Lanham, Maryland 20706

3 Henrietta Street
London WC2E 8LU, England

British Cataloging in Publication Information Available

Library of Congress Cataloging-in-Publication Data

Buller, Cornelius A.
The unity of nature and history in Pannenberg's theology /
Cornelius A. Buller.
p.   cm.
Includes bibliographcal references and index.
1. Nature—Religious aspects—Christianity—History of doctrines
—20th century. 2. Pannenberg, Wolfhart, 1928- —Contributions
in doctrine of nature. 3. History (Theology)—History of doctrines
—20th century. 4. Pannenberg, Wolfhart, 1928- —Contributions
in doctrine of theology of history. I. Title.
BT695.5.B85   1996   231.7'092—dc20   95–42633

ISBN 0–8226–3054–0 (cloth : alk. paper)
ISBN 0–8226–3055–9 (pbk. : alk. paper)

Printed in the United States of America

♾™ The paper used in this publication meets the minimum requirements of
American National Standard for Information Sciences—Permanence of
Paper for Printed Library Materials, ANSI Z39.48–1984.

To Vernelle, Stefan, Lisa, and Jodine

CONTENTS

PREFACE

This treatise is not so much an introduction to Wolfhart Pannenberg's thought as it is a companion for readers of his theological and philosophical works. My aim is to facilitate the reader's understanding of some of the central concerns and notions that guide Pannenberg's writings. While philosophical and ethical questions are broached in this book, and are entailed in the central issue, it is primarily intended to be an explication of Pannenberg's theology.

One of the modern uses of the word *nature* is to refer to a realm of reality that is paradoxically regarded with romantic yearning on one hand and scientifically guided greed on the other. To many people in the West nature is a mysterious other—sometimes useful for recreation and other times useful as a resource for business. Nature is at times regarded as little more than the occasion for human history. It is primarily in opposition to the dualism that opposes human and nonhuman realms that I intend to speak of a unity of reality as Pannenberg describes it. As will become plain, the concept of the unity of reality is developed by Pannenberg in his systematic exposition of the ideas of God as Creator and Redeemer, as well as in his theological anthropology. I believe that Pannenberg's analysis of the contemporary situation provides critical insight regarding the origins of the ecological problematique. His conceptions of God and reality provide a vision for rethinking the character of our relationship to the nonhuman world in the context of the relationship of all of reality to God.

This book is based largely on my dissertation (McMaster University, 1994) and represents several years of research, reflection and writing. It also represents the love and continued patient support of family and friends. I especially wish to name Vernelle, Stefan, Lisa, and Jodine, to whom I dedicate the book. You have taken up your roots and moved with me to Hamilton, to Germany, back to Hamilton, and finally back to Winnipeg. You have shared with me in the joys and the frustrations of this project. Thank you.

I also wish to acknowledge Professors Clark H. Pinnock and John C. Robertson and Professor Emeritus Gérard Vallée. And I especially want to express my appreciation for my friend and former adviser, Professor P. Travis Kroeker, who has been a source of wisdom, direction, and encouragement. Public acknowledgment also should be made for the financial support received from the Social Sciences and Humanities Research Council of Canada, Graduate Studies of McMaster University, and the University of Tübingen, as well as, several members of my extended family. Taken together the support of these persons and institutions made it possible for me to spend the necessary time researching and writing this book. Without the support and direction received from all of these named and unnamed persons and institutions, this work would not yet be completed. If there is in it something to be praised, these have a share. However, since the work is my own, I alone will claim its imperfections and limitations.

ACKNOWLEDGMENTS

Acknowledgment is made to the following:

Westminster Press, Philadelphia, for quotations from *Anthropology in Theological Perspective* by Wolfhart Pannenberg, trans. Matthew J. O'Connell, 1985.

Vandenhoeck & Ruprecht, Göttingen, for quotations from *Systematische Theologie, Band 2*, by Wolfhart Pannenberg, 1991.

Wm. B. Eerdmans Publishing Co., Grand Rapids, for quotations from *An Introduction to Systematic Theology* by Wolfhart Pannenberg, 1991.

Wm. B. Eerdmans Publishing Co., Grand Rapids, for quotations from *Systematic Theology, Vol. 2*, by Wolfhart Pannenberg, trans. Geoffrey W. Bromiley, 1994.

All scripture quotations, unless otherwise indicated, are taken from the *Revised Standard Version*.

INTRODUCTION

NATURE AND HISTORY

Whether one agrees or disagrees with his thought, Wolfhart Pannenberg (b. 1928) is a contemporary thinker who is most worthy of careful study. He is one of the most significant twentieth-century theologians and has engaged in dialogue with a host of philosophers and theologians, both ancient and contemporary. He has made noteworthy contributions to the ecumenical dialogue and also has addressed the interreligious dialogue. He is a careful interpreter of other thinkers, showing clearly where he agrees and disagrees with the most significant figures in the history of Western thought. It is in the context of an impressively wide-ranging and always in-depth analysis of this tradition that Pannenberg develops a most coherent presentation of a Christian conception of reality. But it is not a closed system that Pannenberg presents his readers. By means of historical and critical analysis of philosophical and religious problems Pannenberg draws us into a living tradition of thought. He invites us into a dialogue with a vast range of figures, from Parmenides to Habermas. And to be introduced to this tradition from Pannenberg's point of view is a great benefit. He is a fair and intelligent interpreter and a diligent seeker of truth. But he is more than this. The scope and brilliance of Pannenberg's work are almost without contemporary parallel. Nonetheless, he invites us to think, not simply to accept his position. His major works are must reading for any serious student of contemporary Christianity.

However, Pannenberg's works do not make for easy reading. His thought resists facile summarization and categorization. What makes his thinking so challenging is the synthetic and creative character of his interactions with other thinkers. For example, in a characteristic passage, in which he deals with Heidegger's notions of being and time, he refers critically yet appreciatively to thinkers including Plato, Aristotle, the Stoics and Sophists, Plotinus, Saint Augustine, Immanuel Kant, Friedrich Nietzsche, Wilhelm Dilthey and Alfred N. Whitehead. Within this broad historical discussion Pannenberg clarifies the issues, criticizes Heidegger, and presents his own position.[1] The result is a complex and nuanced position that resists simple classification as Heideggerian, Whiteheadian, Augustinian, or Platonic. But his position shares elements with each of these and others also.

When I visited Wolfhart Pannenberg at his University of Munich office in 1992 I was struck by the appropriateness of two portraits—of Ernst Troeltsch and Karl Barth—hanging on the wall outside his office. Pannenberg, like Troeltsch, Barth, and other great thinkers, has sought to engage the significant issues with a breadth and depth that is arresting. Pannenberg's conception of the unity of nature and history, which is the subject of this book, in part can be thought of as taking up in a new synthesis the opposition of Troeltsch and Barth. Troeltsch is one of the great representatives of the liberal tradition that Barth so vehemently criticized while developing his theology of revelation. Pannenberg's understanding of the unity of nature and history depends upon the unity of the revelation of God both in Jesus Christ and history (a category which for Pannenberg includes nature). Pannenberg sees no radical disjunction between natural and revealed knowledge of God, between reason and faith. On the basis of his understanding of God as Creator he defines the historical process of reality as the history of the revelation of God. Like Troeltsch and other liberal theologians, Pannenberg seeks to do theology in dialogue with philosophy and all the human sciences.[2] That having been said, we must also note that

Pannenberg has a high regard for Barth's emphasis on the self-revelation of God and its unity in Jesus of Nazareth. Pannenberg refuses to accept the liberal skepticism about historical knowledge of Jesus and the historicity of the resurrection. The uniqueness and unsurpassability of the self-revelation of God in Jesus Christ and its contemporary relevance to all aspects of our thinking and living are at the heart of Pannenberg's thought.

Precisely this challenging aspect of Pannenberg's thought can be the source of great stimulation and joy for the reader. Pannenberg's historically conscious means of addressing a problem makes it possible for us to think with him. Thus, we are not only free to challenge his interpretations and conclusions along the way but also are invited to do so. And as we are drawn into Pannenberg's train of thinking we are thus also invited to participate in the ever widening horizons of Western thought. We need not agree with his conclusions, but we dare not make judgments without thinking at least as carefully as he has. And thinking involves critical and appreciative—that is, open—study of the whole tradition that has its roots in Athens and Jerusalem and beyond. When it is true to itself, this tradition is aware of its limits and is open to learning from others. In this tradition, good thinking is rooted in the critical and humble rationality ideally embodied by Plato's Socrates and in the unpretentious curiosity of the child who trustingly and wholeheartedly seeks the Kingdom of God. Fundamental to this tradition of thought is the unity of truth and morality. The challenge of Pannenberg's thought includes moral implications. The truth of the Christian concept of reality challenges us both intellectually and morally. This type of thinking is characteristic of Pannenberg's contribution to theology.

Such thinking does not represent a prejudice for some form of idealism. It is, rather, a methodological recognition of the limits of human knowledge on the one hand and on the other hand, a fundamental trust in reality. It is a recognition that our knowledge of the world has developed in a historical process. It is a recognition of the historicality of our hold on truth without letting go of either that hold itself or of the expectation of greater knowledge yet to come.

Pannenberg's idea that revelation and history are one, that the history of reality is the process of the revelation (realization) of the image of God in creation, is a conception of universal history that draws significantly on Hegel. The idea of the unity of nature and history is implicit in this concept of universal history. Pannenberg's method of developing his thought in dialogue with the whole of the intellectual tradition is intimately connected with this notion of history and revelation. His views of reality and of Western thought, therefore, not only invite us to consider this historical tradition but challenge us to think historically and dialectically in the context of this tradition. Here and elsewhere, Pannenberg's process of thought, his methodology, and his central ideas reflect the positive contributions of Hegel.

However, Pannenberg makes important criticisms of Hegel, and these critical moves clearly distinguish his thought from Hegel's. For example—and this is discussed in more detail in subsequent chapters—Pannenberg does not understand history as primarily a matter of mind. Drawing on the Old Testament, he defines the idea of *spirit* more broadly than does Hegel, to include physical life. Again drawing significantly on the Bible, but also on process thought, Pannenberg develops an understanding of history that is more contingent and open than Hegel's concept of reality.

The central aim of Pannenberg's work is to correct certain inadequacies inherent in modern Western culture. One very significant problem is the dualism expressed in human use and abuse of the nonhuman world. Our culture has produced much artwork that celebrates nature's powers to draw us out of our selves and to bring us into an encounter with *One* who is not identifiable with anything finite. Nevertheless, in the modern age we have not been accustomed to hearing such voices, not, at any rate, when we have been going about our business. In moments of romantic bliss and leisurely rest we have heard rumors and whispers, but we have connected these with the prescientific past. We have relegated these experiences and thoughts to weekends, holidays, and vacations—to our young and to our old. The business of the civilized West has cut us off from metaphysics, goodness, and love. In so doing, it has cut us off from seeing the wholeness of life, from meaning and joy, and most ironical, from the true depth of the life of reason.

My aim is to explore how Pannenberg attempts to show the fundamental unity of all reality. As we shall see, Pannenberg believes that consideration of God as the Creator and Redeemer with the support of a theological anthropology leads to a perception of the wholeness of life. This is significant for conceiving the moral character of existence. In the modern world both theologians and ethicists face the task of overcoming the separation of metaphysics from the realms of science, technology, and industry. An examination of Pannenberg's theological foundation for ethics is especially relevant in light of the contemporary ecological problematique, because he systematically has attempted to think of nature (the physical world) and history (especially the activities of human culture) as a unity. The focus will of necessity remain on theology and the theological foundation for ethics rather than ethics itself because Pannenberg has decided to devote his career to addressing fundamental theological issues. Pannenberg acknowledges the need for a Christian contribution to a theory of justice, which he thinks must precede the development of specific moral codes. He has, however, determined that more fundamental theological issues (e.g., the truth of the Christian faith in God) must be dealt with first.[3]

Nonetheless, this does not imply that Pannenberg's thought is irrelevant to daily living. It is worth emphasizing that thoughtfulness regarding the nature of reality is fundamentally practical. The radical distinction between pure and practical reason is here disputed. The theological and philosophical pursuit of God finds both its motivation and goal in the twofold character of love:

"Love God and love your neighbor."[4] And the love of neighbor includes all creatures. In other words, the claims of fundamental theology regarding God and the world have both explicit and implicit moral content.

Pannenberg's writings address topics that range from the philosophy of science to ecclesiology, and evidence and arguments for his conception of the unity of reality in God can be found anywhere and everywhere in his work. I have chosen to focus on what I consider to be the most significant concepts for Pannenberg's theology. The Trinitarian conception of God as Creator, Redeemer, and Spirit is central to Pannenberg's conception of the unity of nature and history and shapes the character of this concept. This treatise has one chapter on creation, one on Christology, and one on theological anthropology. I do not include a separate chapter on the Spirit, but I do argue that this aspect of Pannenberg's understanding of God is integral to understanding creation, redemption, and anthropology. In each chapter I examine the character of nature, of history, and of their union, as well as the justification of this union.

I hope that this treatise offers a new approach to understanding one of the major German theologians of this century. Pannenberg's philosophy of history and his theology (explicitly on his Christology) have received treatment, but little work has been done on his attempt to ground ethics in theology or on his attempt to think of nature and history in a unity, and no major work has been done on his philosophy of nature. Pannenberg himself suggests that his thought provides a positive contribution to the grounding of environmental ethics.[5] But he has not yet given an explication of that contribution.

As Pannenberg insists, theological and moral claims must be sufficiently true to hold the loyalty of reflective and rational beings. Our thinking must correspond to all we know of reality and must be internally coherent. The intention of this book is to demonstrate that Pannenberg's attempt to rethink the Christian faith in dialogue with modern secular conceptions of reality is in essence an argument for the essential unity of all experience, and that this unity is rooted in the rediscovery of the significance of the divine. This amounts to grounding ethics in the universally religious character of creaturely existence. Pannenberg explicitly notes the variance of his thought from that of the Kantian tradition, which rooted religion in the moral character of existence.[6]

The Problem: Religious and Secular Dualism

Modern Dualism

Our culture is in many ways fundamentally at odds with the realm of nature in which it exists.[7] Unfortunately, it is the destructive consequences of our technoscientific culture that have forced wide-scale recognition of the problematic character of this relationship of human culture to the nonhuman world. According to Pannenberg, the problematic character of the modern relationship of humans to nature is closely connected with the anthropocentrism of the modern turn to the subject.[8]

Francis Bacon, one of the founders of modern scientific methodology, drew a particularly poignant analogy in describing the modern scientist's relationship to the nonhuman world: "We will press nature to the rack until she divulges her secrets." The statement suggests that the practice of science sets in radical opposition the aims of human activity and the good of the nonhuman universe. Bacon considers knowledge to be equivalent to power over nature.[9] Knowledge is the power to shape nature for human use. This anthropomorphic dualism also is expressed by Descartes, who thought of the world as consisting of two opposing realities: *nature*, which he characterized as mindless extension, and *spirit*, which he characterized as unextended mind. According to Pannenberg, this dualism has served to inform both the distinction of human from nonhuman existence and the methodologies of modern sciences.[10]

This opposition of spirit/history and matter/nature reaches back in various forms through history to Mani, certain forms of

Christian asceticism and the gnostics, and is found in non-Western cultures as well. Certain forms of Buddhism, Advaita Hinduism, and Confucianism each could offer examples of a negative regard for physical reality. Nonetheless, certain dominant forms of Western thought from the Enlightenment forward have added a distinctive twist to this dualism. The idea of spirit has been humanized and at times even has been rejected. Western culture in the modern period has had a distinctively materialistic view of reality. Marx's inversion of Hegel's dialectic of the spirit into dialectical and atheist materialism can be regarded as one of the more sophisticated theoretical elaborations of the new materialism.[11] Industrial capitalist versions of modern material culture certainly have shown themselves to be highly complex and vigorous forms of philosophical materialism. In both instances nature is regarded as an other to be exploited for human purposes. In capitalist economies nature is the raw material that the capitalist exploits. In Marxist economies nature is exploited in the interest of the working class.

Jürgen Moltmann points out that Franz von Baader (1765-1841) already warned that "the non-spiritual view of nature which Descartes especially brought into vogue was bound to result in the non-natural view of the mind and spirit, and the godless view of both."[12] That is, on the one hand, the idea of God no longer plays a role either in knowledge of humans or in knowledge of the world and, on the other hand, humans are radically separated from nature. These are two aspects of one view of reality.

In this view the world is construed as a mathematical-mechanical reality.[13] It has no inherent inner rationality but is very much open to rational manipulation. It has no purpose or meaning on its own but receives these through the uses to which humans subject it. Humans, on the other hand, are viewed as fundamentally rational beings for whom nature is but the stage upon which the drama of human history is played. God is not a significant factor in the understanding of either humans or nonhuman nature. Spirit comes to be identified with the rational mind. The apologetic efforts of modern theology to fit its notions of nature, humans, and God to the dominant secular and scientific conceptions of reality have not been able to win a strong public voice in secular society.[14]

Post-Enlightenment Western thought has sought a natural and rational—as opposed to religious and authoritative—ground for morality. Religion and metaphysics came to be regarded as private matters that were neither cognitive nor verifiable. Unfortunately the rational ground of morality and authoritative moral norms soon fell to the criticisms of historical relativity. The upshot, according to Pannenberg, is that morality, like religion, is relegated to the realm of personal conviction.[15] Neither religion nor morality is seen in its depth and fullness. This phenomenon is part of the opposition of modern thought to religion and metaphysics. Value and meaning no longer adhere to facts and events.

Modern culture views nature—and increasingly humans—through the lens of the empirical, technological, and industrial achievements of the mind. Human activity is directed at the methodological manipulation of the physical universe. The progress of empirical human culture (or history) is opposed to the untamed wild (or nature). Nature is the chaos over which human reason progressively asserts itself. The story of this progress is seen as the content of history. The cumulative impact of this "history" is the extension of knowledge and power over the nature that once was known as Leviathan but more and more is finding its way into our museums. However, we are beginning to see that as we destroy the wild we also are destroying ourselves. We have begun to discover that we are on the rack with nature.[16]

Pannenberg's goals as a theologian include overcoming the philosophical separation of spirit and nature. The argument here presented is that Pannenberg explicitly attempts to address this issue and that this effort has ramifications for how nature is viewed and used.

The Scientific Presupposition of Atheism

The principle of inertia, which can be defined as "a force of preservation within" all bodies (Newton), served as the cornerstone of the mechanistic explanation of the universe. Once this principle was combined with the notion that all "bodies always are in some form of movement which they transfer to each other by pressure and push" (Descartes) there was no longer a need to resort to a divine first cause. A mechanical explanation of the universe had been achieved.[17]

With the development of a fully mechanistic view of the cosmos, physics had cut itself off from the idea of a Creator. The universe was conceived as a closed system of matter and process.[18] According to Pannenberg, this methodologically atheistic physics served as the presupposition of an atheistic anthropology. He points out that Ludwig Feuerbach took the decisive step of developing an anthropology that had no need of God to account for the religious aspects of human experience.

Feuerbach accounted for the religious aspect of human nature on the basis of the young Hegel's view that humans are eternal beings. He argued that the idea of God and religion are the products of self-alienation, which is the result of the self becoming the object of its own consciousness. In this estranged act of self-objectification the finite individual becomes conscious of his or her infinite essence. This infinite essence is, however, mistakenly understood by traditional theology as something other than the infinite self-consciousness of the human species, when it is understood as God. In other words, the religious self-consciousness mistakenly regards its own infinite essence as an Other, as God. The methodological atheism of physics serves as a necessary presupposition for Feuerbach's philosophical atheism.[19] The atheistic account of the spirit is interconnected with the atheistic account of nature. In this way Pannenberg traces the origins of modern anthropological atheism to its roots in the development of an account of the physical universe that had no need for recourse to a divine Creator. The conclusion of Pannenberg's historical account of atheism coheres with the argument of Moltmann and von Baader that atheism and the dualism of mind and nature belong together. These theologians argue that because nature and history are correlative realities, when nature became detached from spiritual meaning, history followed suit.

Pannenberg does not, however, try to defend theology from the criticism of modern atheist thought. He acknowledges that various secular points of view have made aspects of the traditional doctrine of God obsolete (especially the combination of the ideas of omnipotence, omniscience, and impassibility). Secular modern culture considers as irrelevant both Christianity and its claims regarding God. Pannenberg confronts Christians and theologians with arguments taken from science and atheism to show that some of their orthodoxies are not valid and are rightly considered impossible or antiquated in the context of modern knowledge of reality.

While Pannenberg is critical of traditional orthodoxy, he is also critical of both the social and the natural sciences. He argues that these sciences provide inadequate views of reality because they have ignored the most fundamental reality. They have ignored the createdness of reality and the God who is Creator. Pannenberg does not expect scientists and philosophers to consider again the claims of Christianity without first becoming convinced of their rationality. This double-edged criticism—of both modern culture and theology—becomes the ground for Pannenberg's positive efforts to reconstruct Christian talk of God in the light of modern science. Pannenberg's self-chosen task as a theologian, in the light of his understanding of modern culture, is to provide reasonable grounds for scientists, philosophers, and anthropologists, among others, to take God into their considerations. In this way he aims to make a contribution not only to theology but to other sciences, as well.[20]

The practice of science has focused on natural and repeatable phenomena. The study of history, which is really the study of events that cannot be directly observed and that are in their details unrepeatable, could be (and at times has been) excluded from science by a narrow or positivist definition of science. Thus, the idea of truth at times has been reduced to truths that can be directly observed and repeated. Yet even this narrowly defined science is at times deprived of any hold on truth, for the observer has come to be regarded as a completely conventional and relative being.[21] Thus, the modern experience and knowledge of reality, as mediated by the natural sciences, has been cut off from history, beauty, goodness, hope, and spirit—everything, in short, that is not cognitively present in some verifiable and repeatable form. And even this hold on physical reality at times has been threatened by more extreme forms of skepticism. Truth, in other words, is not often regarded as a serious category outside of the so-called pure sciences.

In the little volume *Christianity in a Secularized World* Pannenberg gives an account of his understanding of modern Western culture and the task of Christian theology in such a world. Pannenberg argues that while modern culture has made significant progress beyond the medieval Christian world from which it arose, it nonetheless has a limited conception of reality. The modern West has lost not only metaphysics but also its own past and future. The Christian church and its theologians are called upon to address this problematique:

> The opportunity of Christianity and its theology is to integrate the reduced understanding of reality on the part of secular culture and its picture of human nature into a greater whole, to offer the reduced rationality of secular culture a greater breadth of reason, which would also include the horizon of the bond between humankind and God.[22]

It is fair to suggest that the booklet describes one major task that Pannenberg has taken up in his theological enterprise. Pannenberg goes so far as to argue that any natural scientific, philosophical, or human scientific approach to understanding the reality of the world, when done apart from acknowledgment of God as Creator, can only realize approximations of knowledge of the real world. Thus, theology has the task of dialoguing with the sciences regarding the nature of the world. Theology must bring the knowledge of God as Creator to the contemporary scientific discussion of the nature of reality.[23]

The Solution: Reconceiving God and World

The Unifying Unity of Reality

Pannenberg's theology is founded on the assertion that God is the all-determining reality, and the implication of this is that theology must be able to show that all reality is illuminated and best understood when it is seen from this point of view: "the idea of God, if it corresponds to an actual reality, must be able to illumine not only human existence but also experience of the world as a whole, *providing the unity of all reality*."[24] It is fundamental to Pannenberg's task to make us aware of both the unity of reality and the God who is the source of this unity. If theology cannot provide a sound argument regarding the unity of reality then its claims regarding God become questionable. If there is no unity, there is no God, certainly no God in terms of an all-determining reality, no God as understood in the notions of creation and redemption, no God as understood through the interplay of Greek and Hebrew thought, which has guided Western theology and philosophy.

This unifying God whom Pannenberg seeks should not, however, be understood as a being at our disposal. And as God is not directly available to us, so also the unity of all reality—universal history—is not directly available. It must nonetheless show itself, however indirectly, in our experience and knowledge of reality. Pannenberg's account of his own conversion to Christianity is relevant here. He states that on a walk home "an extraordinary event occurred in which I found myself absorbed into the light of the setting sun and for one eternal moment dissolved in the light surrounding me."[25] Since then he has spent many years discovering the significance of what happened to him. He believes that such experiences require rational reflection in the context of what we know about reality—scientifically and historically, as well as philosophically and theologically. Pannenberg connects all experiences and intuitions of unity and wholeness as rooted in God. He also maintains that the idea of wholeness is fundamental to the perception of individual things.

In his contribution to the booklet *Erwägungen zu einer Theologie der Natur* Pannenberg points out that whoever speaks of the world as the creation of God is concerned with the same reality that is the object of the research of the physical sciences: "Exactly that nature which is researched by natural science would have to be claimed by theology as the creation of God."[26] Pannenberg observes that too often theology has regarded the notion of creation as relevant only for the consideration of the beginning of history or for the subjectivity of religious feeling, as in "God has created me." Creation, as Pannenberg uses the word, refers to the whole process of reality, from its beginnings to its ultimate end. His view is that if theology cannot reasonably think of nature in relationship to God then its talk of creation and Creator is mere lip service.[27] Taking God seriously in the modern context necessitates that God be shown to be the source and end not only of humans but also of all of nature. The fact that human history itself emerges naturally means either that both nature and history are related to God or that neither of them are related to God.[28]

Pannenberg's aim in his systematic theology is to present an

> integrated interpretation of God and humanity and the world which we may with good reason regard as true in relation to the knowledge that comes from experience of the world and human life, and also to the knowledge of philosophical reflection, so that we can assert it to be true vis-à-vis alternative religious and non-religious interpretations.[29]

The theologian must be able to make a rationally convincing claim to the truth of Christian doctrine regarding God, world, and human existence.

Recent philosophical thought, according to Pannenberg, has recognized that the positivists' definitions of scientific statements cannot be met by even the best efforts of modern science. Subjective and conventional elements creep into the simplest of claims. Pannenberg's contribution to this discussion attempts to show that any attempt to judge metaphysics as unscientific fails to understand the nature of science. Ultimately, argues Pannenberg, the pursuit of a true understanding of reality cannot justifiably be delimited to the methodologies of the pure sciences.[30] The positivist philosophy of science has failed to show the truth of its claim that metaphysics must be radically distinguished from the pursuit of true knowledge of reality. The pure sciences do not escape the conventionality and subjectivity of other branches of knowledge.

Rather than regarding the failure of positivism as the occasion for greater skepticism, Pannenberg argues for a broader philosophy of science. He argues that truth, albeit in approximations, is available to the theologian, as well as to the physicist, and that scientific theory also has metaphysical aspects. Pannenberg argues that "whatever is true must finally be consistent with all other truth, so that truth is only one, but all-embracing, closely related to the concept of the one God."[31]

Pannenberg argues that during the past one hundred years physics has developed new notions such as (1) events rather than solid bodies constitute the basic principles of the universe, (2) these events are contingent and irreversible, and (3) these events occur within a universal field. This produces an understanding of reality that calls into question the classic modern understanding of inertia. It is no longer possible to regard solid bodies as self-persistent.[32] Pannenberg argues that it has become possible to show that physical reality as it is understood by the natural sciences allows for connection with a Creator. According to Pannenberg, this removes the mechanistic and atheistic premise on which modern philosophical atheism was founded.

As to the Hegelian assumption regarding the eternity of the human spirit upon which Feuerbach relied, it too is no longer self-evident. The mind and soul or spirit tend more often to be reduced by modern science to an epiphenomenon of the body. The religious aspects of human experience no longer can be regarded as misinterpretations of fundamental anthropological experience (an eternal spirit). In other words, it is scientifically no longer possible to base atheism on the notion that humans are in essence eternal spirits. The foundations of philosophical atheism in the tradition of Feuerbach have been destroyed by science. Pannenberg is forced to address the notion of the reduction of spirit to an epiphenomenon of the body. He does so by arguing that the character of human existence and all reality is more fully accounted for when it is regarded as fundamentally religious. This argument is historical, philosophical, anthropological, and theological. Pannenberg also attempts to connect these types of arguments with current scientific conceptions of reality. His systematic attempt to draw all of these branches of knowledge together in the context of his theology is a reflection of the seriousness of his claim that God is the Creator of all reality and that this creation is unified in its determination toward the revelation of the image of God. These notions are developed in the chapters on creation and redemption.

Pannenberg has been able to argue for a transition from empirical to philosophical questioning. This itself is a critique of those philosophies of science that attempt to ghettoize the non-empirical sciences.[33] More than this, Pannenberg's claim coheres with the unity of personal experience of reality. There is no disjuncture between one's empirical questioning regarding the origins of life on earth and one's philosophical or religious reflection regarding the origins of existence. These are certainly different activities.

> The step from the assertions of the generalising sciences to those of philosophy cannot be made by a linear extension of nomological description, but requires a consideration of the language of the generalising sciences and its implications. This follows from the abstract nature of this language.[34]

Nonetheless, they remain linked within the quest for understanding of the unified existence of an individual. There is no need in personal existence to separate completely prayer from scientific research.[35] Science and philosophy are linked in the anticipatory structure of open-ended questioning that they share and can serve to correct each other. This open-ended questioning reflects the characteristic openness of human existence. The unified goal of this questioning is truth, and according to Pannenberg truth is one. Thus, truth further holds together the various forms of questioning and hypothesizing. Truth is the anticipatorily known goal toward which the open-endedness of human existence is directed.

This further implies that the realm of human culture and its history is closely linked to the natural world within which it exists. Questions of truth regarding the nature of the physical world are linked to the philosophical and religious questions as to the meaning of these realities. The questions of truth and meaning draw everything into themselves. No answer to these questions can ignore any aspect of reality. The natural world too has a history, as do both the empirical and religiophilosophical questioning of humans.[36] These histories converge on the anticipated truth and meaning of all aspects of existence. Pannenberg understands this as the goal of existence and argues that it is best understood through the relationship of God to the world.

Personal experiences are not a sufficient basis for claiming the truth of the loving God to whom they point. Pannenberg has recognized the need to bring the claims of the Christian faith into the arena of competing claims regarding the nature of reality.[37] Only in facing the test of coherence with our knowledge of reality can the claim to the truth of God and creation be made with any legitimacy. "[R]ightly understood, the revelation of God as the revelation of *God* is only borne in mind when all other truth and knowledge is organized around it and appropriated by it."[38]

Pannenberg's work has sought to bring a Christian conception of reality into dialogue with secular conceptions of reality, but his efforts are not in the service of proving the truth of certain unquestioned dogmas. Pannenberg's starting point is a concern for truth rather than an attempt to bring contemporary thought and culture into conformity with a particular orthodoxy. The idea of God as it has been transmitted in the history of the Western tradition is treated as a hypothesis that needs testing and clarifying in the light of all that we now know about reality.[39] Pannenberg is interested in arriving at a comprehensive and coherent account of reality, and he is convinced that this is best achieved in the context of a belief in the God of Israel as understood through the Christian tradition.

Pannenberg argues that God is the source of our conceiving of the wholeness, and therefore the meaning, of reality. The meaning of each event and thing is found only in terms of its relationships to all other things and events, and this is completely available only in the perspective of the whole of reality. Each thing is what it is in terms of its relationships, and meaning thus is neither external to the self nor inherent to the self. Each event and thing has its own relationship to the whole of reality, and this whole is grounded by God. Meaning is not that which arises out of the human use of things. This point will be treated further in the first chapter. For the present it is important to note that, according to Pannenberg, the rejection of religion and metaphysics is at the root of both the problems associated with the opposition of human activity to the nonhuman world and the isolation of morality from public life. This isolation compounds the problematic character of the relationship of humans to the natural world.

Theology and Anthropology

One of the significant results of the anthropologization of the arguments regarding the existence of God is the removal of both the natural world and the Kingdom of God from the center of theological concern. Pannenberg recognizes this and attempts to recover the significance of the Kingdom of God as a central theme of theology.[40] He begins with the anthropologized situations of philosophy and theology, but his arguments lead to a fundamental modification of these modern presuppositions. Pannenberg's theological anthropology implies no less than a turn to God, and this entails a turn to the world, which is no longer valued simply in anthropomorphic terms.

Stanley Grenz points out that Pannenberg follows more recent Christian thought in conceiving humans as a unity of body and soul. He adds that Pannenberg builds on the findings of contemporary philosophical anthropology.[41] We shall see that Pannenberg argues that philosophical anthropology needs to broaden its understanding of existence by taking account of the divine Spirit that is the source of both body and soul and of their unity. He argues that the wholeness of human existence is rooted in God, whom he understands primarily in terms of love, goodness, and faithfulness, but also as all-determining.

Kurt Koch also has recognized that Pannenberg's theological efforts to overcome the split and opposition—which Koch calls an *Apartheid* between scientific and theological conceptions of reality—are fundamental to the development of a new understanding of the human relationship to the natural world.[42] He agrees with Pannenberg that the anthropocentrism of modernity is at the root of this problem. This anthropocentrism is both pervasive and powerfully dominant. Koch suggests that this becomes evident in all uses of the term *Umwelt* (environment), which he regards as revealing the anthropocentricity of the speaker. The world is viewed as the stage for human history. Koch concludes that unless the anthropocentrism is first overcome, all talk of environmental ethics remains a smoke screen behind which nothing effective is done to protect nature. He concludes that environmentalism is in reality an expression of concern regarding human well-being and that nature is protected only inasmuch as this protection serves humans. Ultimately environmentalism remains trapped in the anthropocentrism of the modern notion of progress.[43] I agree with Koch regarding the anthropocentrism of some environmental thought, but my argument is that for Pannenberg both the centrality of humans and the conception of the world as *Umwelt* are in themselves neither avoidable nor evil. Nonetheless, it will become clear that Pannenberg's high and positive regard of humans is not equivalent to the anthropocentrism that has characterized modernity.

The strongly antidualist trend of much ecotheology requires making an important distinction. Bronislaw Szerszynski points out that many writers have argued that Christian metaphysical dualism—regarding God as wholly other—is the root of the ecological crisis.[44] These writers attempt to develop a new "identitarian" metaphysics. That is, they regard all appearances of separate things and creatures to be merely appearances. They hold that all reality is one all-encompassing meta-Self. Szerszynski opposes this type of thinking with various critical arguments and proposes that metaphysical dualism does not necessarily lead to an ecological crisis. In short, Szerszynski argues that one has either an identitarian (pantheist?) or a dualist metaphysics.

Pannenberg's attempt to conceive the wholeness of existence as rooted in the nearness of God to creation fits neither of Szerszynski's categories. The unity of nature and history is a rejection of dualism, but it is neither identitarianism nor some form of pantheism. Pannenberg makes clear distinctions and recognizes the existence of real oppositions within history, but he seeks to reach more deeply to the unity that underlies the very possibility of making distinctions. Szerszynski argues that because selves are the products of relationships it is nonsense to argue that all things are really one huge Self.[45] If Pannenberg were to respond to Szerszynski he might point out that the development of the self depends upon the capacity of selves to differentiate other selves and objects, and that this in turn depends upon the recognition (albeit a dim recognition) of a fundamental unity of reality, and, finally, that this unity depends upon an infinite and other source, namely the Creator God.

Conclusion

Wolfhart Pannenberg has noted the disastrous result of the modern opposition of history and nature and has attempted to address the problem in his presentation of a Christian understanding of reality. A healthy relationship of humans to all reality must be rooted in an understanding of reality that transcends the self-interests of modern individualist culture without negating the special place of humans in the world. The bulk of this work presents Pannenberg's attempts to do just this on the basis of his systematic conception of God as Creator and Redeemer and of humans as central figures in the aims of creation and redemption. His conception of God's love incorporates all reality in the process toward the eschatological achievement of the aim of creation and redemption.

This book has several intertwining themes: First, Pannenberg's thought is a thoroughgoing attempt to think of humans and the nonhuman world as together taken up into a divinely grounded unity that includes all histories, whether they be human, organic, geological, or stellar. I use the categories history and nature to represent the two aspects of existence that modern thought and practice have opposed to each other. I employ the unity of nature and history to refer to Pannenberg's effort to overcome this modern split. The terms are taken from Pannenberg's writings. Second, Pannenberg places the eschatological Kingdom of God at the center of his interpretation of reality. Universal history is the key category by which to understand reality, and this history is the process of realizing the eschatological Kingdom of God. Third, the ideas of creation and redemption together with that of the coming Kingdom of God are expressions of the Trinity: Father, Son, and Spirit. Fourth, this is at the same time the foundation of Pannenberg's theological enterprise and the ethics rooted therein. Divine love is Pannenberg's foundation for ethics. Finally, I try to show that divine love provides theological ethics with a sound foundation from which to engage the particular modern problematique of ecology.

NOTES

1. Pannenberg, *Metaphysics and the Idea of God*, trans. Philip Clayton (Grand Rapids: Eerdmans, 1990), 69-90. Hereafter *MIG*.

2. Having said this, I want to point out my disagreement with Oliver O'Donovan's claim that Pannenberg is "rehabilitating Troeltsch," (O'Donovan, *Resurrection and Moral Order: An Outline of Evangelical Ethics*, 2d ed. [Grand Rapids: Eerdmans, 1994], 61). The idea of the unity of nature and history does not fit O'Donovan's categorization of Pannenberg's thought as historicist (*Ibid.*, 59ff.).

3. Pannenberg, "A Response to My American Friends," in *The Theology of Wolfhart Pannenberg: Twelve American Critiques, with an Autobiographical Essay and Response*, ed. Carl E. Braaten and Philip Clayton (Minneapolis: Augsburg, 1988), 330f., and Pannenberg, *Christian Spirituality* (Philadelphia: Westminster, 1983), 65f., 70. Hereafter *CS*.

4. Matt. 22:37-40.

5. Pannenberg, *Anthropology in Theological Perspective*, trans. Matthew J. O'Connell (Philadelphia: Westminster, 1985), 74-79. Hereafter *ATP*.

6. Pannenberg, *Systematische Theologie*, 3 vols. (Göttingen: Vandenhoeck & Ruprecht, 1988, 1991 & 1993), 3:87-93, 104-13. At this point only the first two volumes are available in translation: *Sytematic Theology*, 2 vols., trans. Geoffrey W. Bromiley (Grand Rapids: Eerdmans, 1991, 1994). Hereafter *ST* and *STe* will be used to represent the German original and the English translation.

7. See, for example, Holmes Rolston III, "Environmental Ethics: Values in and Duties to the Natural World," in *Ecology, Economics, Ethics: The Broken Circle*, ed. F. Herbert Bormann and Stephen R. Kellert (New Haven: Yale University, 1991), 74f.

8. Pannenberg, *The Idea of God and Human Freedom* (Philadelphia: Westminster, 1973), 90. Hereafter *IGHF*. Cf. also *ATP*, 74-79 and Pannenberg, "Typen des Atheismus und ihre theologische Bedeutung," in *Grundfragen systematischer Theologie*, 2 vols. (Göttingen: Vandenhoeck & Ruprecht, 1967 & 1980), 1:347-60; *Basic Questions in Theology*, 2 vols., trans. George U. Kehm (Philadelphia: Fortress, 1970, 1972), 2:184-200. Hereafter *GF* and *BQ*. Miroslav Volf, in *Zukunft der Arbeit, Arbeit der Zukunft: Der Arbeitsbegriff bei Karl Marx und seine theologische Wertung* (Grünwald: Kaiser, 1988), 117, refers to Pannenberg as a theologian who has recognized the anthropological focus of philosophical atheism. He points out that the basic question is whether one believes that God is the Creator of the world and of humans.

9. This dualism also is associated with the domination of women by men. Bacon associates women with nature and regards both as analogous types of slaves to men (Cf. Kurt Koch, "Der Mensch und seine Mit-Welt als Schöpfungs-Ebenbild Gottes: Schöpfungstheologische Aspekte der mensch-

lichen Verantwortung für die Natur," *Catholica: Vierteljahresschrift für Kontroverstheologie* 42/1 (1988): 36-37). Koch cites Pannenberg as noting the ethical significance of overcoming the dualistic separation of science and theology from each other. Regarding the impact of Bacon on the domination of nature see, for example, William Leiss, *The Domination of Nature* (New York: George Braziller, 1972), 51-58, 71.

10. Pannenberg, *Wissenschaftstheorie und Theology* (Frankfurt: Suhrkamp, 1973), 76; *Theology and the Philosophy of Science*, trans. Francis McDonaugh (Philadephia: Westminster, 1976), 74. Hereafter *WT* and *TPS*. Cf. also Pannenberg, "Geist und Energie: Zur Phänomenologie Teilhards de Chardin," *Acta Teilhardiana* 8 (1971): 6. Pannenberg points out the significance of this separation of reason and phenomena for the thought of Kant. He also connects this with the grounding of ethics in reason ("Theologische Motive im Denken Immanuel Kants," *Theologische Literaturzeitung* 89, 12 (1964): 897-906. Cf. also Louis Dupré, "The Dissolution of the Union of Nature and Grace at the Dawn of the Modern Age," in *The Theology of Wolfhart Pannenberg*, ed. Braaten and Clayton, 96, and Jürgen Moltmann, who presents a similar argument in *God in Creation: A New Theology of Creation and the Spirit of God*, trans. Margaret Kohl (London: SCM, 1985), 250-52.

11. See Moltmann, *God in Creation*, 45.

12. Ibid., 27. Moltmann cites Baader, *Über den Zwiespalt des religiösen Glaubens und Wissens*, 2d ed. (Darmstadt, 1958), 49. Pannenberg notes that this had far-reaching consequences for theology. It separated the Creator from the creation. See "Gott und die Natur: Zur Geschichte der Auseinandersetzung zwischen Theologie und Naturwissenschaft," *Theologie und Philosophie* 58, 4 (1983): 486f.

13. Cf. Ernst Troeltsch's analysis of modernity in *Historismus und Seine Probleme*, vol. 3, *Gesammelte Schriften*, (Tübingen: Mohr, 1922), 9.

14. Cf. Koch, 35f.

15. Pannenberg, "Christliche Rechtsbegründung," in *Handbuch der christlichen Ethik*, vol. 2, ed. Anselm Hertz, et al. (Freiburg: Herder & Gütersloh: Gerd Mohn, 1978), 330.

16. C. S. Lewis perceptively notes that the power of humans over nature is more accurately regarded as a tool in the service of the power of a few humans over many other humans. See *The Abolition of Man* (London: Harper Collins, 1943), 35.

17. Pannenberg, "The Doctrine of Creation and Modern Science," *Zygon* 23, 1 (March 1988): 5.

18. *IGHF*, 105.

19. "Until Feuerbach, atheism appeared only as an asssertion. Feuerbach, however, through his genetic theory of religion, provided the proof of atheism. The scientific view of the world . . . was only the presupposition for this. That *everything* could be explained without reference to God . . . demands that religion too could be explained without reference to God. Only

thereby is the position of atheism completed." My translation. "Bis zu Feuerbach ist der Atheismus eigentlich nur als Behauptung aufgetreten. Feuerbach jedoch hat durch seine genetische Theorie der Religion den Beweis des Atheismus geliefert. Eben dafür war das naturwissenschaftliche Weltbild . . . nur die Voraussetzung. Daß man *alles* ohne Gott erklären kann . . . das erforderte, daß man auch die Religion selbst ohne Gott erklären konnte. Erst damit ist die Position des Atheismus vollendet" (*GF* 1:348; *BQ* 2:185f.; cf. *ST* 3:575).

20. *WT*, 9, 17f.; *TPS*, 5, 13f.; *CS*, 77.

21. *TPS*, pt. 1.

22. Pannenberg, *Christianity in a Secularized World*, trans. John Bowden (New York: Crossroad, 1989), 57. Hereafter *CSW*. "Die Chance des Christentums und seiner Theologie ist vielmehr [im vergleich mit ein irrationeller Flucht aus der modernen Welt so wie es die exotische Religionnen bieten], das reduzierte Wirklichkeitsverständnis der säkularen Kultur und ihres Menschenbildes in ein grösseres Ganzes zu integrieren, der reduzierten Rationalität der säkularen Kultur gegenüber eine grössere Weite der Vernunft selbst offenzuhalten, zu der auch der Horizont der Gottesbildung des Menschen gehört." *Christentum in einer Säkularisierten Welt*, 75. Hereafter *CW*.

23. "That means that theology, in the dialogue with the sciences, has the task of demonstrating in specific terms the dimension which has thus been omitted from the phenomena which the sciences are investigating, through which these phenomena are associated with God as the creator of the world" (*CSW*, 52). "Das bedeutet, daß die Theologie im Dialog mit den Wissenschaften die Aufgabe hat, in den von ihnen untersuchten Phänomenen die dabei ausgeblendete Dimension konkret aufzuweisen, durch die diese Phänomene mit Gott als dem Schöpfer der Welt verbunden sind." (*CW*, 68).

24. Stanley J. Grenz, *Reason for Hope: The Systematic Theology of Wolfhart Pannenberg* (New York: Oxford University, 1990), 8. Emphasis mine. Cf. H. Richard Niebuhr, *The Meaning of Revelation* (New York: Macmillan, 1941), 62-64. Niebuhr also claims that the idea of God encompasses all reality.

25. Pannenberg, "An Autobiographical Sketch," in *Theology of Pannenberg*, ed. Braaten and Clayton, 12.

26. Pannenberg, *Toward a Theology of Nature: Essays on Science and Faith*, ed. Ted Peters (Louisville: Westminster/John Knox, 1993), 74. Hereafter *TTN*. "Gerade die von der Naturwissenschaft erforschte Natur müßte von der Theologie als Schöpfung Gottes in Anspruch genommen werden." Pannenberg, "Kontingenz und Naturgesetz," in A. M. Klaus Müller and Pannenberg, *Erwägungen zu einer Theologie der Natur* (Gütersloh: Gerd Mohn, 1970), 35. Hereafter *ETN*.

27. *ETN*, 34f.; *TTN*, 73f.

28. "If theology wants to think of the diety of God, then it has to think of God as the power that determines not only human history but also nature.

This demand results in addition from the observation that in human history itself events proceed only naturally; so, either history and nature together or neither one has anything to do with God" (*TTN*, 75). "Will die Theologie das Gottsein Gottes bedenken, so muß sie Gott als die nicht nur die menschliche Geschichte, sondern auch die Natur bestimmende Macht denken. Diese Forderung ergibt sich auch daraus, daß es in der menschlichen Geschichte selbst nur natürlich zugehen kann, so daß entweder Geschichte und Natur oder keine von beiden etwas mit Gott zu tun haben" (*ETN*, 36).

29. *STe* 2:xiv. According to Pannenberg the aim of systematic theology is simply to present a "zusammenhängende Interpretation von Gott, Mensch und Welt . . ., die sich im Verhältnis zum Erfahrungswissen von der Welt und dem menschlichen Leben, sowie zum Reflexionswissen der Philosophie, mit guten Gründen als wahr vertreten läßt, darum auch im Verhältnis zu alternativen religiösen und nicht-religiösen Weltinterpretationen als wahr behauptet werden kann" (*ST* 2:11).

30. *TTN*, pt. 1.

31. *An Introduction to Systematic Theology* (Grand Rapids: Eerdmans, 1991), 6. Hereafter *IST*.

32. Pannenberg, "Theological Questions to Scientists," *Zygon* 16,1 (1981): 68-72, "Doctrine of Creation and Science," 4-18, and *ST* 2:66-69, 99ff.; *STe* 2:49-52, 79ff. Cf. also Pannenberg, "Geist und Energie," 6-9.

33. Cf. Dupré, 97.

34. *TPS*, 70. "Der Schritt von Gesetzeswissenschaften zu philosophischen Behauptungen ist nicht in geradliniger Verlängerung nomologischer Deskription möglich, sondern erfordert eine Reflexion auf die gesetzeswissenschaftliche Sprache und ihre Implikationen. Das hängt mit der eigentümlichen Abstraktheit dieser Sprache zusammen" (*WT*, 72).

35. Sigurd Martin Daecke, "Das 'Interdisziplinäre Geschpräch' von 1972 bis 1978: Eine Zusammenfassung," in *Gott—Geist—Materie: Theologie und Naturwissenschaft in Geschpräch*, ed. Hermann Dielztebingen und Lutz Mohaupt (Hamburg: Lutherisches Verlagshaus, 1980), 131, refers to Michael Faraday's separation of these two realms of his own life, expressed symbolically in keeping separated the keys to laboratory and prayer chamber.

36. See Erazim Kohák, *The Embers and the Stars: A Philosophical Inquiry Into the Moral Sense of Nature* (Chicago: Univeristy of Chicago, 1984), 76-85.

37. Cf. *IST*, 4-7.

38. *BQ* 1:2. "Recht verstanden ist die Offenbarung Gottes als Offenbarung *Gottes* erst dann bedacht, wenn alle sonstige Wahrheit und Erkenntnis auf sie hingeordnet und in sie aufgenommen wird" (*GF* 1:12).

39. *ETN*, 42; *TTN*, 81. Ted Peters' labeling of Pannenberg's theology as "apologetic" depends on a definitional narrowing of the term. Peters ignores that aspect of traditional apologetics that defends orthodox faith. He does so in order to focus solely on rational argumentation regarding the truth of faith

("Truth in History: Gadamer's Hermeneutics and Pannenberg's Apologetic Method," *Journal of Religion* 55 (1975): 36-38). That Pannenberg corrects orthodox positions on the basis of modern perceptions of reality confirms that his methodology is not a traditional apologetic. Rather, it is rooted in a scientific methodology that proposes hypotheses and then tests them.

40. *IGHF*, 16.

41. Grenz, *Reason for Hope*, 91.

42. Koch, 29f. & 32.

43. Koch, 32f.

44. Szerszynski, "The Metaphysics of Environmental Concern—A Critique of Ecotheological Antidualism," *Studies in Christian Ethics* 6, 2 (1993): 67-70.

CHAPTER 1

GOD THE CREATOR

Wolfhart Pannenberg's understanding of creation is distinguished by its Trinitarian and eschatological foci. The connection of eschatology with the doctrine of creation gives his understanding of creation a process character with an orientation to the future. The explication of creation in terms of the Trinity gives each detail within the general eschatological form its place in relation to the love of the Creator. Father, Son, and Spirit create the universe in one mighty act that is only fully seen from the point of view of the eschaton, which is the perfect realization of the inner-Trinitarian love. On the way to the realization of the Kingdom of God, the Trinity works immanently in all reality.

This chapter is an elaboration of Pannenberg's understanding of creation through an analysis of his discussions of the Trinity and of eschatology that is guided by the question of the relationship of nature and history. The question I shall try to answer is how Pannenberg's understanding of a Trinitarian and eschatological doctrine of creation serves to overcome the dualism of nature and spirit.

Although I concentrate specifically on these two aspects of Pannenberg's understanding of creation, I will need to develop some of the basic background concepts involved. Pannenberg seeks direction in the Jewish context within which Christianity developed. The notions of history and revelation are fundamental, as is the radical monotheism of Israel's faith. Finally, some questions regarding pantheism, anthropocentrism, evil, and moral consequences will be treated.

God: Ancient Israel and Modern Atheism

Monotheism, History, and Revelation

According to Pannenberg, the context for the development of the Christian conception of a Trinitarian God is found in the history of ancient Israel. Here are the roots of the notion that there is one God, Jahweh, who is above all gods, and that the so-called gods are merely the creations of the human imagination. There is only one God in whom is to be sought the determining power that governs all reality. This conception of the oneness of the deity and the corresponding nothingness of the gods is a realization that marks a significant progression in Israel's history. The faith of ancient Israel was not always radically monotheistic.

Israel came to know Jahweh through the experience of reality as a process between promise and fulfillment.[1] Through the years Jahweh punished offenses against the covenant codes—the curses came upon covenant breakers; he forgave and healed the repentant people, renewing the covenant for the sake of the Patriarchs; he sent prophets, established kings, and turned enemies away. In the process the people came to know the love, holiness, faithfulness, jealousy, and power of Jahweh. They also came to know the weakness of human love and faithfulness. And in this context they came to know the faithfulness of Jahweh in reestablishing covenant, in offering healing, and in overcoming human frailty.

From the biblical record it is apparent that the Patriarchs, the judges, and the early kings did not share this radical monotheism. Early Israel did not have access to the fuller knowledge that the sixth-century B.C. prophets attained.[2] Jahweh's relationship with the people of Israel is a process. The relationship has a history in which the more recent is no longer the same as the more distant past. Various sorts of encounters drew forth new and ever more complete expressions of faith in Jahweh. Many early biblical references testify to a continued belief in the reality and power of other gods long after the encounters with Jahweh during the exodus from Egypt, the desert wanderings, and the conquest of Canaan. That the monotheistic faith of Israel was achieved in the process of a history of God's relationship with the people is no longer controversial. Whatever Abram believed, it is clear that the understanding of God that developed in the process of ancient Israel's history made an end of both polytheism and monar- chialism.[3]

In the modern world it also must be noted that this understand- ing of God allows for no dualism of nature and spirit. Jahweh was known as the God who rules nature, as well as history. The understanding of Jahweh as the Creator God is only possible if it is accompanied by a faith in the absolute character of God's rule in history. "The cosmic order and origin were traced back to the God of salvation history, and thereby unlimited power came to be seen in God's historical action."[4] Jahweh is the one and the only God who rules in Israel's history, as in all history. Jahweh is the *one* who has brought the cosmos into existence and exercises the *power* that renews the world and keeps all things from returning to chaos and nothingness.

The jealous holiness of Jahweh and its exclusive claim upon the people of Israel led to the understanding that the creation of the cosmos, the renewal and maintenance of the world, and the course of history—all history—are the activities of only one God—Jahweh. The radical monotheism of Israel brought the various aspects of religious life into a unity of worship and serv- ice given to one God. No longer was it legitimate to seek the goodwill of various fragmented powers in the various compart- ments of human experience. Life within the covenant of Jahweh with Israel did not allow for the isolation of religious life from agricultural practice, for example. The covenant stipulations covered all aspects of life, and the blessings and curses attached to the covenant no less so. The misuse of the land could be punished by political exile. Drought would result from the mistreatment of the poor. Land and sky were not isolated from human concourse. A reading of the Old Testament shows that the lives of shepherd and king were equally considered to be under the one rule of Jahweh.[5]

Pannenberg argues that the driving motive for appropriating the cosmological functions of the ancient Near Eastern gods, El and Baal, is to be found in the holy jealousy of Jahweh, as expressed in Exod. 20:3, the first commandment: "You shall have no other gods. . ." and "you shall love the Lord your God with all your heart, and with all your soul, and with all your might."[6] Love is the character of the ultimate relationship of creature with Creator. The biblical statements about God's love and election of the Patriarchs (Abraham, Isaac, and Jacob) form the basis of God's continuing love for the people of Israel. At the heart of the response to God is love. Obedience to God in the context of the covenant is the form that love takes. Pannenberg's focus on the unity of the Trinity, as well as on the participation of creation in this unity, also suggests that love be understood as the central category for understanding the creation-redemption-fulfillment process.

Pannenberg is not, however, simply trying to derive the idea of God from an analysis of ancient Hebrew faith. Rather, the idea of God is treated as a hypothesis that needs to be tested for its truth.[7] The connection between nature and history is sought in the idea of the all-determining Creator. Pannenberg relies especially on a conception of God as the one who acts in history and a conception of history that includes all of reality. These ideas are rooted in the faith of ancient Israel and are expressed in the creation texts of Genesis 1-3, as well as in the prophets who draw all of reality, including the future, together under the creative and free action of God. The unity of the deity seen in Jahweh's action in history (economy of God), which was experienced by

Israel in a promise-fulfillment character—i.e., in God's trustworthiness over time—grounds Israel's conception of the unity of all history.[8]

The experience that the fulfillment of promises was mostly inexact and involved a reinterpretation of the past (the promissory events) pointed beyond the fulfillment of the promises to a more ultimate fulfillment of God's actions in history. In the developments of postexilic apocalypticism, which is a most significant example for Pannenberg, it became evident that God's actions could be understood in the perspective of an ultimate and eschatological future. Thereby, the meaning and determination of history (universal) and all its particularities were understood from the vantage of this eschatological perspective.[9] Pannenberg is concerned to show that this universal history includes nature.

"In both nature and history the universe is then the field of Jahweh's acts."[10] Pannenberg detects in the Hebrew Bible a notion of creation that is defined both from the perspective of origins and from that of history. Close connections are made between God's creation of the world and God's saving acts on behalf of the covenant people.[11] Jahweh comes to be regarded as the only God, as the only one who acts out of the boundless freedom of divine power. There is no room for a dualist understanding of creation—the physical world is not created by some demiurge. The material universe and the human spirit both belong to the one creation of the one Creator.[12] Jahweh brings all that exists into being, and it continues to exist on the basis of Jahweh's continued interest in the welfare of the creation. Jahweh the Creator of all reality is also the God of all history, Israel's as well as that of all nations. Further biblical roots for Pannenberg's understanding of God are found, for example, in a prayer of the early Christian community.[13] In one compact prayer God is acknowledged as Creator, as Sovereign over kings and rulers (i.e., human history), and as Redeemer.

Pannenberg connects his understanding of human with his understanding of natural history in the context of this monotheistic conception of God the Creator. God grounds the unity that is apparent in both human and natural histories. And God's future rule is that which gives the final context and unity by which the diverse and unrepeatable events of all reality are seen to be a history of God's creation and redemption, which culminates in the manifestation of divine love, power, and glory. This is seen in one of the more common ways in which Pannenberg refers to God—"*die alles bestimmende Macht*" (the all-determining power). This phrase should be understood in the context of the Judeo-Christian concept of God as the one and only God who is the Creator, Redeemer, and Perfecter of all reality. It conveys that God is the source and end of all existence and that God is to be reckoned with in all that happens. The phrase is also intended to refer to human experiences of dependence that Pannenberg regards as fundamental and universal.[14]

The universality of God means that all events and realities are determined by God. This means, further, that the activity of God in history is to be sought in the day-to-day events of history.[15] Because (1) God is the creator of all reality, (2) creatures are given an independent existence, and (3) God remains faithful to creatures in spite of the sinful character of their actions, Pannenberg understands all events to be an indirect self-revelation of God.[16] And this means that history in its totality must be understood as the self-revelation of God. The realization of the ultimate eschatological goal of history coincides with God's full and final self-revelation. History reveals the faithfulness of God as Creator, Sustainer, and Redeemer.

The Question of Truth

The question of the truth of the Christian faith is significant in the context of the claim that God is the all-determining reality. It is the question regarding the Christian faith's

> power to encompass all reality—even that of modern science, the technological control of nature, and the forms of individual life—and to

claim them all as evidence for the content of the Christian message. The question about the truth of the Christian message has to do with whether it can still disclose to us today the unity of the reality in which we live, as it once did in the ancient world.[17]

For Pannenberg questions of truth are ultimately questions of the absolute truth, which can only be one truth.

According to Pannenberg, the Hebrew notion of *emeth* (truth) is fundamentally historical. It is the ever repeated reliability and faithfulness of persons in relationships, which is a fundamentally moral conception of truth. It is oriented to the future—truth will show itself in future faithfulness.[18] Pannenberg argues that *emeth* takes up and refines the central aspect of truth that the Greek notion of *aletheia* had in view.

[T]he Greek dualism between true being and changing sense-appearances is superseded in the biblical understanding of truth. Here, true being is thought of not as timeless but instead as historical, and it proves its stability through a history whose future is always open.[19]

The truth is not reached in abstraction from the flux of history but is disclosed in new ways at new junctures in history. Thus, both the historical and the abiding aspects of truth are included in the concept of *emeth*.[20]

Pannenberg argues that the Hebrew notion of truth has continued to shape Western thought. He sees this in the context of the problem of how true knowledge of nonhuman reality is possible and how this possibility is related to the knowledge of God. Pannenberg argues that Nicolas of Cusa's conception of thought as a creative productivity underlies the construction of hypotheses, which is fundamental to modern scientific thinking. Knowledge is attained through creative subjectivity, which construes hypothetical models of reality, which are then experimentally tested. In Cusa's view of this attainment of knowledge, the problem of explaining the adequation of creative reflection to the world is answered by the conception of the image of God. God is the Creator of the world and humans are the creators of an intellectual world, and, thus humans are the likeness of God. Since humans are the image of God, their ideas will reflect the things created by God.[21]

The unity of creative subjectivity and external reality is a central aspect of the unity of nature and history. History is the unrepeatable sequence of creative human activity. It is a category of the human mind/spirit. It tells the story of human culture, as well as the story of the nonhuman world within which it lives. Nature, the nonhuman world, is the fundamental external reality within which humans live, about which they think, and upon which they act. Apart from the consideration of a greater unifying reality, it has become problematic to consider these inner and outer realities as a unity. According to Pannenberg's analysis of the epistemological process, only the Creator can be the true ground of both subject and object and thus can be their unity. God is the one truth which is the source of both humans and the world which humans examine and come to know. I have used this somewhat dualist way of speaking intentionally. It is not part of the ordinary experience of modern people to think in terms of a unity. Our secular culture tends to separate the inner (human) world and the outer (nonhuman) world. Pannenberg's theological construal of the world argues that these two worlds are really the one world created by God, and that this is evident through a consideration of epistemology.

One of the aims of Pannenberg's *Theology and the Philosophy of Science* is to establish that it is not possible to make a sharp distinction between the historical sciences and the natural sciences. Pannenberg argues that all the hypotheses and results of scientific investigation are anticipatory because all knowledge is yet incomplete and must remain so as long as the future remains unknown or open.[22]

The substance of Pannenberg's claim that the natural sciences, like the human sciences, are historical and limited is found in recent arguments in the philosophy of science. These discussions have shown the weaknesses of positivism and logical positivism.

They have shown the inescapably historical character of all scientific investigation. At the same time, they have broken the barriers that existed between the natural and the metaphysical sciences. Pannenberg notes that it can no longer be argued that because the human sciences are inexact they have no valid claims to truth, for such a judgment also would fall upon the natural sciences. Modern physics, to take as an example the science regarded by some as the most successful of all modern sciences, is remarkably accurate in its descriptions of the real world, but it must acknowledge minute discrepancies between its general laws and individual instances of the realities these laws intend to describe. More than that, in quantum physics it has been argued that the free decisions of experimenters as to the measuring instruments used for particular experiments lead to mutually exclusive results. According to the physicist A. M. Klaus Müller, there is, in other words, an inescapable element of contingency in the results of experimental science. Müller states that "physics, at this level of reflection, therefore, no longer simply describes properties of existing objects, but only the results of experiments."[23]

As long as the question of truth remains significant to scientific inquiry, in spite of the anticipatory nature of science's general laws, the distinction between these anticipatory laws and the actual realities described can be explained by referring to the traditional metaphysical distinction between essence and appearance. Pannenberg, however, redefines *essence* in a historical manner. This means that one must draw a distinction between the way in which a particular object appears in a particular time and place and what the object finally will prove to be when it is wholly known.[24] This is an indication of the connection that Pannenberg makes between metaphysical reflection and scientific inquiry. It reflects, at the level of epistemology (the adequation of human thought to the natural world), the unity in God of nature and history.

The Being and Coming of God

Some of the results of Pannenberg's interaction with various atheist positions warrant a brief discussion, for in this interchange Pannenberg seeks to show the correspondence of his understanding of God (which he draws largely out of the biblical tradition) with modern perceptions of reality. This is an important task for any theologian who wishes to claim the universality of God's rule. For when theologians make such claims they are making claims about the same world that other thinkers also claim to understand.

Pannenberg points out that atheists such as Feuerbach argue that "the experience of freedom excludes belief in the existence" of a God who is "understood as an omniscient and omnipotent being complete and perfect at the beginning of the created world."[25] Pannenberg agrees with the atheist criticism that such notions of God (he regards them as characteristic of much of medieval theology) cannot be reconciled with the experience of human freedom. Pannenberg's constructive response is to reformulate the notion of God by placing these characteristics of God in the future. God is identified with the power of a sure future. Pannenberg develops an understanding of God that distinguishes between the immanent and the economic reality of the Trinity. This distinction allows Pannenberg to regard the reality of God both as a process of becoming perfect and as eternally perfect.[26] "What turns out to be true in the future [regarding God] will then be evident as having been true all along."[27] The absolute power of God's love is eternally realized within the inner-Trinitarian relationship of Father, Son, and Spirit. However, this characteristic of God, in its relation to the created universe, is only fulfilled in the universe through the process of its mediation and realization through Christ and the Spirit.[28]

The fundamental difference between Pannenberg's notion of God and that of the medieval theologians is that Pannenberg replaces the notion of an eternally *perfect* and *unchanging* deity with the idea of a God who is eternally *faithful* to creatures. Pannenberg no longer speaks of God as unmoved and unchanging. The monarchy of the Father and the unity of the Trinity are determined by the realization of God's rule in creation through the work of the Son and the Spirit.[29] But the work of the Son and the Spirit is to reveal the God who *is* in eternity.[30] This, he argues, makes it possible to hold without contradiction both that God is eternal and that God's relationship with the creation involves a contingent history. It is thus in the relationship of the economic to the immanent Trinity that one can speak of God becoming something that God previously was not.

> If eternity and time coincide only in the eschatological consummation of history, then from the standpoint of the history of God that moves toward this consummation there is room for becoming in God himself, namely, in the relation of the immanent and the economic Trinity, and in this frame it is possible to say of God that he himself became something that he previously was not when he became man in his Son.[31]

Pannenberg can state this even more strongly. God freely decides, in entering into a history with his creation, to allow himself to be determined by this history. As E. Frank Tupper puts it, Pannenberg speaks of God's being only in terms of God's relationship to history.[32] The being and deity of God are intertwined with God's rule, which is the expression of divine power and love in history.

Pannenberg also points out that history is determined from the point of its ultimate completion, which is the Kingdom of God. The Kingdom of God, however, represents most perfectly the determination of reality by the power of the all-determining God.[33] The apparent circularity of this conception of the relationship of God and creation may be clarified by a careful distinction of perspective. If one attempts to consider reality from the perspective of God, then all is determined by God. If one distinguishes from this the perspective of the historical experience of God's determination of reality, then it becomes clear that humans, through the freedom they have as independent creatures, participate in the determination of reality, which is to say, they have a determining role in the expression of God's power in history.[34] In other words, God determines the creation to be inter-dependent with God's self. Pannenberg's distinction of immanent and economic Trinity appears to be intended, at least in part, to deal with this difficulty. It enables one to hold both that God is already and always has been God and that God will one day become ruler of reality in such a way that present doubts regarding that rule (and goodness) are overcome.[35]

In this context Pannenberg asks his now well-known question: "God does not yet exist, but will come to be?" (Gott ist noch nicht, sondern wird erst sein?)[36] Later formulations of this thought, which primarily speak of God as the power of the future, seem somewhat less radical. But even here the intention is to highlight the idea that the perceived (by creatures) reality of God is dependent on the manifestation of God's power to bring the creation to perfection.[37] Pannenberg states that Jesus' death and resurrection exemplify the nature of God's relationship to history. The death of Jesus calls into question both the truth of Jesus' role as God's agent and the power of God. The resurrection of Jesus retroactively confirms what was true of both all along. In a like manner the eschatological realization of God's rule will confirm what always has been true about God.[38] The claims that God is love and is Creator remain open until sin, hatred, and evil are overcome by God's rule.

Pannenberg here clearly considers the reality of God in terms of a process understanding of reality. But there is one significant point at which Pannenberg parts company with process theologians. He refuses to incorporate time into the idea of God.[39] Regarding God's being, Pannenberg argues that the ultimate (eschatological) truth regarding God's immanent being will prove to be consistent with the economy of God in time and space, on the way to the Kingdom.[40] John O'Donnell argues that Pannenberg understands the immanent Trinity completely in terms of the economy of the Son's activity in the world. He interprets Pannenberg to hold that "there is no immanent Trinity standing behind the economic Trinity. There is no eternal essence lying behind the manifestations. Rather the essence comes to appearance in the action."[41] Unfortunately, O'Donnell has taken a comment of Pannenberg's out of its context. He refers to Pannenberg's *Systematische Theologie* where Pannenberg states that the essence of a thing comes into appearance in its existence (*Dasein*).[42] O'Donnell interprets this to signify an identity of essence and appearance in the *Daseinsmoment*. In so doing O'Donnell misses an important qualification in the sentence he quotes: "In it (the particular moment of existence) the essence of a thing *merely* comes into *appearance*."[43] I emphasize *merely* because it makes clear Pannenberg's intention. God's essence is never, during the course of history, fully revealed in the appearances of divine power in individual events. According to Pannenberg, God's self-revelation in history is always indirect. This becomes completely unambiguous when Pannenberg states explicitly that God's essence comes into appearance (*Erscheinung*) in history in only anticipatory ways.[44] In the case of God, it is always the same reality that appears in history. God appears as the all-determining reality who both transcends history and is its future unity. Nonetheless, O'Donnell rightly sees that Pannenberg regards God's being or essence as coming, and that God's appearances are fundamentally identifiable with God's being.[45] What God is eternally will come fully to appearance in the Kingdom of God. Furthermore, the (incomplete) appearance of God in history is, nonetheless, the true appearance of this future reality. When God's rule has become fully realized, then the true character of all the anticipatory appearances of God's rule will be known.

O'Donnell also argues that Pannenberg makes the same error in judgment regarding the idea of God that process thinkers make, which according to O'Donnell, is the sacrifice of divine omnipotence and omniscience to save creaturely freedom. O'Donnell's point is that Pannenberg need not have accepted the atheist outcome of certain medieval ideas of God's omnipotence and omniscience, which excluded the possibility of human freedom. However, when O'Donnell states that "in a strict sense, we cannot speak of any foreknowledge in God," he already has taken a significant step with Pannenberg.[46] O'Donnell fails to see that Pannenberg's location of the realization of the rule of God in the future is not a removal of God's rule from the present. God's power is present as the ultimate future. Pannenberg conceives the relationship of time and eternity in the context of the relationship of the immanent and economic Trinity. It is in this context that we need to consider Pannenberg's remarks regarding the futurity of God's existence. The dependence of God's future on the freedom of creatures is related to the becoming of God that Pannenberg locates in the relationship of the economic to the immanent Trinity. God (economic) is not manifest to creatures as God (immanent) in power and authority except from the perspective of the future full participation of creatures in the Kingdom of God. We do not yet see face to face.[47] This does not mean, as O'Donnell supposes, that according to Pannenberg God is not present at the origin of the universe. It appears that for O'Donnell the real problem may be that Pannenberg's thought does not provide for an authoritative enough church, one that possesses "the guarantee of the church's certitude to stand in the truth."[48] Pannenberg argues that God has a history of becoming the one God of all people. This is a history in time. Nonetheless, God remains the same from eternity to eternity.[49] In the end God will reveal that it was always the one true God who appeared in the events of history.[50] During the course of history the church's certitude depends on truth that must nonetheless remain open and controversial.

Jerry Norris Beam argues that if "God is simultaneously present to all times" then God would "know the future as actual before it occurs."[51] However, the real point about the simultaneity of God's presence is that God encompasses time but is more than time and space. Pannenberg speaks of God's continuing presence (*fortdauernde Gegenwart*).[52] God does not know the future as actual before it occurs. Rather, as the future occurs God is present to it. God is present to all times as their mutual future wholeness.[53] In Pannenberg's formulation the past is not lost to God, but past, present, and future are together grounded in the eternal act of creation.[54] God's *faithfulness*, not divine impassibility, is characteristic of God's presence to all time. Humans experience history as fragmented and multitudinous times and places. Time and space are a unified reality only in the presence of the faithfulness of the redeeming Creator. God's creative activity is immediately present to each creaturely moment.[55] In this context Pannenberg also notes that the unity of God's creative activity is open to questioning. This is addressed by the connection of the eschatological Kingdom with creation. Creation is from the coming Kingdom.

The distinction between Pannenberg's notion of God and a medieval one is a significant point, which if missed can result in a serious misinterpretation of Pannenberg's thought. If one *fails* to note that Pannenberg has effectively eliminated the notion of God's unchangeableness from his theology and that it has been replaced with an understanding of the eternal faithfulness of God, then it may be possible to suggest that Pannenberg's God needed to create a universe in order to realize his absolute monarchy.[56] This misinterpretation becomes even more distorted insofar as one fails to note that Pannenberg defines the content of God's eternal faithfulness as creative love.[57] However, Pannenberg's attempt to maintain both the all-determining power of God and the rootedness of human freedom in God's determination of human existence is most clearly formulated within a Trinitarian conception of God and creation, at the heart of which is God's faithful love.

The Trinity and Creation

Freedom in Self-Differentiating Acknowledgment

The doctrine of creation regards the free activity of God as the source of the existence of the universe. However, this is not to say that the world is needed by God in order for God to be active. God is eternally active within the inner-Trinitarian dynamic of love.[58] The correlate of the non-necessity of God's action, says Pannenberg, is that the universe is contingent; it does not exist necessarily.[59]

In creating the world (*Welt*, here understood as everything that exists in time and space, and this understood as a unified reality)[60] the inner relationship of the persons of God is turned outward. In other words,

> The action of the one God in relation to the world is not wholly different from the action in his trinitarian life. In his action in relation to the world the trinitarian life turns outward, moves outside itself, and becomes the determinative basis of relations between the Creator and the creatures.[61]

This understanding of the act of creation already expresses that the relation between God and the creation is (or is intended to be) characterized by the love and unity of the persons of the Trinity with each other. It regards the creation as one reality, unified in the creative act of divine love. It also expresses both the distinction of the creation from the Creator and the (intended) unity of creation with its Creator.

Pannenberg more specifically understands the initial differentiation of the created universe from God in terms of the relationship of the Father to the Son. The eternal Son, says Pannenberg, responds to the love of the Father with an eternal self-differentiation (*Selbstunterscheidung*) from the Father.[62] The character of this self-differentiation is an acknowledgment by the Son of the Father as God. This self-differentiation is the starting point for the otherness of the creation from the Father. The independent existence of creatures is rooted in this differentiation. Pannenberg sees the relationship of Father and Son reflected especially in the relationship of humans to the Father. However, the entire universe participates in this relationship, for it is the ground of the possibility of its existence.[63] Pannenberg consistently highlights the special place of humans in creation but does not allow for a dualism of nature and spirit. The opposition of the human and the nonhuman worlds is not possible on these grounds.

Pannenberg points out that Hegel's conception of the inner-Trinitarian relationship (and the dependence of creation on this relationship) is grounded in logical necessity. The necessity of the self-expression of God in the creation of a world is connected with the principle of *Anderssein* (being different or other), which serves as the generative force or productive principle in Hegel's conception of reality. God necessarily brings forth a world that stands in difference to the divine reality. This bringing forth of a world is seen by Hegel as an unfolding (*Entfaltung*) of the idea of the absolute subject. The creation of the world necessarily follows upon the absolute subject taking seriously the principle of differentness (*Andersheit*).[64]

Pannenberg modifies Hegel's conception of the Trinity in conceiving the Son's act of self-differentiation as a free act, and not the necessary *Entfaltung* (in the *Anderssein* of the Son from the Father) of the idea of the absolute subject.

> Thus creation is a free act of God as an expression of the freedom of the Son in his self-distinction from the Father, and of the freedom of the fatherly goodness that in the Son accepts the possibility and the existence of a creation distinct from himself, and of the freedom of the Spirit who links the two in free agreement.[65]

The world is not the necessary and finite result of God's infinite otherness. God freely brings a world into existence.[66] Pannenberg can say that creation is "an utterly non-necessary product of a completely free action." This means that the existence of the world is completely contingent and that God's actions are completely free.[67]

Pannenberg points out that this correction of Hegel's concept of the idea and its necessary unfolding has implications for the understanding of reason. Reason remains historical but has only an anticipatory relationship to the totality of reality. Pannenberg replaces the necessity of Hegel's *Begriff* (idea or notion) with a *Vorgriff* (anticipation) of the truth that will be known only when history is complete.[68] The relativity of reason corresponds both to the contingency of God's activity and to the determination of the Creator to make humans free creatures. It also corresponds to the human experience of the historicality of reason and of the resulting anticipatory relationship to truth.

In this conception of the Trinity, the Son distinguishes himself from God the Father, and in so doing he becomes the source of everything that is distinct from the Father.

> The eternal act of the Son's self-differentiation from the Father would then contain the possibility of the separate existence of creatures. As the self-distinction of the Son from the Father is to be regarded as an act of freedom, so the contingency in the production of creatures would be in continuity with such freedom. In this way one could think of the Son as a generative principle of otherness, from which ever new creatures would come forth.[69]

Creation is rooted in the character of the relationship of the Son to the Father. This is a relationship in which the Son's self-differentiation from the Father has the character of a freely given deference to the Father as Father. This acknowledgment of the Father by the Son is best understood by the symbol of love and as mediated by the Spirit.[70]

It should be noted that while Pannenberg uses biblical symbols that emerged in a patriarchal society, these symbols point to a reality that transcends the limitations of patriarchal notions of reality. Feminine images were also used of God. All such symbols are open to distortion and are subject to the limitations asso-

ciated with the inadequacy of human understanding and goodness. Both masculine and feminine images need to be corrected
by pointing out their symbolic character. They need to be corrected by removing the biases that adhere to them in various historical settings. Neither maleness nor femaleness are essential to
the symbols. What appears to be essential to Pannenberg's use of
Father and Son is the free deferential devotion and love of a child
for the parent. This could be further developed to show that it
entails notions such as security, unconditional love, discipline,
guidance, sustenance, dependence, and more. Definitely
excluded is any notion of biological or sexual propagation. The
Son in his self-differentiating love for the Father *is* in *eternity*
both one with the Father and the source of finite reality. The Son
is this through the Spirit.

In freely differentiating himself from the Father, the Son acts
in accord with the Father. There is no tenor of disunity in the
relationship. The Spirit provides the unity that makes the differentiation possible.[71] In the same way the creation receives its
independent existence as a free act of the Trinity. It receives its
independence in the form of a free creaturely existence in distinction from the Creator. And just as in the relationship of the Son
to the Father, this freedom is not (necessarily) in discord with the
Trinity. God determines creaturely existence to be free existence, to be independent. The independence of the creature corresponds to the independence of the Son.

That there are a multitude of forms of existence within the
created order is part of the self-differentiation of finite creatures
and is grounded in the independence of the Son. This does not
necessarily nor ultimately contradict the unity of creaturely existence. The differentiation of creatures from each other is experienced through their underlying unity with each other. The strife
and conflict that too often characterize creaturely relations are a
consequence of loss of communion with God.[72] Having lost this
communion the unity of creaturely life in the Spirit is also lost
from view. Communion with God through participation in the

Spirit is only possible on the basis of agreement of creaturely self-differentiation with the self-differentiation of the Son. The Son's independence from God is most fundamentally constituted both by his recognition of the Father as God and by his continued harmony with the Father.[73]

Creaturely independence includes a capacity for misuse of freedom. Sin is the name for such misuse. One of the themes of eschatology and redemption is that God not only aims to overcome sin but has the power to do so.[74] God is all-determining and could determine creatures in an almighty way but instead chooses to enter into a history with humans. "God could rule almightily over us without our participation. He could handle humans as things. But inasmuch as God enters into a history with humans in order to reveal himself to them, he accepts them as a you (*Du*)."[75] This, says Pannenberg, amounts to the condescension of God to act in less than almighty ways for the purpose of allowing humans independent personhood. The characteristic of faithfulness here is connected with both omnipotence and condescending self-revelation. Independent human persons choose not to recognize God as Lord and Creator, and yet God chooses to remain Creator and to allow humans to continue to exist as persons. The faithfulness of God is at the root of the preservation of creation and the redeeming self-revelation of God. The upshot of human abuse of creaturely freedom, on the one hand, and God's condescending faithfulness (expressed both in the preservation of creation and in God's self-revelation), on the other hand, is the process that we experience as the history of the universe.

What Pannenberg means by the understanding of reality as history is based in his understanding of God and of the relationship of God to reality. God is the Creator "who acts freely and unrestrictedly not only in laying the foundations of the universe but also in the subsequent course of events."[76] This means that God's continuous creation of reality is characterized by contingency, for God's acts depend upon nothing except God's love.

It is not possible for us to predict the future on the basis of models of causality using our knowledge of the past and the present. God continues to act freely in history, introducing new and unexpected realities. The emergence of "regularities and persistent forms of created reality" gives expression to God's identity and faithfulness.[77] "The continuity of this creation can be characterized as the continuity of a history of God being engaged in with his creation," the end of which is perfect participation of creatures in the inner-Trinitarian love.[78]

History is the relationship that God enters into with the creation, for only in a gradual process, apart from overwhelming power, is it possible for God to determine all things toward their ultimate goal and at the same time to preserve creaturely independence. History encompasses all that occurs in the span between the fecund promise of creation and its ultimate fulfillment in the eschatological Kingdom of God. Within this span God acts in unexpected and new ways.[79] The fulfillment need not coincide exactly with the promise. For the fulfillment allows for the independent actions of creatures. History moves irreversibly forward, and God's fulfillment remains faithful to the promise by taking up the promise and revealing it in a new light.

All history finds its unity in the fact that all reality is the creative work of God. Pannenberg emphatically parts company with the efforts of Barth, Bultmann, and others who would isolate the history of God's activity (*Heilsgeschichte*) from the mundane events of (secular) history (*Geschichte*).[80] Pannenberg traces the separation of natural and supernatural realities, which underlies the separation of *Heilsgeschichte* and *Geschichte,* to the attempts of the medieval theologians to relate Christian theology and Aristotelian philosophy in a systematic account of reality. It is true, says Pannenberg, that in Thomas Aquinas's thought, nature was understood as determined by the supernatural. In seeking to harmonize Christian theology and Aristotelian physics Thomas distinguished two epistemological realms. However, Thomas's distinction between natural and supernatural realms of perception proved sufficient to ground the further separation of the realm of nature from that of the supernatural.[81]

Pannenberg is not attempting to return to an understanding of reality in which nature is understood in Greek terms or alternately in a new synthesis of Greek and Christian views of nature. His view is that Greek notions of reality have become obsolete. He is critical of both the idea of eternal ideas and the concept of an unmoved mover, both of which were variously taken up by Christian theologians.[82]   In contrast, he regards the Judeo-Christian understanding of God as the Creator of all reality—who is active in history, redeeming and remaining faithful to creation, who establishes the possibility of conceiving the unity of reality—as fundamental to the process of understanding all reality.   For Pannenberg this is also true for the historian and the scientist.[83]   In the context of this treatise it is important to point out that Pannenberg claims that the Christian understanding of creation can be tested and shows itself true in the context of modern conceptions of reality.   Furthermore, the Christian conception of creation provides a corrective to the nature-history dualism of modern thought.[84]

In the passages cited in this section, Pannenberg mostly uses the word *Geschöpf* when he speaks of the independent existence of *creatures*.   In summary, it is clear that he especially has human creatures in mind.   It also has become apparent that he does not have humans in mind apart from the rest of creation. Humans are one with created reality, and humans best represent the independence of existence in distinction from God and are best capable of bringing to expression creaturely recognition of God as God.   Such expression is most fully achieved in full consciousness of the representative character of this activity.   That humans are most able consciously to acknowledge God as God does not signify a separation of humanity from the rest of creation.   Rather, it signifies the unity of humans with the universe and indicates the special role of humans in acknowledging the otherness from and dependence on God of creaturely existence.

Love

Creation can be thought of as moving toward the end of participation in the companionship (*Gemeinschaft*) of the Father and Son through the Spirit. Pannenberg wishes to make the positive point that the appearance in history of the relationship of the Father and Son in the person of Jesus represents the actual mode of drawing the diversity of creatures into this divine relationship. The Father's love for the Son is eternal, and the Son is the primary object of the Father's love.

> The love of the Father is directed not merely to the Son but also to each of his creatures. But the turning of the Father to each of his creatures in its distinctiveness is always mediated through the Son. . . . [T]hey become the object of the Father's love because the eternal Son is manifested among them.[85]

It is not that the love of the Father for creatures corresponds with the love for the Son, but that the creatures are drawn into this eternal love. They come to participate in the relationship of Father and Son.

Just as the love of Father and Son for each other is mediated by the Spirit, so the Spirit's work is bound up with the Son's mediation between creatures and the Father. The participation of creatures in the love of the Father for the Son amounts to the transcending of the finite realities of existence. It is a transcendence of one's own finitude to "participate in God."[86] Pannenberg argues that the aim of God's creative activity is the development of independent creatures. This independence, however, is closely connected with participation in God. Apart from participation in the love of God as mediated by the Son and the Spirit existence has no powers of persistence or of the self-transcendence that is so central to human existence.[87]

The Future of Creation

Unity and Independence

Pannenberg argues that creaturely life is a process of increasing complexity and increasing capacity for self-transcendence. This process is also characterized as the expression of an increasing participation in the life of the Spirit. The goal of this evolutionary process is the realization of self-differentiation from God. Self-differentiation is dependent upon participation in the unifying Spirit of God.[88] Thus, the goal of creation is a complete realization of the independent life within unity that the Trinity itself enjoys. Creaturely existence (imperfectly) mirrors the self-differentiation of the Son from the Father and the unity of both through the Spirit. The goal of the process of creation is the perfect participation of creatures in this differentiated unity of Father, Son, and Spirit.

The independent existence of creatures is not to be swallowed up in an ultimate undifferentiated oneness. Pannenberg affirms that through that aspect of creation that is not only preservation but also the introduction of new and unexpected realities, God cares for each individual member of creation.[89]

> Every creature is itself an end in God's work of creation and therefore an end for his world government as well. But the way in which he has the good of individual creatures in view, namely, with regard for his care for all other creatures, can be very different from what the creatures themselves seek as their good.[90]

This is the point at which protests could arise regarding the nature of God's loving care for the world. Pannenberg answers that the Christian answer to this problem is the resurrection hope. Christian faith goes beyond trust in God for daily care to a hope that anticipates a final answer to all the absurdity of evil, suffering, and death. It is the ultimate realization of God's rule as expressed in the image of the coming Kingdom of God that will prove the justice and love of God's handling of history.[91] According to this hope, every aspect of reality in the totality of its history will be included, and each individual will receive justice from God. In the biblical visions of God's Kingdom the animals and plants, the sun, moon, and stars are included in this hope.[92]

Pannenberg notes that the presence of evil contradicts the claims of theology regarding God's preservation and immanent involvement in the world. However, at the heart of the expectation regarding God's reign over the world is the expectation that "even the consequences of creaturely revolt from the Creator finally have to serve God's purpose for his creation. God's skill in government shows itself in his constant ability to bring good even out of evil."[93] This remains the Christian hope until the eschatological realization of God's perfect government, that is, until nature and history are taken into the Kingdom of God.[94]

The hope for an eschatological completion (which will justify God and overcome all evil) is fundamental to Pannenberg's understanding of creation. Creation is characterized as determining reality from its future completion.[95] Creation is not primarily understood as an event associated with the primordial establishment of the universe. It is understood as a process that has its determining source in the ultimate unity of all reality with the Creator. The activity of God "should be envisioned in terms of a *continuous creative activity,* corresponding to the unity of one single, eternal act of creation that comprises the entire history of the universe."[96]

The idea that creation is associated only with the beginning of the cosmos and that the universe can be understood by analogy to a machine (i.e., that all events can be understood by means of causality) is, according to Pannenberg, contrary to the biblical belief in creation. If creation were understood as an act that was completed at the beginning of time, then all subsequent events would have to be understood in terms of the causal forces of previous events. It appears that Pannenberg's intention is to think of the relationship of God to all events in cosmic history in more direct terms than such a one-time conception of creation allows for.

> [T]he divine act of creation does not occur in time—rather, it constitutes an eternal act, contemporaneous with all time, that is, with the entire world process. Yet this world process itself has a temporal beginning, because it takes place in time.
>
> In this statement eternity is elucidated as contemporaneous with all time.[97]

This facilitates the argument of Pannenberg that reality is one creation of God.

According to Pannenberg, time is itself part of the created process. Creation is an act outside of and encompassing time and matter. Time and matter are inseparable. From the point of view of the eternal act of creation, every time and place is present in one unified reality. From the point of view of humans there are anticipatory experiences of this eternal simultaneity. The expansion of consciousness to experience a process, albeit a short one, as a unified event is analogous to the relationship of God to created reality.[98] Pannenberg describes this as a participation in eternity, and similarly finds such an anticipation in the activity of human understanding. Understanding draws knowledge together in preliminary wholes, which are derived from the anticipation of the ultimate whole that is only available from the end of the process.

Finally, it should be noted that there is neither panentheism nor pantheism in Pannenberg's thought.[99] God is not in time. Only the object of God's action exists under the limitations of processes in time. "The free origin of a lasting creation has to be viewed as the expression of an intention to create this reality that is different from his own, which has its basis in the eternity of the Creator."[100] The universe, humans included, is other than God and is intended by God to remain other, even in the eschatological unity of God's rule.

Determinism of the Future?

Pannenberg is critical of Alfred N. Whitehead's notion that God does not so much create the world as redeem it.[101] He states that there is a dualism of matter and spirit at the root of Whitehead's conception of God and world. God is conceived of neither as creating the physical universe *ex nihilo* nor as acting freely with divine power. Matter is thought of as self-originating, as independent of God.[102] Some process thinkers have in turn criticized Pannenberg for not allowing for the freedom of creatures.[103] They argue that a God who acts with such power as Pannenberg describes negates the freedom of creatures. The problem appears to lie in the active definition of freedom. Lewis Ford, for example, defines freedom as "freedom from God."[104] Pannenberg certainly does understand humans as having freedom to turn from the divine source and goal of their existence, but he would characterize this as the ultimate loss of freedom.[105] For Pannenberg true freedom is not a possession, but is given by God and is best realized in communion with God.

Pannenberg points out that Whitehead's process thought attributes to God the task of giving events (creatures) the *ideal* (initial aim) toward which they create themselves. Whitehead's God has powers to lure and to convince but not to create. Pannenberg argues that in regard to the idea of creation, Whitehead's God is further removed from the biblical notion than is Plato's demiurge.[106] On the other hand, Pannenberg does note the affinity of Whitehead's ideas of the luring and convincing of God with biblical notions of divine patience and love. Pannenberg concludes, in distinction from his interpretation of Whitehead, that these ideas, in the biblical tradition, always already presuppose that God is the one Creator of all reality. Pannenberg wishes to grant no quarter to the ontological dualism he perceives in Whitehead's thought. Events do not come to be (achieve concrescence) apart from the creative and determinative love of God. According to Pannenberg, patient and loving redemption of creatures is rooted in the powerful act of love by which the Creator grants creatures their independent existence.

Lewis Ford argues that it is unnecessary to presuppose either an end to history (which Pannenberg especially connects with the power of God) or a whole within which parts can be perceived in relation to one another. He argues that "the power of the present must unify both the power of the past ('flesh') with the power of the future ('spirit')."[107] Here it appears that process thought has only a limited capacity to provide either hope or answer for the individual who is crushed under the brutal realities of history. The claims that "straightforward apocalyptic hope is an idle dream" and that God's forever future reign provides "the opportunity for realization here and now, however fragmentary" appear to disregard those whose hopes for "here and now"[108] —and very lives as well—are cruelly annihilated in the course of history. According to Ford, the power of the past is the causal efficiency of past events and that of the future is the luring power of its possibilities. These possibilities are provided by God. The power of the present is located in the subjectivity of individual events. This formulation of reality is grounded in Whitehead's atomism, which considers "the ultimate elements of reality in terms of single occasions contingently following each other."[109] Pannenberg agrees that reality should be thought of in terms of events that are contingent rather than causally determined from the past, but he counters that this conception of reality already presupposes a whole within which the various temporal events can be understood.[110] According to Pannenberg, individual events are only understandable in contexts. Some conception of reality as a whole—as in Einstein's conception of the universe as a field—ultimately provides a cosmology that does justice to this logical necessity.[111] The realization of final wholeness is more fully expressed by Pannenberg with reference to the biblical conception of communion with God in the context of the eschatological Kingdom.[112]

A further criticism of Pannenberg's thought by the process thinkers is that his notion of a God who has created *ex nihilo* runs into the difficulty of accounting for evil.[113] Pannenberg responds by pointing out that the difficulty with the process answer to evil (limiting the power of God) is that God can no longer be depended on to overcome evil. Other powers must be assumed to stand over against God. Pannenberg prefers the difficulty of not having a way of accounting for evil in a world created *ex nihilo* by a loving God to that of a dualist metaphysics.[114] He finds it more compelling to admit that the problem of evil is beyond the capacity of humans to comprehend than to accept a limitation of God—a limitation that implies the existence of other powers that are in some way equal to and independent of God.

The real difficulty of some forms of process theology is that they offer no hope beyond death.[115] Death effectively eliminates the future. The individual is sacrificed to the eternal process. Furthermore, if individual occasions are responsible for the creation of atomistically conceived moments of reality, then the individual (ironically) loses intimate connection with the material universe. This is so because no individual has real and direct contact with more than a minute portion of reality. Individuals are dependent on others to provide such contact. Only if God is regarded as creating the world and if each one is immediately related to God as the source of her or his existence, is the individual, through the mediation of God, intimately related to all of reality. This is so, Pannenberg argues, because God is the unifying unity of the world. Apart from God there is no *world,* no whole that allows one to make anything of the individual members and events of the world.[116] It appears that the process thinker is left with hope and love that do not carry individuals to a future beyond death. It would seem that love, when it loses both its eschatological power to transcend death, as well as its determinative power in the creation of the world, becomes an abstraction. The Whiteheadian process thinker would need to show how love can be thought to have intimate contact with the world and personal contact with individuals who seem to have no future beyond death.

From this discussion it has become evident that Pannenberg thinks of God as the determining power of the future. God is regarded as all-determining in the sense of creating out of the future unity of creation with God. Although some process thinkers have argued that this concept of God eliminates creaturely freedom, Pannenberg incorporates Whiteheadian notions that focus on human freedom. Pannenberg's idea of the determination of all things from the future is not a deterministic causality in reverse.

Pannenberg also reflects on the possible correspondence of his theological-philosophical claims regarding God's all-determining and future power to the current scientific understanding of reality. For example, Pannenberg notes the correspondence of the idea that God is the unity and ground of reality with the notion that divisions in space or in time presuppose an infinite and undivided field within which divisions can exist. In modern physics, time and space are not regarded as separate realities. Their unity is expressed in the notion of field.[117] Pannenberg argues that there is a fundamental correspondence between the biblical notion of God as creative and empowering Spirit and the modern field concept that "suggests the idea of dynamic movement, of force, together with spatial and temporal extension, but without requiring a material element."[118] He argues that it is possible to imagine God "in terms of the *comprehensive field of eternity*, comprising time and space through its futurity in relation to all potential events."[119] God is here viewed as the ground and unity of all existence. And existence is viewed as a process that has its unity in a future that represents the full realization of participation in the unity of Father and Son through the Spirit.

Pannenberg differentiates his notion of the determinative power of the future from the closed character of teleology.[120] In Aristotelian teleology the end unfolds as the necessary result of the beginning. Determinative power comes to be located in the "seed" of a thing. Pannenberg's position is different. It focuses on the determinative power of the end of a process on the stages of the process.

In a similar vein, Pannenberg argues that Teilhard de Chardin's understanding of the teleological Omega point is an extrapolation of the latter's concept of evolution. This is understood as the expression of the energy that is the inherent possession of bodies. Pannenberg argues that energy needs to be thought of in connection with the Omega, which is reconceived by Pannenberg as the creative power of the future.[121]

The idea that the goal of the process already guides the process is an important notion that Pannenberg shares with Whiteheadian process thought.[122] He has, however, modified the notion of process with the ideas of creation and ultimate whole and with the field concept.[123]

> In the process of its growth the plant or animal is always this plant or this animal, although its specific nature indeed comes fully to light only in the result of its genesis. By way of anticipation it is in each instant already that which it only becomes in the process of its growth. . . . By anticipating its essential form in the process of its growth, a being's substantial identity is linked together with the notion of process.[124]

This means that what a thing is cannot be determined merely from the appearance of the thing at any stage of its process. The idea or substance of a thing is only known from the point of view of the end of its process. According to Pannenberg, it is not evolutionary causes that guide reality to the Omega point. The eschatological rule of God is the efficient cause of the coming unity of reality.[125] The end of the totality of reality, Pannenberg says, remains open, even though it has become a determining reality through the proleptic appearance of the Son's relationship with the Father in the destiny of Jesus of Nazareth.

Whole and Part

Pannenberg argues that the relationship of the categories part and whole has a fundamental significance for the human and the natural sciences. In the natural sciences the category of the whole underlies general notions such as body or point, as well as more specific notions such as atom and molecule. A whole is a unit composed of parts and is itself a part or element of larger wholes. The concept of whole is also implicit in descriptions of systems, for example in formulas.[126] In the human sciences the category of the whole is central. Humans are themselves individual wholes and "every individual appearance occurs within a context that itself is unique and that itself forms (in a certain sense) a whole in which the individual appearance has a specific, unexchangeable place."[127]

Pannenberg contends that "various levels of meaning-totalities are to be differentiated" and that these "are again related to one another as parts and wholes."[128] For example, words have meaning on their own, but in the context of a sentence their meaning becomes specific to their relations to the other words of the sentence. Similarly, a sentence can have a context that shapes its meaning. Taken together sentences, paragraphs, chapters, and volumes combine to form a meaning-totality that must be taken into account in the determination of the significance of any part of that whole. A similar structure of whole-part relationships exists in the determination of the meaning of individual events. Each event must be understood within its particular social system (semantics), is relatable to ever widening contexts, and is ultimately relatable to the totality of history. In history "the significance of individual appearances changes with time," for the whole that serves to determine the meaning of the part is a process that, as a whole, will only come into view at its end.[129]

According to Pannenberg, the individual experience and communication of meaning is first possible because there is a whole that gives the individual meaning. The notion of meaning is preliminarily determined by the relationship of whole and part. In this relationship the part is not understandable apart from its context within the whole, and the whole context of reality is determinative here.[130] For meaning does not first of all appear in the realm of human existence. The uniqueness of human existence is the capability and the drivenness of human beings beyond the scope of finite experience and knowledge to seek for coherent structures of meaning—ultimately for one system of meaning that includes and transcends all particular human experience.

Pannenberg elaborates his understanding of meaning in relation to Ernst Troeltsch and Jürgen Habermas, who seek the source of meaning in the "mechanisms of the process of communication."[131] According to Pannenberg, Troeltsch fails to realize that the dialectical relationship between the anticipations of partners in communication requires a prior consciousness of a unity of meaning. Pannenberg points out that Troeltsch's understanding of the willingness to communicate and the possibility for agreement that underlies such willingness implies that there is an anticipation of a future position that would grant the positions of the dialogue partners enduring value. If there is no hope for such a solution, then the dialogue would either lose the character of a genuine dialogue or simply never begin. The final solution represents a larger whole that is able to take previous differences into itself. Such solutions are not predetermined unities but are open to the process of dialogue and need only be partially realized in any agreement that is achieved. Pannenberg adds:

> But in every case the totality of meaning present in this sort of agreement has "metaphysical" dimensions. At least potentially, it integrates the semantic structures of the experiences and possibilities of action of the individuals involved in the communication [process] and so constitutes the unity of the social environment. Troeltsch was therefore right to let the question of the "objectivity" of historical knowledge lead him to the question of the relation of the individual to the whole in reality in general.[132]

Pannenberg argues that this leads Troeltsch to consider the relationship of the individual to the whole and that he then sees that the relationship of parts to the whole implies a unity that goes beyond the realm of psychology and sociology. He agrees with Troeltsch that this points toward a metalogical level at which every particular requires an explication that depends upon a common determination.[133]   Pannenberg agrees with Troeltsch's understanding that reflection on the process of communicative action and the question of meaning drives beyond the limits of the two social sciences in question and that it overcomes the Cartesian opposition of nature and spirit, as well as the opposition of the human and natural sciences.[134]

Pannenberg agrees with Habermas regarding the function of an anticipation of a still open future for the hermeneutical process of understanding.   But he argues that Habermas has failed to recognize that this open future is a totality of meaning that goes beyond a particular society.

> Society is not the embodiment of all reality and meaning [the position Pannenberg attributes to Habermas], but needs itself in its particular current form to be rooted and corrected by an absolute confidence of meaning which can transcend both conflicts between individual and society [Habermas's aim] and the tension between man and nature.[135]

Pannenberg continues that this all-encompassing horizon of meaning is what the religions of the world have aimed to provide.   Such a context of meaning provides for the foundation of societies by furnishing meaning and order that is not merely conventional or arbitrary.   Religions have provided means for understanding the relationship of the individual to society and for making that relationship meaningful.   This is because religion points beyond the limitations of particular concrete realizations of social order.   They provide, in other words, a vision that can serve a critical function.   Religion gives the individual a way of meaningfully relating to society even when society has become oppressive and arbitrary.

Pannenberg argues that Wilhelm Dilthey's concept of *structure* provides a way of understanding the relationship of the individual to the whole of reality.[136]   The concept of structure shows that while the whole is not merely the sum of its parts, neither is this additional element completely mysterious.   The concept of structure refers to the manner in which the whole provides the locations of the parts and relates them, not merely to each other, but to each other in the context of their individual relationship to the whole. Pannenberg argues that meaning and structures of meaning do not first of all appear in the human realm and are not limited to the realm of organic life. In his analysis humans are unique because of their capacity to experience structures of meaning (*Sinnzusammenhänge*) that transcend in an unlimited way the reality of individual existence (*Dasein*).[137] In other words, an individual is able to experience his or her life as meaningful precisely in experiencing the relatedness of individual existence to a structure of reality that transcends the individual, culture, and nature, and hence is capable of providing meaning and unity to all reality.

Pannenberg regards reality as a process that moves through time from a beginning to an end. In natural processes (such as are described by the natural sciences) the end of the process (its results) are determinative for understanding the process. Pannenberg argues that this is also true for those realities that are the focus of the human sciences. The whole within which the parts of any process are understood is accessible only through the end of the process. And since many of the processes we try to understand are unfinished, and remain unfinished as long as the future remains open, the end is only available by means of anticipations.[138]

The whole and the end of temporal processes are not available to us except by means of (anticipatory) extrapolations. However, the open character of history makes it impossible to determine the ultimate end of anything by means of extrapolation from what is known of the past and the present. The process is open to the appearance of unforeseen, new realities. These new realities, argues Pannenberg, are never fully explainable on the basis of the past alone. The parts, because of the unity of individual existence, bear within themselves a *Vorgriff* (an anticipation) of the end. This anticipation of the end of reality plays a fundamental role in all human understanding (*Verständnis*): the end that is anticipated is a meaningful structure that includes the self within the whole of reality.[139] Thus, according to Pannenberg, the proleptic presence of ultimate truth is needed to claim that any present understanding of reality is an anticipation and approximation of that truth.[140]

Pannenberg notes that this totality of meaning (*Sinntotalität*), like the question of truth, depends on correspondence to reality, coherence with all that is known, and the consensus of competent observers.[141] Both natural and human sciences are directed toward the expression, as near as is possible, of a systematic understanding of the whole of reality, logically and without contradictions.[142] These systematic claims to truth must be open to revision. They are anticipatory claims.[143]

The whole refers to the world or the universe or universal history. It is not God, for it is not self-constituted. Rather, it presupposes a unifying ground that is "distinct from the totality of the finite" that this whole represents.[144] Pannenberg conceives God as distinct but not absolutely distinct from the world. God is the source of both the unity that can be understood as a whole and the individual creatures that make up this totality of reality. Pannenberg points out that this conception of God as the "unifying unity of the world" must preserve the distinctness of God from the world.[145] God is neither the sum nor the highest instance of reality. God is the source of all reality, as well as of its unity.

Exactly how God is understood as the "unifying unity" that will come fully into view only at the end of the process of creation, while also overcoming the often brutal realities of individual existence, is answered by the Son in the person of Jesus. The perfection of the unity is not a reality that is available within history apart from Jesus of Nazareth's resurrection. The unity remains a future reality, but toward that reality all creation moves. Pannenberg argues that God determines reality from the future unity of the Kingdom. Within the limitations of reality "it remains true that the actual process of history devours individuals and empires rather than bringing them to harmonious completion as parts of a meaning-whole."[146] The independent existence of creatures is finite. Creaturely transcendence of this finitude depends on the special work of the Spirit. Just as the Spirit is the unity of Father and Son so the Spirit creates the unity of creation and redeeming Creator. The incarnation of the Son in Jesus of Nazareth brings the goal of creation into the historical process itself. The Spirit of God brings the ultimate purpose of existence near to each individual by revealing the unifying power of love, and this in the resurrection of Jesus.

Pannenberg argues against all attempts to get beyond this proleptic and anticipatory presence of the whole. He characterizes his own position as insisting upon the recognition of the anticipatory and therefore necessarily abstract character of

> all knowledge of the whole in a world that has not yet been completed and reconciled to the whole. To this corresponds the consciousness of the difference of the world from God—a difference that, to be sure, must not be hardened into a dualism since this would result in making God himself finite; yet one that, as the condition of the unity of any creature with God, will not be transcended and eliminated even in the eschaton.[147]

Pannenberg is careful to preserve the individual's significance as an end in him or herself. And he does so without sacrificing the unity of reality. His understanding of the Trinity as the differentiation of persons within loving unity is his model for conceiving the relationship of the world to its Creator.

Nature and History

Contingence and Regularity

According to Pannenberg, the inexact or preliminary character of the formulation of natural laws is rooted in the nature of reality.[148] The lawfulness (*Gesetzmäßigkeit*) of nature is limited by the contingency of natural events.[149] This is the result of the unique and irreversible character of nature's processes. The application of natural laws is necessarily relative to time and space.

Pannenberg argues that this corresponds to the idea of creation, which itself implies that all of reality is contingent on the free action of God.[150] This, says Pannenberg, also corresponds to ancient Israel's experience of God's actions in its history. It corresponds to the idea of prayer. History is not predetermined, but is open to the appearance of new and unexpected realities, which are the creative work of God. Pannenberg's point is that in the observations of both the natural sciences and the religious traditions, reality is characterized by contingency and that this corresponds to the idea of a God who is God of all reality.

The contingency that Pannenberg has in mind is the unexplainable element, in terms of causality, in the appearance of new realities in history. When something new appears in the world, something that cannot be explained simply in terms of past events, something that from that time on displays a dependable continuity, then the creative work of God has become visible. This creative and contingent activity is the basis of the durability of new realities. Pannenberg describes the appearance of new forms of orderliness as the creative action of divine love.[151]

Years later, in his *Systematic Theology*, Pannenberg makes the point regarding contingency more confidently and with more support. The dialogue between physics and theology has progressed, and Pannenberg is able to point to some agreement regarding the notion that contingency is a phenomenon at the boundary of the nomological (natural) sciences. There is agreement that the laws of physics, as well as the reality—"the open process character of natural events"—that these laws seek to describe, are contingent.[152] Pannenberg points out that contingence appears only as a lack of determination in events and realities. Thus, it is not possible for science to develop nomological descriptions of contingence. It represents the starting point for philosophical and theological reflection regarding the nature of physical reality. From a theological point of view, the philosophical concept of contingency can be regarded as the creative activity of the God of love.

Pannenberg argues that the contingency of reality does not conflict with the constancy of form in which events occur.[153] Natural laws are abstracted from the individual realities they describe.[154] They are based on static observations of contingent events. Thus, the scientist works in a situation in which the validity of the general laws and hypotheses of science are dependent on the contingency of both the events themselves and the decisions of the experimenter.[155]

Not only the contingent character of reality but also its regularities must be definable as the work of God. The dependence of regularity on contingency must be verifiable from within a natural scientific description of the world. Only in this way will it be possible to regard God as the Creator of the world—in both its contingency and its regularities.[156] We have seen that Pannenberg connects the contingency of reality with the creative freedom of God. He also connects the basic regularities of nature—which allow for the rise of life in ever new and more complex forms—with God's trustworthiness in preserving creation. Finally, he connects the cosmic process and the one-way irreversibility of time with the God of history (i.e., with the biblical notion of the God who makes promises and fulfills them).[157] This linking of theology and science takes place at the level of philosophical and theological reflection and would never lead to evidence of God's existence that would be acceptable to the natural sciences. The function of such reflection is to show the coherence of a scientific description of the world with a Christian description of the world as the creation of the God we read about in the Bible.[158]

If one regards the laws of nature as themselves grounded on contingency and functional within open systems—i.e., these laws describe realities that did not always exist and will at some point in time cease to exist, and therefore the laws are historically relative—then it is no longer nonsense to admit that God can act in ways that brings about new and unexpected realities. On the other hand, the natural laws describe the existence of regularities that make the independent existence of creatures possible. Thus, these regularities express the faithfulness of God toward the creation.[159]

One consequence of the view that the universe had a beginning is that unless one wishes to regard the natural laws discovered by science in terms of eternal ideas, of which the natural universe then is a slightly imperfect copy, one must regard these laws as themselves part of the changing cosmos. Pannenberg tries to follow this line of thinking in arguing that God's faithfulness or trustworthiness is the ground of the regularities that natural laws describe. The regularities that do occur in nature do so in the context of a contingent universe in which all events have an element of contingency. Even causality, argues Pannenberg, cannot simply be accepted as we normally think of it. He agrees with Hume's analysis that causality does not so much describe the power of A to bring about B (in the context of a hypothesis "if A then B"), as it describes a relationship between A and B. This reliable relationship, says Pannenberg, must have had a first occurrence at some point within time. Only after the first occurrence of B after A did this relationship become a regularity, describable by laws. Therefore, it should be thought of as depending on B. "In this sense, the connection of events between the two is constituted backward from B."[160] Pannenberg also intends this as an argument in support of the ontological priority of the future, but he is here arguing that the relative or contingent nature of reality, even in its regularities, is not self-explanatory. It leads beyond itself to philosophical and religious questioning.

The unity of history and nature is found in the trustworthiness of God, which provides for the continuity and wholeness within which it is possible to distinguish (*einteilen*) relationships between individual realities.[161] Pannenberg characterizes the trustworthiness of God as the sameness of God in that God remains true to his earlier works ("*in seinem Festhalten an seinem früheren Werken*").[162] This gives reality its form and unity.[163]

Anthropocentrism?

Pannenberg points out that apart from humans the world can, therefore, be described in terms of natural laws. Its continuity is lawful (*Gesetzlich*) rather than historical. Both human and natural worlds have the character of a unique and irreversible process. Both are historical processes in this sense. However, the nonhuman world has no awareness of this historicality. Pannenberg suggests that one can perhaps speak of a historical form of relationship that bridges the evolution of organic life from nonorganic forms of reality, and that this is connected with an increasing significance of individual existence with the more complex forms of organic life.[164] Furthermore, humans too are part of the processes of nature. Pannenberg concludes that this universal process has a history that must be understood in anthropocentric terms. "Only in this sense is it possible to speak of a history of nature. This is not a history of nature by itself apart from the human being; rather, it is a history of nature directed to the human being."[165] But this history does not have its unity in or through humans. The unity of all history is grounded only in the experience of the divine ground of all reality.[166]

History and nature are united only in God, "who has ordained the contingent sequence of forms [of existence] toward the human being so that this sequence can be conceived as a meaningful connection of occurrences backward, a sequence that is shaped and perfected by human recognizing and acting."[167] It is not through human perception and mastery of nature that the world process receives its history. God is the one who provides the continuity and regularity that allows for regular relationships to exist. In this way it is possible for new events to shed light on earlier events and relationships. Thus, a larger context of events is grounded.

This understanding of history is theocentric, but it continues to regard humans as the most significant creatures.

> It is first with the emergence of humans and with the appropriation of nature through humans that the world process as a whole working backwards from humans achieves its coherence in itself. This happens through human knowledge of nature, as well as through the dominion over nature which is connected with it.[168]

This statement reflects Pannenberg's positive regard for the scientific investigation of reality. It could perhaps be misunderstood as a justification of the continued abusive domination of nature. However, this statement must be read in the larger context of the essay in which it occurs and of Pannenberg's other works. The central point of this essay, the overcoming of the dualism of nature and spirit, is a significant step in providing grounds for countering the negative consequences of this dualism. Furthermore, Pannenberg's understanding of dominion is anything but a justification for the abusive use of nature. Thus, the statement affirms the role of human dominion in taking all non-human reality into the central theme of creation: the creaturely realization of the inner-Trinitarian love. This certainly results in a reconception of the idea of dominion.

In the essay "Theology and Science" Pannenberg's theological reflections on modern conceptions of the universe conclude with a discussion of the anthropic principle.[169] Here he argues that the

> process of cosmic expansion looks like the instrument of the Creator to produce the conditions for the emergence of increasingly complex and increasingly independent creatures—all the way to the self-organization of organic life and to the emergence of human beings at the end of the evolutionary process.[170]

In the "Big Bang" model of the universe the continuing expansion of the universe after the initial explosive expansion created the necessary space and allowed for the cooling off that is essential for the emergence of a multitude of life forms. This is one of the basic factors that contributes to the theory that the development of the universe appears to be governed by a final cause—the emergence of intelligent life. Pannenberg admits the speculative nature of these hypotheses.[171] Nonetheless, he is able to point to a remarkable correspondence between several variations of this modern view and his interpretation of the biblical account of reality.[172] From minute aspects of the conditions of the Big Bang, to many other incidents in natural history, virtually negligible differences would have made the emergence of human life impossible. This suggests to Pannenberg, looking back reflectively from the perspective of human history, a purposiveness to the entire process. Previous events and their meaning are taken up into a more complete view of reality. This reflective activity of Pannenberg itself corresponds with the backward-working purposiveness that Pannenberg perceives in the Christian expectation of communion with God. In other words, Pannenberg, the twentieth-century theologian, can be seen as participating reflectively in the process of taking nature into the religious (ultimate) meaning of history. Pannenberg's argument is that the future has an ontological priority, which is seen in the reinterpretation of past events in the light of later and more universal horizons. He also argues that this can be shown to correspond with significant aspects of the anthropic principle.

This implies that the meaning of nature cannot be exhausted, and may be entirely missed, by the abusive practices of modern culture. In other words, if nature is conceived primarily in the utilitarian and often arbitrary manner of modern materialist culture, then its broader significance—even for human history—cannot be perceived. Pannenberg's contention is that this broader significance most clearly becomes available in the context of a theological conception of universal history.

Pannenberg regards reality as determined from the point of view of a future communion of creation with God. This companionship finds its fullest expression in the relationship of humans with God through Jesus of Nazareth. Pannenberg intends to bring to expression the notion that the process character of reality is grounded in the Trinitarian character of the act of creation: the Father creates, the Son redeems, and the Spirit brings eschatological completion.[173] The act of creation is understood to encompass all reality, from its beginning to its end. And it proceeds from the eschatological realization of perfect communion of creatures with the Creator.

Pannenberg's emphasis on the role of the Spirit in creation also focuses on humanity: "The Lord God . . . breathed into his nostrils the breath [*nephesh*] of life."[174] Pannenberg is careful to point out that this does not relate primarily to mind or intelligence. The work of the Spirit is to create a living soul, and soul signifies the living being. This living being is a creature that is alive through its dependence upon God, who is the source in terms of both origin and continuation of this existence.[175] In a manner that distinguishes human beings from the other creatures, the Spirit uniquely makes humans into living beings.

Pannenberg follows the biblical tradition in claiming that the fulfillment of creaturely existence is to praise God and that this is especially to be fulfilled by humans.[176] He argues that this focus on humans is the conclusion to be drawn from both the modern scientific and the biblical understanding of the sequential emergence of forms of life, culminating with the emergence of human life.[177] If Pannenberg indeed intends to overcome the modern dualism (and he does claim this as his intention), how can he also wish to show a correspondence between this presentation of a Christian conception of reality and that of the modern sciences, which emerged in the context of Cartesian dualism?

To show such a correspondence would be a problem if the modern sciences themselves continued to operate under the assumption of the dualism of nature and spirit. However, the strength of Pannenberg's efforts to overcome this dualism from the point of view of theology and philosophy is augmented by the fact that modern science has itself begun to reject such dualism. Even the anthropic principle, which at first glance appears to mark the conceited height of anthropocentrism, upon reflection may show itself to negate the opposition of spirit and nature. For it seems that if one understands humans to be at the pinnacle of an evolutionary process, one certainly cannot then radically distinguish humans from the rest of the creatures and realities that make up the process. Humans together with all nonhuman reality make up one process. Humans are seen in their dependence on the process, and this means dependence on all parts of the whole that the process is. What gives the anthropic interpretation of the universe the persuasive power it possesses is the narrowness of the window of possibility for the evolution of reality as we know it. This narrowness implies that each part of the whole is significant to the existence of the whole. And this further implies that each part must be regarded as an end in itself. It also implies that each part cannot be regarded as an end apart from a similar valuing of all the other parts. That there is differentiation among the parts does not negate the fundamental significance of each part.

To this analysis of Pannenberg's notion of creaturely unity I would add that, in addition to the biblical focus on humans, it also must be noted that the Bible contains curious remarks such as Jesus' statement that "the very stones would cry out" the praises withheld by the people.[178] That the heavens and the earth participate in declaring the praises of Jahweh[179] implies a continuity of purpose, and even of existence, between what we normally regard as two very different types of being: inorganic and human. Modern science and the Bible regard humans as the highest level of organic life. Yet there is a unity of existence in the origin, continuation, and purpose of existence. In a manner that is consistent with this, Pannenberg regards humans as the apex of the creaturely world. Humans have the capacity to express most consciously, freely, and with greatest creativity the praises of God. Humans have a language with which they can praise the Creator on behalf and alongside of the whole creation. That St. Francis of Assisi names other creatures his sisters and brothers and admonishes them to praise their Creator and Redeemer is not merely a charming notion of a somewhat strange but saintly character. Seen in the context of this argument, it could be received as a realization of a fundamental truth about the character of reality.

Moral Implications

Pannenberg also points out the significance of the moral implications of this understanding of God's relationship to the world. Before spelling out these consequences, it may be useful to restate the main points of his understanding of creation. First, creation is a threefold (origin, preservation and immanent divine self-involvement, and perfection), unified process. It is the work of the Trinity, with each person contributing to the process. The Father brings a world into existence out of nothing. The Son redeems the world. The Spirit brings everything to its fulfillment. Second, the relationship of this world to the Father is cast in terms of the relationship of the Son to the Father through the Spirit. Creatures have their value in a manner like to that of the Son. Participation of creatures in the oneness of the Trinity depends on their participation in the Son's loving acknowledgment of the Father as God. Creatures are independent and are free either to acknowledge or not to acknowledge the Father as God. Loving acknowledgment and participation are one, and praise is the form of acknowledgment.

Acknowledgment of God involves the acknowledgment of the multitude of other members of the creation, each standing independently within the relationship of the one creation to its ultimate goal—participation in the Son's relationship with the Father.[180] Inasmuch as creatures fail to acknowledge God they also fail to acknowledge the independent good of others. In other words, they use other creatures and things to serve their own less than ultimate ends. This could also be stated in reverse order, although it is the acknowledgment and love of God that remains prior. Inasmuch as a creature uses others as a means apart from these others' independent intrinsic relationship to God, the creature fails to acknowledge God. These formulations express the twofold nature of love[181] as it is seen through its application in 1 John 3:11-24 and 4:7-13: The one "who does not love [his or her neighbor] does not know God; for God is love."[182]

It needs to be pointed out that acknowledgment of God as God, as found in Pannenberg, is understood only in terms of the acknowledgment by the Son of the Father as Father. This self-differentiation is a humble act of love and devotion. It is not the acknowledgment of the demons who shudder in fear but neither love nor obey.[183] The eternal Son's loving acknowledgment—through the Spirit—of the Father is the central and founding reality.

Pannenberg regards "mutually acknowledging" love as the foundation of the positive laws that make community life possible. In love "God's future gains power over individuals and enables them to fulfill their destiny in relation to one another. Here the creative freedom of the imagination is alive."[184] Pannenberg suggests that the "imagination of love" motivates "truly rational behavior" in the quest of love to overcome concrete social problems.[185] Through the development of creative solutions new forms of community can be founded. In this way loving acknowledgment functions as the root of laws that enable, rather than oppress, members of a community. Pannenberg appears to point beyond the human world to include the non-human world as part of the universal community of God's creation in which this imaginative power of love is active.[186] Whether such inclusive wholeness is his intention in this particular essay is not crucial. There are many other works in which Pannenberg is explicit regarding his intention to include all reality in the eschatological creation of God and, hence, in the religious and moral aspects of human destiny.

Thus, in Pannenberg's understanding it is not eternally valid laws or ordinances of creation that ground morality and law. It is the eschatological power of love that always seeks to bring redemptive and freeing possibilities to concrete situations and that grounds social norms. According to Pannenberg, only the faithfulness of divine love "is the basis for permanence and reliability."[187] Creative and eschatological love is the foundation of ethics, but it is always an ethic in transition toward and submission to the realization of the eschatological Kingdom of God. Pannenberg insists that, within history, there are no legal and political realizations of love that can be permanently institutionalized.

The discussions of the priority of meaning and of the whole for the individual are significant for the consideration of political morality. Pannenberg argues that if one considers meaning as the production of individual action and communication, as does Habermas for example, then there is no possibility for the criticism of political systems, for these must then also be considered to be the expressions of individuals and groups of individuals. In this case political systems would never be more than the expression of those who happen to have more power than others. Political systems of norms must then be ultimately experienced as oppressive and capricious. Each political system, says Pannenberg, requires legitimation through "*Weltbilder.*" These visions of the world as a meaningful whole provide both the legitimation of and the opportunity for criticism of any particular social order. The fact that the truth of worldviews remains controversial and open to revision does not alter the fact of their priority over individual constructions and experiences of meaning.[188] Such worldviews must aim to integrate all of reality to overcome individual capriciousness. This is, however, always only possible in a preliminary (*vorgängige*) manner.

Pannenberg favorably cites Jürgen Moltmann's interpretation of the universal historical perspective. For both Moltmann and

Pannenberg the "still outstanding end of all things" is understood as the salvific opening of the future to the whole of the mortal world. The individual, society, and nature (nonhuman reality) are included in this salvation. Pannenberg agrees with Moltmann's political application of this understanding of the end of history.

> Because this anticipation of the end of history, as an "anticipation of the deliverance of all things, discloses a future for our mortal bodies, for society, and for nature," it includes, as Moltmann rightly stresses, the political idea of the "liberation of every enslaved creature" and this becomes his starting-point for a "political hermeneutic."[189]

Pannenberg does not explicitly take up a political hermeneutic. He does, however, agree with Moltmann's political application of the anticipated salvific and unifying end of history to all creatures. Pannenberg, however, expresses concern that a specifically political hermeneutic will lose sight of its own limitations and become a tool of oppression.[190]

The significant point here is that Pannenberg sees religion and/or quasi-religious systems of thought as providing for a horizon of meaning that goes beyond the conflicts between individuals and between human culture and the nonhuman world. Religion provides a horizon of meaning that seeks to overcome all the conflicts between the various aspects of reality. All systems, processes, events, and individuals are included in the horizon of meaning provided by religion. This is not to say that every religion and philosophy or every particular form of any one of these fulfills this function equally. Pannenberg's argument is that the Judeo-Christian understanding of creative and redemptive divine love best fulfills this function.

Pannenberg also has argued the contextual—historical, social, and beyond that universal—nature of all scientific endeavors. At one important level the context is that of the worldview or paradigm. Each attempt to express a systematic analysis of some aspect of reality moves within paradigmatic models for understanding reality as a whole. Some of these attempts push beyond the limits of operative paradigms and result in the need to revise the paradigms in question.[191] In these pages Pannenberg analyzes T. S. Kuhn's work on the idea of paradigm change. Pannenberg's own efforts, it appears, are aimed at just such a revision, namely, to contribute to the overthrow of the modern opposition of nature and spirit that has played such a significant role in post-Enlightenment thought.

This has significant moral implications. A new, more comprehensive view of reality along the lines suggested by Pannenberg would include the consideration of religious and moral aspects of experience as inescapably real and as inseparable from those pursuits of scientific curiosity that are directed at the physical universe. A paradigmatic model for a systematic integration of experience that includes these "spiritual" realities and that does not permit a dualism of spirit and nature implies that human actions in and upon the physical world are subject to a demand for correspondence to these spiritual realities. The compartmentalization of life into mutually exclusive and even opposed aspects does not correspond to the unity and wholeness that the scientific endeavor, in any field whatsoever, both presupposes and strives for. The anticipatory vision of ultimate truth provides for the necessary openness to criticize all social and political failures to measure up to that vision. It also provides, in the form of experienced wholeness, the ground for human curiosity to pursue systematic understanding.

It is clear that the conception of systematic and reflective understanding that is operative in Pannenberg's thought is informed by a special theological notion of unity. The systematic understanding that Pannenberg refers to is connected with a divine unity that includes all reality in itself and is identified with truth. All attempts to develop systematic structures of understanding, say in a particular field of knowledge, which attempt to integrate various bits of information into a meaningful structure, are efforts that can be combined with parallel efforts in other fields of knowledge. These models of reality can be further integrated in ever larger wholes until all that is known and experienced of reality is included.

Pannenberg's vision of unity moves in this direction and beyond the best achievements of humans toward a unity that, not only in knowledge but in reality, will include absolutely everything, subsuming all contradictions that have arisen along the way. Pannenberg's argument is that this ultimate unity is already a fundamental element of experience and that it makes knowledge possible. Differentiation presupposes unity. Knowledge, even partial knowledge, of particular aspects of reality presupposes a unity of experience and reality within which such knowledge can arise.

Pannenberg's system is an open-ended understanding of reality. It allows room for an open future that is determined neither by the past nor by logical necessity. It leaves room for the creative freedom of God and of humans. Pannenberg's idea of unity is founded on the Judeo-Christian idea of a God who creates all reality in love. Love is the power that is both the presently experienced unity of reality and the determinative power of the future realization of this unity. The future is open because divine love has determined humans to be capable of participating in love's creative work.

There is also a significant implication here for the methodology of the natural sciences. A. M. Klaus Müller points out that Pannenberg's argument—that the element of contingency that is present in both the practice of science and in the real world—results in a need for further evolution of the philosophy and practice of the empirical sciences. This, says Müller, is necessary not merely for the sake of further advancing knowledge or satisfying scientific curiosity but also because it is dangerous to continue to ignore the repercussions of a technical and physically standardized approach to the world.[192] Müller then cites the example of modern medicine, which treats individual humans as a category of physics. Medicinal practice today consequently ignores what it is that makes individuals human. There is, therefore, a critical element in Pannenberg's argument that the world as a whole is an irreproducible process and that contingency is a fundamental element of this process. Pannenberg's argument implies the need for a critical reflection on the fundamental assumptions and practices of the modern natural sciences and the technological branches of human activity that are dependent on these sciences. The mechanical positivist conceptions of the universe ignore the individual and process character of real objects/events in time and space. This has had certain negative consequences in specific applications such as medicine, agriculture, and industry, where some of the repercussions of our technology have had extremely negative effects.

But the critical force of Pannenberg's argument regarding contingency is not sufficiently felt until the source of contingency is considered. We have seen that Pannenberg regards contingency as rooted in the free and loving creativity of God. Pannenberg understands the contingent process of reality to be created from the goal of unity with the love of God. Each creature is loved and valued by God from this point of view. New creatures come (contingently) into existence as part of the whole toward which all creation is moving. The perspective of divine love and valuation needs to inform the generalizing character of the natural sciences. Pannenberg's understanding of reality calls for love to characterize the relationships of humans with each other and with each creature. The quest for general laws that govern existence must be humanized by love for individual creatures.

Pannenberg's argument has unexplored implications regarding the application of the results of experimentation to the alteration of the natural world and in the production of goods for public consumption. Experiences of the past several hundred years, in which the results of science have been rushed into production, show the truth of Pannenberg's observation. Scientists have not always known enough about their discoveries to be aware of all the repercussions and implications of these gains in knowledge.

Certainly it must be acknowledged that financial interests, fear, vengeance, greed, and other human vices have played a major role in the practical application of scientific knowledge.[193] However, our awareness of this must not obscure the fact that the positivist opposition of scientific methodology to nonhuman nature itself bears responsibility for the existence of a blindness to the limitations of modern science. Scientists have begun to recognize that all our knowledge remains very limited. This is especially true of the complex and far-reaching interrelationships that compose the world of living creatures.[194]

David McKenzie agrees that Pannenberg's argument implies a fundamental and critical acknowledgment of the limitations of scientific methodology. He concludes that "Pannenberg asks for a critical approach even to the revered natural laws of modern science."[195] Pannenberg's argument is that there is no perfect knowledge of any reality. The fact that reality is a process and that the process is unfinished and its end unknown requires the acknowledgment of the incompleteness of the endeavor, to become aware of the entire context within which any one event or reality is to be understood. This also indicates that the end of the process, if one accepts Pannenberg's arguments regarding the goal of history, can serve a critical and a motivational function.[196] In other words, in light of the concepts of creation and world and the ultimate goal of unity with divine love, broader questions of relationships, interdependence, and value must be addressed at various levels of scientific inquiry. These types of questions become even more significant when the large-scale application of new discoveries is considered.

Conclusion

Although Pannenberg's understanding of the Trinity and of creation is characterized by careful reasoning and argumentation within the context of a thorough familiarity with the theological and philosophical tradition, it would be a mistake to think of it as rationalistic. Pannenberg is aware of the limitations of metaphysics, but he has not conceded to Heidegger and others that metaphysical thinking is no longer possible. His claim to truth is a claim that admits its historical relativity but stands on the systematic coherence and correspondence to the experience of reality that the presentation is able to achieve. Pannenberg does not operate purely within the assumptions of a particular school of thought. He does not simply dismiss conflicting positions regarding the character of reality. He engages in a critical dialogue that he hopes is open to the discovery of truth beyond the limitations of any one dogma. Through this open and critical dialogue he hopes to establish the truth of the Christian claim regarding existence and God. This in turn would establish moral thought.

Pannenberg's theology is Trinitarian, and as such it focuses on the inner-Trinitarian relationship of Father and Son as mediated by the Spirit. Creation, redemption, and fulfillment are conceived in terms of this relationship, which is characterized by the love of the Son for the Father. Just as both the Trinitarian process and the Trinity are one reality, so the creation is one totality. For only if the Creator is one is it possible to think of creation as a united and uniting process. Reality is a totality that entails a process spread out through time-space, and within it are found a multitude of finite processes. What makes one reality of these multifarious processes is the unifying love of God, which is not only the origin but also the "final destiny and consummation" of all creation.[197] Each process is linked to all other processes and to the whole of reality in its immediate participation in the creative love of the Trinity. Pannenberg has described reality as fundamentally religious and moral, and he has sought to eliminate any dualism that would limit human responsibility to what is merely one aspect of a world that is only first known in its unity.

NOTES

1. In 1959 ("Heilsgeschehen und Geschichte") Pannenberg applied the notion of a process beginning with the divine promise and moving toward its fulfillment to describe the idea of history. Later he modifies this by pointing out that the promises are themselves transformed by unforseen events, and thus their fulfillment can only be "affirmed in a way that deviates from their original literal meaning." This is cited from Pannenberg's "Response to the Discussion," *Theology as History (New Frontiers in Theology*, vol. 3), ed. James M. Robinson and John B. Cobb, Jr. (New York: Harper & Row, 1967), 259. The idea of *Überlieferungsgeschichte* is understood by Pannenberg as fundamentally informing the conception of promise and fulfillment. This change came before the publication of Pannenberg et al., *Offenbarung als Geschichte* (Göttingen, 1961)—the English translation is *Revelation as History*, trans. David Granskou (New York: Macmillan, 1968). Hereafer *OG* and *RH*. The change is elaborated in "Kerygma und Geschichte," in *GF* 1:79-90; *BQ* 1:81-95. See *GF* 1:9; *BQ* 1:xvii; and Polk, *On the Way to God*, 61.

2. See for example Gen. 31:19 and Isa. 66:1-2.

3. For a fuller account of the development of monotheism see, for example, Gerhard von Rad, *Old Testament Theology*, vol. 1, trans. D. M. G. Stalker (London: SCM, 1975), 203-12. See also Pannenberg, *GF* 1:268-71, 308f.; *BQ* 2:85-88, 134-36.

4. *STe* 2:11. "Durch Zurückführung auch der kosmischen Ordnung und ihres Ursprunges auf den Gott der Heilsgeschichte wurde die Unumschränktheit der in seinem geschichtlichem Handeln sich manifestierenden Macht dargetan" (*ST* 2:25).

5. See for example Lev. 25-26; Deut. 10-11; Amos 5.

6. Deut. 6:5; *ST* 2:25.

7. *ETN*, 42; *TTN*, 81.

8. *ETN*, 46; *TTN*, 85.

9. *ETN*, 46f.; *TTN*, 86.

10. *STe* 2:11. "Das Universum ist in Natur und Geschichte gleichermaßen das 'Handlungsfeld' Jahwes" (*ST* 2:26).

11. Isa. 43-48.

12. *ST* 2:29; *STe* 2:15.

13. Acts 4:24-30.

14. *ST* 2:224-28; *STe* 2:194-99.

15. *GF* 1:77; *BQ* 1:79.

16. *OG*, ix-xv.

17. *BQ* 2:1; *GF* 1:202. Cf. also the introduction to *WT*, 7-26; *TPS*, 3-22.

18. *GF* 1:203f.; *BQ* 2:3.

19. *BQ* 2:9. "[D]er griechische Dualismus zwischen wahrem Sein und wechselndem Sinnenschein [ist] im biblischen Wahrheitsverständnis überholt . . .: Hier ist das wahre Sein selbst nicht als zeitlos, sondern als geschichtlich

gedacht, und es erweist seine Beständigkeit durch eine Geschichte, deren Zukunft immer noch offen ist. . ." (*GF* 1:208f.).

20. *GF* 1:209; *BQ* 2:9f.

21. *GF* 1:213-14; *BQ* 2:15-17.

22. *WT*, 72f., 43f.; *TPS*, 70f., 42f.

23. "Die Physik auf dieser Reflexionsstufe beschreibt daher nicht mehr einfach Eigenschaften von seienden Objekten, sondern einzig die Resultate von Experimenten." Müller, "Über philosophischen Umgang mit exakter Forschung und seine Notwendigkeit," in *Erwägungen zu einer Theologie der Natur*, 23.

24. *WT*, 44; *TPS*, 42f.

25. *IGHF*, 93.

26. *ST* 1:354f.; *STe* 1:326f.

27. Pannenberg, *Theology and the Kingdom of God* (Philadelphia: Westminster, 1969), 63. Hereafter *TKG*.

28. Cf. Pannenberg, "Probleme einer trinitarischen Gotteslehre," in *Weisheit Gottes—Weisheit der Welt*, ed. W. Baier (St. Ottilien: EOS, 1987), 333. Pannenberg is critical of Moltmann's notion of the monarchy of the Father. Pannenberg's own Trinitarian theology seeks to understand the three persons of the Trinity in relational equality.

29. *ST* 1:354ff.; *STe* 1:326ff.

30. *ST* 1:359; *STe* 1:331.

31. *STe* 1:438. "Wenn Ewigkeit und Zeit erst in der eschatologischen Vollendung der Geschichte koinzidieren, dann ist unter dem Gesichtspunkt der Geschichte Gottes auf jene Vollendung hin Raum für ein Werden in Gott selbst, nämlich im Verhältnis von immanenter und ökonomischer Trinität, und in diesem Rahmen ist es dann auch möglich, von Gott zu sagen, daß er selber etwas wurde, was er zuvor nicht war, als er in seinem Sohne Mensch wurde" (*ST* 1:472f.).

32. E. Frank Tupper, *The Theology of Wolfhart Pannenberg* (Philadelphia: Westminster, 1971), 193f., 199. See also Grenz, *Reason for Hope*, 50.

33. See Michael Schulz, "Zur Hegelkritik Wolfhart Pannenbergs und zur Kritik am 'Antizipationsgedanken' Pannenbergs im Sinne Hegels," *Münchener Theologische Zeitschrift* 43, 2 (1992): 208f.

34. Cf. Polk, *On the Way to God*, 270-80, 287. Polk argues that Pannenberg does not allow for human self-determination. He cites a recorded conversation with Pannenberg (10-21-82) in which Pannenberg states the following: "If the human person is a *creature* of God, so [sic] everything that belongs to that creature, including its self-creative, self-determining potential, is already an effect of the work of the Creator" (the conversation is cited in *On the Way to God*, 313n262). Polk can be criticized for failing to note the change in perspective when speaking of divine and human determination. In this context one should perhaps interpret Pannenberg in a manner similar to Mary Potter Engel's interpretation of Calvin (*John Calvin's Perspectival*

Anthropology [Atlanta: Scholars, 1988], 1-10). Potter notes that seeming contradictions in Calvin's assertions regarding predestination on one hand and human responsibility on the other hand are attributable to changes in perspective from divine to human (139-44).

35. *GF* 1:393; *BQ* 2:242.
36. *Ibid.*
37. See Pannenberg, "Probleme einer trinitarischen Gotteslehre," 338f.
38. *ST* 1:359; *STe* 1:331.
39. See Tupper, *The Theology of Wolfhart Pannenberg*, 204f.
40. *TKG*, 63.
41. John O'Donnell, "Pannenberg's Doctrine of God," *Gregorianum* 72, 1 (1991): 87-90. The quotation is from page 88.
42. *ST* 1:387; *STe* 1:357.
43. "In ihm [dem einzelnen Daseinsmoment] kommt das Wesen der Sache *nur* zur *Erscheinung*" (*ST* 1:387). O'Donnell omits the "*nur*." The emphasis of *Erscheinung* is Pannenberg's. Bromiley translates as follows: "The essence simply finds manifestation or appears in it" (*STe* 1:357). Bromiley does not show Pannenberg's emphasis of *Erscheinung* (manifestation).
44. "The individual manifestation is distinct from the essence. . . . If the manifestations are to be viewed as a series, their totality can be defined only in anticipation of the completed sequence. . ." (*STe* 1:358). ("Die einzelne Erscheinung ist vom Wesen verschieden. . . . Sind die Erscheinungen als eine Reihe aufzufassen, so ist deren Totalität nur durch Antizipation ihrer ganzen Abfolge . . . bestimmt") (*ST* 1:388). See also Pannenberg, *Ethics*, trans. Keith Crim (Philadelphia: Westminster, 1983), 191.
45. O'Donnell, 91.
46. Ibid., 95.
47. 1 Cor. 13:12.
48. O'Donnell, 97.
49. *OG*, 97; *RH*, 133f.
50. Ibid., 98; 134.
51. Jerry Norris Beam ("A critical assessment of Wolfhart Pannenberg's relation to Process Thought," Ph.D. Baylor University, 1985, 23n27) argues that Pannenberg, to be fully consistent, should become a process thinker, that he should fully incorporate time into his notion of deity, and that he should no longer speak of God as acting powerfully (100-115, 145f.). Beam believes that Pannenberg's argument that God is free and powerful and that God is in this way the ground of creaturely freedom is self-contradictory. If there is an end to history, says Beam, then there can be no freedom within history. Pannenberg should drop eschatology. Pannenberg should talk about God as one does about finite humans (117). Beam neglects Pannenberg's efforts to ground human freedom in God's freedom. He simply states that Pannenberg's notions of God and human freedom are contradictory on the basis of the assumption that if one's ontology is not completely shaped by the open-endedness of

Whitehead's ontology, then it must be a deterministic conception of divine omnipotence (38f., 156, cf. also 164, 179, 186f.).

52. *ST* 2:63; *STe* 2:46.

53. *TKG*, 63.

54. *ST* 2:58; *STe* 2:42.

55. Pannenberg speaks of "the immediacy of the divine action in creation to every creaturely present" (*STe* 2:142) ("die Unmittelbarkeit des göttlichen Schöpfungshandelns zu jeder geschöpflichen Gegenwart") (*ST* 2:167).

56. Cf. the claim of Beam, "A critical assessment," 114.

57. *ST* 1:473; *STe* 1:438.

58. *ST* 2:18; *STe* 2:4f.

59. *ST* 2:15; *STe* 2:1.

60. All parts of the universe are primarily understood from the point of view of their wholeness as a world, and not from the point of view of the often conflicting diversity of the parts. Cf. Stanley Grenz, *Reason for Hope*, 83.

61. *STe* 2:5. "Das Handeln des einen Gottes im Weltverhältnis ist nicht ein völlig anderes als in seinem trinitarischen Leben, sondern in ihm wendet sich dieses trinitarische Leben selber nach außen, tritt aus sich heraus und wird zum Bestimmungsgrund der Beziehungen zwischen Schöpfer und Geschöpf" (*ST* 2:19).

62. Stanley Grenz, *Reason for Hope*, 46-54, has a useful discussion of Pannenberg's Trinitarian conception of God. To enter into the various levels of argumentation that Pannenberg engages in would take us too far afield. My purpose is to show how Pannenberg grounds the unity of nature and history through his central theological positions.

63. *ST* 2:37, 360f.; *STe* 2:22f., 319f.

64. *ST* 2:43; *STe* 2:28.

65. *STe* 2:30. "So ist die Schöpfung freier Akt Gottes als Ausdruck der Freiheit des Sohnes in seiner Selbstunterscheidung vom Vater und der Freiheit väterlicher Güte, die im Sohn auch die Möglichkeit und das Dasein einer von ihm unterschiedenen Schöpfung bejaht, sowie auch des Geistes, der beide in freier Übereinstimmung verbindet" (*ST* 2:45).

66. Cf. Charles Villa-Vicencio, "History in the Thought of Reinhold Niebuhr and Wolfhart Pannenberg" (Ph.D. Drew, 1975), 35. Villa-Vicencio writes: "To Hegel the otherness of God must by necessity assert itself in finiteness. Yet against a charge of Neo-Platonist emanation, Pannenberg affirms Hegel's consistent distinction between creation and emanation, the basis of which distinction is found in the fact that God is a subject. There is no mere reflection of the absolute idea but a free bringing into being of a natural world."

67. Pannenberg, "Theology and Science," *Princeton Seminary Bulletin* 13, 3 (November 1992): 301, cf. *GF* 1:337; *BQ* 2:171.

68. Pannenberg, "Glaube und Vernunft," in *GF* 1:248-50; *BQ* 2:60-63. See also Michael Schulz, "Zur Hegelkritik Pannenbergs," 210.

69. *IST*, 42.

70. Cf. Philip. 2:1-11.

71. *ST* 2:47; *STe* 2:32.

72. *ST* 2:46; *STe* 2:31f.

73. *ST* 2:49; *STe* 2:34.

74. *ST* 2:75f.; *STe* 2:57f.

75. "Gott kann zwar allmächtig ohne uns über uns verfügen, die Menschen als Sachen behandeln. Aber insofern Gott eine Geschichte mit den Menschen eingeht, um sich ihnen zu offenbahren, nimmt er sie als Du." Pannenberg, "Person," in *Religion Geschichte und Gegenwart*, 3d ed., vol. 5 (Tübingen: 1961), 232.

76. Pannenberg, "Theological Questions to Scientists," 71.

77. Ibid.

78. Ibid., 72.

79. *GF* 1:24; *BQ* 1:18.

80. *GF* 1:22-78; *BQ* 1:15-80.

81. *GF* 1:20; *BQ* 1:13f.

82. Pannenberg, "Christentum und Platonismus: Die kritische Platonrezeption Augustins in ihrer Bedeutung für das gegenwärtige christliche Denken," *Zeitschrift fur Kirchengeschichte* 96 (1985): 151, 159-61; *GF* 1:343-45; *BQ* 2:179-82.

83. Cf. *GF* 1:77f.; *BQ* 1:79.

84. According to Stanley Grenz, Pannenberg conceives of the religions as attempting to provide a unified understanding of reality (*Reason for Hope*, 36). See Pannenberg's *ST* 1:133-205, where his discussion of religion focuses on the relationship of humans with God (or powers). Cf. John O'Donnell, "Pannenberg's Doctrine of God," 82.

85. *STe* 2:21. "Die Liebe des Vaters richtet sich nicht nur auf den Sohn, sondern auch auf jedes einzelne seiner Geschöpfe. Aber die Hinwendung des Vaters zur Besonderheit eines jeden seiner Geschöpfe ist immer schon durch den Sohn vermittelt. . . . Weil in den Geschöpfen der ewige Sohn in Erscheinung tritt, werden sie Gegenstand der Liebe des Vaters" (*ST* 2:36).

86. Pannenberg refers to this as "die eigene Endlichkeit transzendierende Teilhabe an Gott" (*ST* 2:47; *STe* 2:33).

87. *ST* 2:47f.; *STe* 2:33.

88. *ST* 2:48f.; *STe* 2:33f.

89. *ST* 2:63-70; *STe* 2:46-53.

90. *STe* 2:53f. "Jedes Geschöpf ist für sich selber Zweck im Schöpfungshandeln Gottes und so auch für seine Weltregierung. Doch die Weise, wie Gott das Wohl des einzelnen Geschöpfes im Blicke hat, nämlich unter Berücksichtigung auch der den übrigen Geschöpfen gebürenden Fürsorge, kann sehr verschieden sein davon, was das einzelne Geschöpf selber als sein Glück erstrebt" (*ST* 2:70f.).

91. *ST* 2:71f.; *STe* 2:54f.

92. Isa. 11; Rev. 21.

93. *STe* 2:58f.

94. *ST* 2:76.

95. See especially chapters 4 and 5 of Pannenberg's *Metaphysik und Got-tesgedanke* (Göttingen: Vandenhoeck & Ruprecht, 1988). Hereafter *MG* (chapters 4 and 5 of *MIG*) for his argument in support of the ontological priority of the future.

96. Pannenberg, "Theology and Science," 302.

97. *TTN*, 100. "Nicht der göttliche Schöpfungsakt geschieht in der Zeit,—er umfaßt vielmehr als ein ewiger, aller Zeit gleichzeitiger Akt den gesamten Weltprozeß; aber dieser Weltprozeß selbst hat einen zeitlichen Anfang, weil er in der Zeit verläuft.

In diesem Satz ist Ewigkeit als Gleichzeitigkeit zu aller Zeit erläutert" (*ETN*, 60). The last sentence is my translation.

98. *ETN*, 61; *TTN*, 101.

99. Pannenberg speaks of the Trinity as eternal and as the source of crea-tion. Although he insists that we develop our theology from the point of view of the incarnation of the Son in Jesus, he regards the incarnation as the result of the eternal self-differentiating love of the Son for the Father. In other words, God's Trinitarian life is interdependent with creation through the incarnation only insofar as the Trinity has determined it to be so. Cf. Stanley J. Grenz and Roger E. Olson, *20th Century Theology: God and the World in a Transitional Age* (Downers Grove: InterVarsity Press, 1992), 182-84.

100. *STe* 2:20. "Der freie Ursprung einer dauerhaften Schöpfung muß als ausdruck einer in der Ewigkeit des Schöpfers begründeten Intention auf eine von ihm verschiedene Wirklichkeit hin gedacht werden" (*ST* 2:35, cf. 20f.; *STe* 2:6f.).

101. Pannenberg, "Atom, Duration, Form: Difficulties with Process Philosophy," trans. John C. Robertson, Jr., and Gérard Vallée, *Process Studies* 14, 1 (Spring 1984): 24f.

102. *ST* 2:29f.; *STe* 2:15f. Pannenberg refers to Whitehead, *Process and Reality* (New York: Harper, 1960), 528f. He quotes from page 526 of this work: "He [God] does not create the world, he saves it. . ." (30n46). Pannen-berg also refers to Lewis S. Ford, *The Lure of God: A Biblical Background for Process Theism* (Philadelphia: 1978), 20ff.; Ford, "An Alternative to *creatio ex nihilo*," *Religious Studies* 19 (1983): 205-13; and J. Cobb, *God and the World: The One Who Calls* (1969), 42-66. Pannenberg acknowledges Cobb's attempt to "correct" this problem by "subordinating the principle of creativity to God as the supreme entity." However, Pannenberg indicates his dissatisfac-tion with this sort of correction, which he claims would have "far-reaching consequences for the network of concepts in Whitehead's philosophical system" (Pannenberg, *Ethics*, 180; *Ethik und Ekklesiologie* (Göttingen: Vandenhoeck & Ruprecht, 1977), 171. Hereafter *EE*.

103. See Lewis S. Ford, "God as the Subjectivity of the Future,"

Encounter 41 (1980): 290; and Pannenberg and Ford, "A Dialogue About Process Philosophy," *Encounter* 38, 4 (Autumn 1977): 319.

104. Ford, "The Nature of the Power of the Future," in *The Theology of Pannenberg: American Critiques*, 85.

105. Pannenberg, "Response to American Friends," 325. Pannenberg answers that freedom of decision normally relates to finite objects and that God is never fully known. Those who seek freedom from God may well not know what they are turning from. The nature of reality is that creatures are intended to "participate in communion with the eternal God." They are capable of turning from this communion and falling under the judgment of God. Ted Peters agrees that Pannenberg's future ontology provides the true ground of human freedom ("Pannenberg's Eschatological Ethics," in *The Theology of Pannenberg: American Critiques*, 254f.).

106. *ST* 2:30; *STe* 2:16; and "Gott und die Natur," 491.

107. Lewis S. Ford, "A Whiteheadian Basis for Pannenberg's Theology," *Encounter* 38, 4 (Autumn 1977): 315.

108. Ibid.

109. *TKG*, 66.

110. Pannenberg and Ford, "A Dialogue," 323; Pannenberg, "Atom, Duration, Form," 22f.; and *Ethics*, 190f.

111. Pannenberg and Ford, "A Dialogue," 318.

112. Cf. *ST* 2:30; *STe* 2:16.

113. Cf. John B. Cobb, Jr., "Pannenberg and Process Theology," in *Theology of Pannenberg: American Critiques*, 70, 73f. Cobb claims that process thinkers are sensitive to women and to the suffering and oppression of others, and that Pannenberg, on the other hand, is only concerned with eschatology. It appears that Cobb has failed to recognize the eschatological grounding of Pannenberg's ethical thought. Pannenberg makes this point in "A Response to My American Friends," 330f. In the same volume see also Ted Peters, "Pannenberg's Eschatological Ethics," 241, 243f. Peters's argument directly contradicts Cobb's undocumented claim, and Pannenberg notes his agreement with Peters's analysis ("Response to My Friends" 331).

David Polk, *On the Way to God*, 287, 293, makes a similar error in interpreting Pannenberg. He thinks that Pannenberg's notion of the Kingdom allows for no judgment of evil.

114. *ST* 2:31; *STe* 2:16f.

115. Beam's (op cit.) work provides a clear example of this problem. Ted Peters argues that John Cobb's process theology is able to offer nothing more than *meaning* to the individual who suffers evil. No hope is given for the realization of perfect communion with God (Peters, "Pannenberg's Eschatological Ethics" 244f.).

116. See the following section, "Whole and Part."

117. "Theology and Science," 305f.

118. Ibid., 307.

119. Ibid.

120. *ST* 2:20f.; *STe* 2:6f.

121. "Geist und Energie," 9.

122. Cf. "Atom, Duration, Form," 27-29.

123. Cf. "Geist und Energie," 7, 11n4.

124. Pannenberg, "Atom, Duration, Form," 27f.

125. See *MG*, 76f.; *MIG*, 105f.

126. Pannenberg, "The Significance of the Categories of 'Part' and 'Whole' for the Epistemology of Theology," *Journal of Religion* 66, 4 (October 1986): 373f. Pannenberg is arguing that the concept of the whole is implicit in scientific explanation of the world. He recognizes that it is not in the foreground of "scientific description of natural processes" (374).

127. Ibid., 375.

128. Ibid.

129. Ibid., 377.

130. Pannenberg argues against Jürgen Habermas's conception that a *Sinntotalität* arises out of individual communicative action (*WT*, 101-4, 133; *TPS*, 100-3, 131).

131. *WT*, 116; *TPS*, 114.

132. *TPS*, 115. "Die in solchem Einverständnis präsente Sinntotalität hat aber in jedem Falle 'metaphysische' Dimensionen: Sie integriert zumindest virtuell die Bedeutungsstrukturen der Erfahrungen und Hand-lungsmöglichkeiten der am Kommunikationsprozeß beteiligten Individuen und konstituiert damit die Einheit der sozialen Lebenswelt. Troeltsch hat sich darum mit Recht von der Frage nach der 'Objektivität' geschichtlicher Erkenntnis auf die Frage nach dem Verhältnis des Einzelnen zum Ganzen in der Wirklichkeit überhaupt führen lassen" (*WT*, 116).

133. *WT*, 116f.; *TPS*, 114f. Pannenberg uses Troeltsch's term (Troeltsch, *Historismus und seine Probleme*, 678).

134. *WT*, 117.; *TPS*, 115f. Pannenberg again refers to Troeltsch, *His-torismus* 107.

Pannenberg prefers the eschatological focus of Ernst Troeltsch's ethics to the conventionalism of Habermas's focus on the individual. For Troeltsch the eschatological Kingdom of God represents the ultimate good to which all preliminary goods and goals must submit (*WT*, 111; *TPS*, 109). However, says Pannenberg, Troeltsch's notion of *Zweck* (goal), combined with his neglect of the presence of the Kingdom of God in Jesus' history, prevents Troeltsch from overcoming the relativism of his position (Cf. Ernst Troeltsch, *Historismus und seine Überwindung* [Berlin: Pan Verlag Rolf Heise, 1924], 60, 68, 82, and see below the chapter on Christology). For Troeltsch the Kingdom of God is completely beyond the horizon of the future. Troeltsch, according to Pannenberg, fails to recognize the constitutive significance of the future for the meaning of historical reality (*WT*, 115; *TPS*, 114). Cf. also *GF* 1:252-54; *BQ* 2:65-68.

135. *TPS*, 203. Diese [die Gesellschaft] ist nicht der Inbegriff von Wirklich-keit und Sinn überhaupt, sondern bedarf ihrerseits in ihrer jeweiligen konkreten Gestalt der Verankerung und Korrektur durch ein absolutes Sinnvertrauen, das sowohl die Konflikte zwischen Individuum und Gesellschaft als auch *den Gegensatz zwischen Mensch und Naturwelt übergreift"* (*WT*, 203f.). Emphasis mine.

136. Pannenberg refers to Wilhelm Dilthey, *Gesammelte Schriften VII*, 230.

137. *WT*, 131-33; *TPS*, 129-31.

138. *WT*, 150-52; *TPS*, 149-51.

139. *WT*, 162f.; *TPS*, 161f.

140. Philip Clayton, "Anticipation and Theological Method," in *Theology of Pannenberg: American Critiques,* esp. 131, 141. Clayton argues that Pan-nenberg's notion of anticipation or prolepsis needs further philosophical clarification. This is a foundational concept for Pannenberg, and it is some-what controversial, as Clayton shows. Pannenberg's interaction with process thinkers is also relevant here.

141. *ST* 1:18-36; *STe* 1:8-26.

142. Cf. *WT*, 220; *TPS*, 220f. Pannenberg defines the concept of *Erklärung* as the foundation of both human and natural sciences. It is the theoretical and systematic function "best described in the language of systems-theory as the function of fitting parts into a total pattern of meaning" (*TPS*, 153). ("Es ist das die systemtheoretisch zu beschreibende Funktion der Einordnung von Teilen in das Ganze eines Sinnentwurfs") (*WT*, 154).

143. Pannenberg also takes up his argument regarding the significance of the proleptically present end of history (here in the form of the totality of his-tory) in dialogue with recent discussions of hermeneutics. Pannenberg argues that Gadamer's description of the "task of interpretation as an attempt to fuse the horizons [*Horizontverschmelzung*] of the author and the interpreter presup-poses the totality of history . . . as its ultimate frame of reference" (*TPS*, 284). ("So habe ich selbst . . . zu zeigen versucht, daß die Aufgabe der Interpreta-tion als Horizontverschmelzung der Verstehungshorizonte von Autor und Aus-leger die Totalität der Geschichte als ihren letzten Bezugsrahmen voraussetzt"). To this Pannenberg adds that every experience of meaning implies a totality of meaning (*Sinntotalität*) that is only available as an anticipation of a future reality (*WT*, 286, and see *GF* 1:142-49; *BQ* 1:162-71). See also Pannenberg, "History and Meaning in Lonergan's Approach to Theological Method," *Irish Quarterly Review* 40 (1973): 112-14.

144. "Part and Whole," 378.

145. Ibid., 380.

146. "Theology and Science," 381.

147. Ibid., 385.

148. *ETN*, 38f.; *TTN*, 76-78.

149. *ETN*, 59; *TPS*, 98f. Pannenberg defines contingency in relation to

that which in its individuality has not necessarily arisen from the past (*ETN*, 75n11; *TTN*, 116n11).

150. *ETN*, 40; *TTN*, 79.

151. *ETN*, 58; *TTN*, 98.

152. *ST* 2:88; *STe* 2:69f.

153. *ETN*, 44f.; *TTN*, 84.

154. Pannenberg has the support of Erwin Schrödinger and other physicists in arguing that the regularity of nature is grounded on contingency (Schrödinger uses *Zufall* or chance (*ST* 2:84f.; *STe* 2:66). Pannenberg refers to Schrödinger, *Was ist ein Naturgesetz? Beiträge zum naturwissenschaftlichen Weltbild* (1962), 10.

155. *ETN*, 56f.; *TTN*, 96f.

156. *ST* 2:88f.; *STe* 2:69f.

157. *ST* 2:89f.; *STe* 2:70f.

158. *ST* 2:90; *STe* 2:71.

159. *ST* 2:92; *STe* 2:72f.

160. *TTN*, 108. "In diesem Sinne konstituiert sich der Ereigniszusammenhang zwischen beiden von B her nach rückwärts" (*ETN*, 67).

161. *ETN*, 69; *TTN*, 109.

162. *ETN*, 72; *TTN*, 113.

163. "The establishment of such relationships—through ever renewed reversion from the later to the earlier—bears the stamp of a personal power, not the mark of a merely structural regularity. Thus, and perhaps only thus, does the unity of events, in the context of the preservation of their contingency, become understood." Translation is mine. ("Die Herstellung solchen Zusammenhanges aber durch immer erneuten Rückgriff vom Späteren auf Früheres trägt den Stempel einer persönichen Macht, nicht den einer bloßen Gesetzesstruktur, und so—vielleicht nur so—wird die Einheit des Geschehens unter Wahrung seiner Kontingenz verständlich") (*ETN*, 72; *TTN*, 113).

164. *ETN*, 70f; *TTN*, 111.

165. *TTN*, 111f. "In diesem Sinne erst läßt sich von einer Geschichte der Natur sprechen, nicht von einer Geschichte der Natur für sich, ohne den Menschen, sondern von einer Geschicht der Natur auf den Menschen hin" (*ETN*, 71).

166. *ETN*, 71; *TTN*, 112.

167. *TTN*, 112. "Dieser Weg [der Weg der Geschichtsstiftung] hat seine Einheit erst recht nur unter der Voraussetzung Gottes, der die kontingente Abfolge der Gestalten auf den Menschen hin geordnet hat, do daß sie von ihm her rückwärts als sinnvoller Geschehenszusammenhang erfaßbar wird und durch sein Erkennen und Handeln gestaltet und vollendet wird" (*ETN*, 71).

168. Translation is mine. "Erst mit der Entstehung des Menschen und mit der Aneignung der Natur durch den Menschen erlangt der Weltprozeß als ganzer, rückwirkend vom Menschen her, seinen Zusammenhang in sich selbst. Das geschieht durch die menschliche Erkenntnis der Natur ebenso wie durch

die damit zusammenhängende Herrschaft über sie" (*ETN*, 71; *TTN*, 111).

169. The anthropic principle argues that minute changes in the nature of the universe would have made the evolution of sentient organic life impossible. This appears to suggest that human consciousness is the goal of evolution.

170. "Theology and Science," 309.

171. *ST* 2:93f.; "Theology and Science," 309f. Physicist Stephen Hawking in *A Brief History of Time: From the Big Bang to Black Holes* (New York: Bantam, 1988) acknowledges the generally accepted validity of the anthropic principle in its weak form (124f.). Pannenberg's theological reflections are based on the weak form of the principle.

172. Pannenberg, "Doctrine of Creation and Science," 3-21.

173. *ST* 2:20 and cf. 34f.; *STe* 2:6, 20.

174. Gen. 2:7.

175. *IST*, 43. See *ST* 1:403-16; *STe* 1:372-84 for Pannenberg's critique of Spirit as *nous*, and also *ST* 2:104; *STe* 2:84 for a summary of this argument. Stanley Grenz points out that this is one of the significant differences between Pannenberg and Hegel. Pannenberg understands Spirit in terms of the Hebrew *ruah*, not in terms of German Idealism (*Reason for Hope* 91, 108f.).

176. Rev. 19:1ff.; John 17:4; *ST* 2:73f.; *STe* 2:55f.

177. "Theology and Science," 307f.

178. Luke 19:40.

179. Ps. 19:1ff.; Ps. 98:4.

180. *ST* 2:373f.; *STe* 2:333f.

181. Mark 12:29-34.

182. 1 John 4:8.

183. James 2:19.

184. *Ethics*, 54.

185. *Ethics*, 54f.

186. *Ethics*, 56.

187. *Ethics*, 31.

188. *WT*, 103-5; *TPS*, 101-3.

189. *TPS*, 285. "Da die Antizipation des Endes der Geschichte zugleich 'als Antizipation der Erlösung des Ganzen . . . zukunftseröffnend für den sterblichen Leib, für die Gesellschaft und für die Natur' ist, schließt sie, wie Moltmann mit Recht betont, auch die politische Thematik der 'Befreiung der ganzen geknechteten Kreatur' ein, die bei ihm zum Ausgangspunkt einer 'politischen Hermeneutik' wird" (*WT*, 287). Pannenberg's quotations of Jürgen Moltmann are taken from M. Moltmann, *Perspektiven der Theologie* (1968), 135.

190. Pannenberg is leery of "rational" and "definitive programs." He argues that revolutionary objectives quickly turn conservative, for they too easily identify themselves with the highest good and thus insulate themselves from all criticism. This critique of political theology should be understood in the context of Pannenberg's commitment to the improvement of life in the

world (*TKG*, 114). Cf. *Ethics*, 134f. where Pannenberg connects the hopes of Christian eschatology with the Old Testament prophets' politically concrete expectations for a reign of peace. Also see Pannenberg, "Christianity, Marxism, and Liberation Theology," *Christian Scholar's Review* 18, 3 (1989): 215-26. He argues that Marxist and Leninist economic analyses are simplistic and are firmly rooted in ideological programs.

191. *WT*, 57ff., 221; *TPS*, 55ff., 221f.

192. Müller, "Über philosophischen Umgang," 24.

193. See Gene E. Likens, "Toxic Winds: Whose Responsibility?" in *Ecology, Economics, Ethics*, 148, 150. Likens provides several examples that show how concern for personal financial gain produces a willingness to pollute the environment.

194. See, for example, Edward O. Wilson, "Biodiversity, Prosperity, and Value," in *Ecology, Economics, Ethics*, 10.

195. David McKenzie, *Wolfhart Pannenberg and Religious Philosophy* (Washington: U. P. of America, 1980), 88. In this context McKenzie shows the connection of Pannenberg's argument regarding the possible truth of the resurrection. "If one can avoid absolutizing them [the natural laws], then from the side of science the incompatibility between the Resurrection and natural science is also removed" (Ibid.).

196. *TKG*, 80f.

197. *Ethics*, 179; *EE*, 169f.

CHAPTER 2

GOD THE REDEEMER

In the Jew Jesus of Nazareth many Christians believe the eternal Son of God, the second person of the Trinity, has appeared in unity with the creaturely world. In other words, they believe that Jesus was in one person the unity of Creator and creature. He was God incarnate. "In the process of the transmission of his eschatological revelation, God is immanent in history and determines its unity from within, from the inner-historical event of Jesus' history, and thus proves himself as God, as the all-determining reality."[1] For Wolfhart Pannenberg this fundamental claim of the Christian tradition is central: "in Jesus Christ—and in him alone—the one God of the universe is present to save his creation from sin and decay."[2] Pannenberg's Christology is the focus of this chapter.

Pannenberg understands history as the process of God's creative immanence overcoming the failings of creatures and carrying creation forward into its eschatological source—the Kingdom of God. The aim of creation is the unity of creatures with the Creator, and history is the process toward that goal. History is revelation. And if history and God, creation and Creator, are not opposed to one another, are not each the radical "other" to the other, but are interdependent and have intertwined destinies, then neither is any kind of creaturely reality radically other from the rest of creation or from God. This chapter shows how Pannenberg understands Jesus of Nazareth as the incarnation of the "unifying unity" of all reality.

As in the understanding of creation, Pannenberg seeks direction in the Jewish context within which Christianity developed. The notions of history and revelation continue to be significant. The unity of nature and history, of matter and spirit, can be understood in the context of Pannenberg's rejection of Karl Barth's dialectical opposition of God and world and in Pannenberg's corresponding depiction of revelation as history.[3] According to Pannenberg, the difference of his thought from Barth's could also be depicted as a new appreciation of God as Creator of all reality and a uniting of the notions of creation and redemption.[4]

The task of this chapter is to analyze how Pannenberg's elaboration of this central Christian claim contributes to the argument that the relationship of nature and history should not be construed dualistically. How, in other words, does the appearance of the eternal Son in history serve to overcome the modern dualism of nature and spirit? This question, rather than a complete treatment of Pannenberg's Christology, will guide the following discussion. This chapter will examine the following aspects of Pannenberg's understanding of Jesus the Messiah: the Hebrew context of the appearance of the Son, the message of the Kingdom, the resurrection, the unity of creation and redemption, and, briefly, the Christian community.

The Hebrew Context

A separate study would be required to investigate fully the hermeneutical and theological reasons for Pannenberg's emphasis on the importance of taking full account of the Jewish context of Jesus' resurrection when attempting to understand the significance of the latter event for the meaning of history. This study will indicate only several of Pannenberg's major arguments. First, the Jewish experience of God's action in history had lead to a unique understanding of both history itself and of the relationship of God to history. Jesus was a Jew, and Jesus' destiny made him the ultimate, if proleptic, revelation of God's action in history. The particular nature of this revelation connects it intimately with its Jewish context. Second, Pannenberg is concerned to reject completely the separation of *Heilsgeschichte* from *Geschichte*. Theologians who make such a distinction place merely historical realities at the periphery of the events that constitute *Heilsgeschichte*. Pannenberg regards this as an unacceptable isolation of the Christian *Traditionsgeschichte* from secular history.

Ancient Israel and the Concept of History

Pannenberg's understanding of Israel's concept of history and its influence on modern conceptions of history is argued in the context of a modern debate. Karl Löwith, one of Pannenberg's teachers, has argued that the modern Western linear conception of history has its roots largely in the faiths of ancient Israel and nascent Christianity.[5] Pannenberg interprets Löwith both as rejecting the idea of progress, which Löwith regards as a secularization of both the Christian faith in providence and the Christian expectation of an eschatological telos of history, and as preferring the Greek view that history is the constant reoccurrence of a cycle of cultural development, rise, and fall.[6] Hans Blumenberg targets Löwith's argument that progress is the secularization of Hebrew and Christian beliefs and argues to the contrary that the modern age, including its belief in progress, grew out of a new secular self-affirmation of culture against the Christian tradition.[7] Pannenberg suggests that Blumenberg's argument depends on the idea of an original opposition of eschatology against history and that this can be traced to certain arguments of Bultmann and even of Löwith. Pannenberg argues that because the Old Testament view of history is the background for New Testament eschatology, the latter cannot dualistically be opposed to reality. In other words, both apocalyptic eschatology and the linear notion of history grow out of the experiences of ancient Israel. "[E]schatology, as the future of history, is part of the understanding of reality as history."[8] Eschatology is a development of the Hebrew notion of history and belongs to it fundamentally. Pannenberg argues that his revision of Löwith's argument, conceiving Christian eschatology as an extension of the Old Testament view of history as the activity of God on behalf of his people, is sufficient to defend it against Blumenberg's main argument, namely, that modern historical thinking does not have its roots in Christianity.

As to Blumenberg's assumption that progress and providence are heterogeneous notions, Pannenberg refers to Löwith's response to Blumenberg.[9] Löwith argues that the idea of progress is only possible within the horizon of the Christian ideas of eschatology and *Heilsgeschichte*, which together open up the possibility of an orientation to the future. Löwith adds that the notion of humans as free creative beings is a thinkable development only in the context of the Judeo-Christian notion of the free Creator God. Just as progress replaces the promise-fulfillment character of eschatological hope, so humanity replaces God in the early modern notion of reality. Freedom is conceived as the self-grounded possession of each individual, and human freedom together with future oriented hope are foundational to the development of the secular notion of progress. Thus, according to Löwith, the modern notion of historical progress is doubly rooted in Judeo-Christian notions.

For Löwith, however, there is an opposition of *Heilsgeschehen* and secular history, a dualism of faith and reality. Reality is characterized by the circularity of history, while faith, in its expectation of an eschaton, has a linear conception of reality. He regards these as irreconcilable views of reality. One is empirically grounded and the other is invisible, is inner.[10] Pannenberg accepts Löwith's argument that the ideas of progress and human freedom are rooted in Christianity, with its Jewish background. He does not, however, accept either Löwith's dualist portrayal of eschatology or the accompanying isolation of the ideas of salvation and hope (*Heilsgeschehen und Heilser-wartungen*) from empirical reality. This is rooted in Pannenberg's view of the continuity from ancient Israel's view of history, to Jewish apocalyptic eschatology, and to the eschatological hopes of the Christian faith. Pannenberg also finds the historicality of our existence to be rooted in the nature of our physical existence. Anthropology is a discipline that can confirm the Hebrew-Christian understanding of existence as historical and as future oriented. In other words, Pannenberg argues that reality is not cyclical but is future oriented, just as faith and salvation are. Pannenberg argues this most pointedly in identifying revelation and history.

According to Pannenberg's conception of history, the methods of modern historical consciousness can, therefore, be understood as themselves having evolved within a conception of reality that is rooted in the transmission of the Hebrew experience of God's promises and the hopes for their ultimate fulfillment. This implies, therefore, that the modern hermeneutical task of interpreting the texts of ancient Israel constitutes a reflection on one's own roots.

The simplicity of this process, however, is broken by the historical and cultural distance (Lessing's ditch) between the ancient and the modern periods. Pannenberg argues that an awareness of a universal historical context can provide a horizon within which the connection of the present with ancient Christianity can be mediated. The truth of this depends on whether reality in its fundamental properties is to be understood as historical. Is it possible "to understand the history of nature and of humanity in their unity as the history of God?"[11]

The context of this quotation is a discussion of the question of the Protestant Reformation's Scripture Principle and is focused on modern attempts to understand and apply early Christian concepts in a modern context. What makes this problem especially relevant to my interpretation of Pannenberg's thought is that his question points to the unity of nature and history in God as the justification for the application of historical consciousness to the hermeneutical enterprise. Pannenberg explains that the hermeneutical problem of bringing the horizons of text and interpreter together raises the question of universal history.[12] The reality of historical distance between ancient text and modern reader points to the need for some conception of history that bridges the historical distance inherent in the situation. The possibility of a modern reader understanding an ancient text suggests that history has a certain unity.

Pannenberg draws on Hans-Georg Gadamer's hermeneutical philosophy of existence, but he argues that Gadamer has short-circuited his analysis by attempting to avoid the notion of universal history.[13] He argues that language is an insufficient category to account for human existence and for the connections among various horizons of experience within the total horizon of universal history. Pannenberg argues that the application of the notion of universal history need not fall into the speculative claims that Hegel made. The notion of universal history (or the idea of the whole of reality) can take full account of the provisional character of all human knowing. He also argues that apart from anticipations of the whole of reality, even though these always remain provisional, it is impossible to do justice to the entire meaning context of any particular event. In other words, according to Pannenberg, an ultimate hermeneutical context is required by the question of meaning.

In this context Pannenberg expresses both appreciation and criticism for positions taken by Dilthey and Heidegger. He agrees with both that the wholeness of existence is always anticipatorily presupposed in all attempts to understand reality and goes beyond both in arguing that this anticipated wholeness cannot be the moment of one's death, but that it reaches out beyond death to a greater whole.[14] The ultimate reality that Pannenberg connects with this whole is God as revealed in Jesus' destiny.[15] It is in the resurrection of Jesus, according to Pannenberg, that the ultimate whole of existence is most fully anticipated and appears proleptically. The horizon of understanding within which Pannenberg understands God and the whole of existence to be most fully present in history is that of Jesus' destiny as prolepsis of the goal of all reality.

Pannenberg points out that the notion of universal history has its roots in the Hebrew and Christian understanding that all of reality is understood as linear and as moving toward an end.

> It is through Jewish apocalyptic and Christian theology of history that the subject of universal history has been transmitted to modern philosophy of history, and it is questionable if the subject of universal history could be understood as a unity apart from the biblical ideas of God.[16]

This statement needs to be interpreted in the context of his controversy with Löwith and Blumenberg. Pannenberg's idea of an open-ended universal history draws together the arguments that Christian eschatology is not opposed to history and that reality is linearly future oriented, which he forwarded in the context of that debate. He suggests, further, that once modern thought had come to separate itself from its Judeo-Christian roots the concept of universal history was lost. Yet the problem of the universal character of history did not disappear. In fact, this question, according to Pannenberg, has become the "last horizon" of the modern natural sciences.[17] The pursuit in physics of a "grand unified theory" could perhaps serve as an example of the significance of this last horizon.

We see that Pannenberg points to both the hermeneutical problem of bridging Lessing's ditch and the situation of the empirical sciences as raising the question of the unity of nature and history within universal history. The notion of universal history, in other words, entails conceiving human and natural history in an overarching unity. Thus, we see that Pannenberg looks to ancient Israel, apocalyptic in early Judaism, and the eschatological hope of early Christianity, for the rise and definition of the concept of universal history.

Contrary to Löwith he argues that the Judeo-Christian concept of history remains essential to modern conceptions of reality. Against Blumenberg he notes the continuity of the modern age with its Christian roots and argues that only through taking up aspects of the Christian understanding of reality will modern thinkers be able more adequately to conceive of reality. Having accepted Dilthey's criticism of Hegel that the absolute is not available in history and agreeing with Gadamer that knowledge is always historical, Pannenberg renews the argument that the concept of universal history, and the idea of God that makes the notion possible, is implicit in all understanding. He agrees with Heidegger that understanding reaches out in anticipation of a final whole within which to understand existence but argues that this whole is to be found beyond the limits of death. Pannenberg offers an account of reality that is grounded in an anticipation of the unity of all reality in God.

His theological conception of universal history draws especially on the classical Hebrew prophets. But it takes distinctive shape in the context of a wide-ranging dialogue. Pannenberg's interpretation of the biblical texts takes place in the context of the tradition that has transmitted the text to him and his culture. The following section considers another modern argument about the reception of that tradition.

History and Myth

Pannenberg takes issue with Bultmann's conception of the relationship of myth to history and to the recording of actual events. Pannenberg's argument is important in the context of this book because it shows his concern for the unity of event and meaning.[18] It also reflects his intention to show that the relationship of God to history, while indirect, is open to rational and critical methods.

On the one hand, Pannenberg contrasts mythological structures of meaning with history-centered conceptions of the quest for meaning. Israel, he claims, is unique in the development of a view that meaning is not found in "nuances of a mythical prehistoric event."[19] In the ancient world, according to Pannenberg, "Israel is distinguished by the fact that it experienced the reality of its God . . . more and more decisively in historical change itself."[20] Experiencing meaning through cultic reenactment of foundational mythologies is contrasted with experiencing meaning through the ever new and unpredictable actions of God in the history of Israel. The root of this distinctive experience of meaning is in the unique idea of a living God who through various actions is directing history toward a goal.[21] The mythical view of reality is overcome by a historical view that itself is attained through the experience of God acting decisively in history.

On the other hand, in "Christentum und Mythos" Pannenberg attempts to counter dialectical theology's negative interpretation of myth.[22] He accepts Malinowski's definition of myth as fundamentally related to a primeval event (*Urereignis*). Myth functions as "grounding and foundational history."[23] Myth is conceived as a generative primeval event that is fundamentally connected with ritual performance in the present.[24] What Pannenberg gains by accepting this definition of myth is a ground upon which to criticize what he regards as the less carefully defined use of *myth* in Bultmann's demythologization program. According to Pannenberg, Bultmann's use of myth includes writings of various genres other than could be included in Malinowski's definition of myth. For Bultmann myth is a story told in human and mundane terms about the gods.[25] Since Malinowski's definition was available to Bultmann, Pannenberg argues that he has grounds to seek other motives in Bultmann's use of an older and less well defined category. Pannenberg suggests that this older category furthers Bultmann's theological agenda, which is defined by the latter's commitment to the dialectical program of radically separating the divine from mundane phenomena. For dialectical theology all mythological elements are regarded as negative because they speak of the Other in terms of the mundane.

Pannenberg is critical of this negative preevaluation of myth, for it shuts out from the modern world the meaning of the myths.

> The stereotypical opposition, from Heyne to Bultmann, of the structure of allegedly "mythical" ideas to the recognition of true causes, forces, and laws of nature, reveals that it concerns a counter idea to the modern conception of the world, which was grounded through [the work of] Galileo and Newton, and which today functions with the designation of "classical" natural science. This counter idea of a mythical state of consciousness was originally certainly not to have a polemical but a hermeneutical function.[26]

Pannenberg wishes to make it possible to reread the ancient myths apart from the polemical preunderstanding of the dialectical theologians, a preunderstanding that has functioned as a hindrance to understanding the message of the myths. But beyond attempting to clear the way for a less biased reading of ancient myths, this represents a fundamental shift from dialectical theology's approach to the Bible. Pannenberg argues that the mythical elements of the New Testament, such as the notion of the Redeemer who descends from heaven to save humans, are myths used in the service of accounting for historical events and their meaning.[27] The heroic Redeemer myth, for example, is put to service in telling the story of a historical person, Jesus of Nazareth.[28] It serves to tell that in this person the eternal Son of God became human, as well as to indicate the significance of this event. Pannenberg intends to overcome the separation of event and meaning that has characterized not only dialectical theology but much of modern historiography as well.

The linear conception of history, as it developed in ancient Israel, has an internal structure of meaning that takes its character from the manner in which the acts of God relate to each other.

Within a reality characterized by ever new workings of God, history emerges in that God issues promises and fulfills these promises. History is the span of events between promise and fulfillment, inasmuch as through the promise it receives an irreversible orientation toward its fulfillment.[29]

This conception of history is later modified by Pannenberg. He recognizes that the promises of God do not always come out exactly as foretold.

Hopes are seldom fulfilled in the way in which they were originally imagined. Often they are completely disappointed. Sometimes they are surprisingly fulfilled, more or less differently than one would have expected. Nevertheless, the person who experiences such a surprising fulfillment perhaps still senses that his real hope was fulfilled beyond expectation in an unpredictable way.[30]

The modification of the promise-fulfillment relationship does not change the fact that for ancient Israel and for Christians history is unrepeatable. Its events follow each other linearly and take place in the context of the expectancy created by the character of promise included in past acts of God.[31] Pannenberg refers readers to Deut. 7:8f. in which the Exodus event is set in the context of promises made to the forefathers of the redeemed people. The passage is significant to Pannenberg because it also points to the deeper meaning of promise and fulfillment: these events have the ultimate goal of revealing God to the people of Israel.[32] God reveals God's self as different from the powerless gods of nature. What these gods of natural realities, of moon and cycle, are powerless to do—provide abundantly, grant fertility, send rains, and so on—Jahweh has the power to do.[33]

But the recipients of this revelation are not only the people of Israel. The understanding of God and his actions expands to include all people. The claim that there is only one God and that the gods of Israel's neighbors are powerless creations of the human imagination has meaning beyond the borders of Israel. Ezek. 36:36 makes it clear that "the nations . . . shall know" that Jahweh is the one who speaks and accomplishes what he has spoken. Israel's consciousness of the implications of monotheism and its experience of history become ever more encompassing.[34]

Apocalypticism and Messianic Expectation

On the basis of the Hebrew Bible Pannenberg defines history as "the reality of humans and their world . . . as the irreversible flow of always new events." He adds that in contrast to the modern anthropocentric notion of history, the Hebrew Bible regarded history as "the action of God in the contingence of events" and this as "constitutive for the connection and meaning of the flow of events." And most significant, Pannenberg further notes that in ancient Israel the concept of history did not lead to an "opposition of nature and history, as it has developed in modern Western thought."[35] Pannenberg quotes Gerhard von Rad's remark that the "actuality of God's action" was constitutive for Israel's understanding of nature and history.[36] This unity of nature and history, according to Pannenberg's understanding of ancient Israel, belongs to the preexilic period of Israel's history. Various disasters such as the exile led to a tension between the belief in Jahweh's lordship over all reality and actual experience. This tension is finally overcome, or at least is taken into, the resurrection hope of Christian eschatology, which is grounded in the resurrection of Jesus.[37]

The development of a future-oriented expectation of a definitive and universal acknowledging of God in exilic prophecy and the subsequent development of apocalyptic opened a universal perspective for the character and meaning of Jesus' destiny.[38] The notion of universal history first arose in the context of the exile and in the further postexilic disappointments. Central to apocalyptic hopes was the expectation of the coming Kingdom of God, which includes the resurrection hope, the just judgment of the world, and the renewal of the creation. These hopes arose in the context of, at times extreme, national failure and disaster. The hopes signified an expected end of history as it is known, and in this expectation is rooted the notion of universal history.[39] The end includes the whole of reality, through all time and space.[40] The meaning and purpose of individual existence is here understood to be given in a context in which God judges the meaning of all human and natural history as one history. For it was no longer possible to conceive of justice and peace within the confines of history and existence as available to mundane experience.

These universalized hopes received their ultimate signification through the destiny of Jesus, especially through his resurrection as the final validation of his claims regarding the nearness of the Kingdom of God. Here, too, it must be noted, the fulfillment differed significantly from many people's expectations. Israel's apocalyptic hopes for justice and peace had a strongly political orientation. The connections of the messianic expectations with the Davidic monarchy suggested a renewal of Jewish hegemony in the ancient Near East. The title Messiah and its Greek translation, Christ, are closely connected with Israel's eschatological expectations.[41] However, Jesus did not fulfill these expectations. Rather, his message made the final break between narrowly national hopes and truly universal expectations for the reign of God.

His message and destiny did this by taking the national hopes into a universal vision and transforming them in the process. Pannenberg argues that the Hebrew Bible, Jewish apocalyptic, and Jesus' message recognize the antagonism of human evil toward God but do not admit of a dualistic conception of reality. Both Jewish and Christian faith, argues Pannenberg, are grounded in the notions of "creation and reconciliation of the world, *this* world in the course of its historical time."[42] The easy opposition of hopes for a heavenly realm on one hand and mundane reality on the other hand belong neither to apocalyptic nor to the eschatological character of the Kingdom of God. According to Pannenberg, images such as renewal, transformation, resurrection, new creation, and new age should rather be interpreted in continuity with reality as we know it. They are certainly new and unexpected, not predictable on the basis of what we know, but they always, in Pannenberg's understanding, take the old into themselves through transformation.

Hans Dieter Betz argues to the contrary that the

> apocalypticist can allow history no revelatory character; the eschaton cannot signify the goal, but only the end of history. He only escapes a complete metaphysical dualism in that he understands God as the one who has the power to soon make a permanent end of the present evil aeon.[43]

Betz grants that apocalyptic asks the question of the relationship of revelation to world history but contends that it sees nothing but negative possibilities for the answer.[44] Betz is right regarding the presence of dualism in some apocalyptic thought, but it should be noted that Pannenberg's conception of the inexact relationship of fulfillment to promise requires a more nuanced conception of the relationship of his theology to apocalyptic thought than Betz has allowed. The claim that Jesus' message regarding the Kingdom is the answer to the hopes of apocalypticism does not depend on an exact correspondence of the message of Jesus to the apocalyptic hopes of ancient Judaism. Pannenberg himself points out that Jesus' message of the Kingdom of God did not conform to the expectations that had developed in Jewish apocalyptic. The question is, therefore, whether Pannenberg is correct in arguing that both Jewish apocalyptic and the eschatological message of Jesus can be seen as developments of the Hebrew view of history. And in this Pannenberg appears to be justified.[45]

Jesus and the Kingdom of God

God is the Loving Father

Pannenberg argues that Jesus' message of salvation comes in the context of a situation in which the people of Israel could no longer be certain of God's loving rule. The failure of the Hasmoneans was followed by a Roman hegemony that was often cruel and that certainly was not favorable to the national political aspirations of the messianic and apocalyptic hopes of the people. In addition to its seemingly obvious lack of presence in the political realm, God's rule appeared to have turned against Israel. This is how Pannenberg interprets the message of judgment announced by John the Baptist. God does not look in favor upon the state of affairs in Judah. The message of the community at Qumran is also one of judgment and censorship. The temple and its priests are rejected. Pannenberg suggests that in the light of these voices it is possible to see the people of Israel as forming a community of the damned, an *Unheilskollektiv*.[46] It is in this context that Jesus announces the gracious and loving presence of the Kingdom (*Basileia*) of God (Matt. 6:33). The message of judgment became the point of departure for Jesus' message of the nearness of the Kingdom of grace and love, albeit only for those who responded with complete trust in the future of God's rule.[47]

It is instructive that the gospel writers make a point of depicting Jesus bringing the gracious message of the Kingdom to the religious outcasts. Jesus shares meals with tax collectors and sinners.[48] Pannenberg regards this as among the most profound marks of the redeeming love of God.[49] When these are invited to share in the joy of redemption, they respond with appropriate openness and are transformed by the presence of the Kingdom.

The "extraordinary intimacy in Jesus' way of speaking about God as Father and in addressing him as Father" is regarded by Pannenberg as that part of the heart of Jesus' message and life that makes possible the later affirmation of the Christian community that Jesus is the eternal Son of God.[50] The heart of Jesus' message is that God is the loving Father of all creation. The intimacy and confident security that characterizes healthy and loving familial relationships is the central symbol of the intimacy of Jesus and God, which in turn is the central symbol of the message of the Kingdom.

But this message already presupposes that God is one and that all reality is determined by the Creator. Pannenberg contends that the message that God is our Father is a further explication of the understanding that there is only one God and that this God requires undivided devotion. The jealous love of Jahweh and the first commandment of the Decalogue are central.[51] That God is the eternal loving Father would have no meaning if this message were not about the Creator of all reality.

Pannenberg argues that Jesus sees as evidence of the nearness of the coming Kingdom that the love of God seeks to save the lost (e.g., tax collectors and sinners). Jesus connects this love with the goodness of the Creator: "Love your enemies and pray for those who persecute you, so that you may be sons of your Father who is in heaven; for he makes his sun rise on the evil and the good, and sends rain on the just and the unjust."[52] Pannenberg says of this passage: "The goodness of the Creator becomes *redeeming* love in the sending of Jesus to *announce* the nearness of God's lordship."[53] Pannenberg argues further that Jesus' message began with the announcement of the nearness of the Kingdom of God. This was first of all, according to Pannenberg, a message of grace and love. But participation in the Kingdom is dependent on repentance (turning to God). When sinners and tax collectors, among others, do turn and receive the Kingdom and participate in its joy, then the creative love of God approaches its goal.[54] It could be said, in other words, that the aim of God's love in the creation and redemption process is the creaturely joy of participation in the Kingdom of God.

The content of Jesus' message regarding the nearness of the Kingdom is the "loving and saving presence of God as it is reflected in the providence of the Creator for each of his creatures."[55] The perfect realization of God's rule is future, but it is already present to those who believe.[56] Participation in this loving presence, that is, in the Kingdom itself, is open to all upon meeting its only condition: "ultimate trust" in and "exclusive concern" for God.[57] To those who open themselves to the message of the Kingdom—in the terms Jesus expresses in Matt. 6:3: Seek first his Kingdom—God's dominion becomes present reality.[58] They already have a share in the joy of the eschatological salvation that is coming. Those who reject the Kingdom of God, and the love and justice that it intends, will be subject to the consequences of turning away from participation in the life and joy of the Trinity. In other words, they become subject to the judgment of God, which falls upon all who reject justice and love.[59]

The joy and salvation that accompany the Kingdom are portrayed in the image of an eschatological wedding feast.[60] Jesus uses the image of the groom, who ensures that all the needs of each wedding guest are cared for and thus enables the guests to participate fully in the joy of the couple. Beyond this the redeemed creation comes to be portrayed as the eschatological bride of Christ. Creatures are joined to the Father through their unity with the Son. The realization of this unity is the occasion for a celebration that Jesus—and later his followers—describes in images drawn from the most joyous and personal of feasts known to him.

There is no ultimate opposition between the promised Kingdom and the *natural* (i.e., created) situation of humans. The message of the Kingdom is one in which peace and joy, not judgment and destruction, are the ultimate and true reality. Pannenberg rejects all supernatural dualism. An eschatological future that is dualistically opposed to the world can only mean a threat of ultimate destruction. It cannot be the hope of the fulfillment of creation.[61] This does not negate the freedom of creatures to turn finally away from, or even against, the destiny of creation. Pannenberg's point is that the world is created from and toward the eschatological Kingdom. Therefore, the Kingdom cannot be dialectically opposed to the world, as its crisis and judgment.[62] That the Kingdom will (and already does) purge away all sin and evil is not hereby denied.[63] This is part of the process of creation from the *telos* of participation in the love of God.

Pannenberg conceives of reality as unified. It is unified by the Creator who also redeems. There can be no final opposition between reality as we know it and the eschatological Kingdom. This is seen in the meaning of the resurrection of Jesus. History is the process of realizing the resurrection generally.[64] Of his own approach to theology he states:

> The new, eschatologically-oriented theology must liberate itself from such remnants of a reactionary supernaturalism, which are reactionary because they arise as a reaction against the problematic of the Enlightenment. Then it will perhaps be able to encounter with less prejudice talk of future, prolepsis, and totality, when presented purely phenomenally.[65]

Pannenberg points out that the response of opening oneself to the rule of God is the response that Jesus calls for. It is a call to trust in the coming of the Kingdom. But it is also a participation in that Kingdom, for it is already present in Jesus. The message of judgment delivered by John the Baptist is preparatory for Jesus' message. Jesus makes this explicit in his encounter with the religious leaders of Jerusalem.[66] They had not listened to John the Baptist, and so neither were they ready to receive the message of grace.[67] Therefore, they must again hear the judgment that they are a community of the damned.[68] Openness to the Kingdom, to the love and grace of God, is itself dependent upon a recognition of the corruption and neediness of the human condition. The gospels depict the encounter of Jesus with the religious leaders of Israel as a conflict. Jesus is not recognized as a messenger of the Kingdom. The reason for this appears to lie in the refusal of these leaders to accept the judgment of Qumran, John the Baptist, and ultimately Jesus, that their community had turned away from God. They saw no need to turn, to repent, and therefore they were able to receive neither the Messiah nor the proleptic presence of the Kingdom.[69]

They were not prepared to perceive the significance of the special relationship of the Son and Father, as given in Jesus' life. They failed to recognize in Jesus the "unquestioning subordination" of the Son to the Father. They failed to participate in this self-effacing love. This is "a spontaneous and unbiased subordination that voluntarily arises from intimate acquaintance."[70] The ultimate trust and concern that are the condition of participation in the presence of the loving Creator, therefore, can be further characterized as a participation in the subordination of the Son to the Father. In this way "others before and after Jesus could and can participate in that form of relating to God as Father."[71]

For Jesus this was the essence of his personal identity. It came naturally to him to relate to the Father in this way. This is not the case with other creatures. They must "turn to God from their earthly concerns and worries before they can live in that relationship."[72] Does this reintroduce a dualism between the world and the Kingdom? No, for in Pannenberg's thought the Kingdom is definitely not the *Krisis* of judgment. The Kingdom is not the ultimate condemnation of the world. Pannenberg does not say to turn from the world, but to turn from the worries and concerns that are focused on the world, that is, from concerns that are not based on trust in God and are not rooted in participation in the filial relationship of Jesus to the Father. It is not the world itself that one must turn from, but a wrong orientation of creatures to God and to the world that must be rejected. According to Pannenberg's way of conceiving the relationship of the Kingdom to the world, to turn to the Kingdom means to turn to the (good of the) world.[73] There is no ontological dualism between God and creation. But a creature's attitudes toward God and world can falsely oppose the world and God.

The aim of Jesus' life and message is to facilitate the participation of creatures in his relationship with the Creator. This is a message of hope and love. And rather than standing in opposition to creaturely reality, it stands as the ultimate goal of creation.

Jesus' condemnation and death reflect the denial of his claim by the religious authorities. They deny and reject his message. His death, however, corresponds most deeply with the eternal self-differentiation of the Son from the Father. "The remoteness from God on the cross was the climax of his self-distinction from the Father. Rightly, then, we may say that the crucifixion was integral to his earthly existence."[74] Jesus sacrificed his life in the interest of the Kingdom and its proclamation. He completed his earthly life in perfect obedience to the purposes of God. This obedience is the natural expression of the Son's acknowledgment of God. It is a selfless concern not for creatures, but for the "glorification of God," and has the coming of the Kingdom as its goal. But the coming of the Kingdom of God to creatures entails the drawing near of God to creatures. Pannenberg argues that it is only in his perfect love for the Father that the Son selflessly loves and redeems creatures. It is the salvation of creatures that have turned away from the source and goal of life. "Precisely thus the way of the Son is also an expression of the love of God for us."[75]

The Resurrection and the End of History

The death of Jesus was the judgment of the religious rulers on his life and teaching. He was condemned as one who did not acknowledge God as God.[76] When God raised Jesus from the dead he overruled the judgment of these rulers. Jesus' resurrection is the vindication of his life and teaching. This means, furthermore, that those who condemned Jesus are themselves guilty of not acknowledging God. Jesus, in other words, died in their place.[77] The forgiveness and nearness of God comes to sinners through Jesus' willingness to undergo himself the punishment that is due to sinners—those who fail to acknowledge and love the Creator.

The resurrection of Jesus of Nazareth is determinative in Pannenberg's theology. The resurrection of Jesus determines that Jesus is the Christ. It is the seal of divine approval on his life and teaching and especially on his death. The resurrection, in other words, is closely connected with Jesus of Nazareth. Not as an isolated event, but in intimate connection with the life, teaching, and death of Jesus, it is the foundation of the Christian faith.[78]

Resurrection (*Auferstehung, Auferweckung*) is a metaphor that draws on the image of waking from sleep. It depends on the metaphorical language that speaks of death as "sleep."[79] A third metaphor, "new life," refers to the qualitative transcendence of the life of the resurrected Jesus from that of normal creaturely experience. The new life is spiritual, but it remains associated with a body. It is eternal and is closely connected with the Kingdom of God. That death, resurrection, and new life are not available to the experience of the living itself implies that they are metaphorical forms of speech. This does not imply, however, that the metaphors of resurrection and new life do not refer to real events in the destiny of Jesus.

The concept of resurrection to a new and eternal life is bound up with the eschatological hopes of Jewish apocalyptic. Pannenberg argues that the apocalyptic context enabled the disciples to perceive the resurrected Jesus as resurrected. The risen Jesus had not simply been revived. The disciples were not subject to multiple group hallucinations. Nor was it an apparition that appeared to them.[80] On the other hand, Pannenberg points out that the resurrection of Jesus is inseparable from the anticipated ultimate and general resurrection of the dead expressed in apocalyptic hopes. This means that the resurrection of Jesus remains controversial until such an ultimate event occurs.[81] It also reveals the proleptic character of Jesus' life and resurrection.

> The Easter message of Christianity corresponds to the proleptic aspect of the history of Jesus in that as the proclamation of a specific event in the historical past, it always presupposes the universality of a changing and fulfilling of the reality of humanity and the world that is still in the future.[82]

Jesus' relationship with God, as characterized by his life and death, and his resurrection are regarded as the appearance of the end of history before history's end. As the proleptic appearance of the end of history and of the Kingdom of God, it is both the answer to the expectations of Jewish apocalyptic and the promise that the fulfillment is near.

Pannenberg maintains that the resurrection hopes of the first Christians are relevant to the hopes of modern people and that the claim that Jesus of Nazareth rose from the dead is believable. According to Pannenberg, the hope for resurrection, as understood in first-century Jewish apocalypticism, resonates with the modern anthropological conception of human openness, which is an openness that reaches beyond the bounds of death.[83] He also holds that the structure of the proleptic character of the resurrection of Jesus finds parallels in the structure of all human relationships to the future.

Central to Pannenberg's claims is that "[h]istoricity does not necessarily mean that what is said to have taken place historically must be like [be analogous to or homogeneous with] other known events."[84] The process of reality (history) is open to the appearance of new and unexpected events. Nonetheless, Pannenberg is clear that no final claim regarding the truth of the resurrection can be made until the resurrection is realized in fullness in the eschaton.[85]

The resurrection makes possible "a certain preliminary perception of the divine plan for history."[86] Pannenberg quotes Rom. 1:3-4 as expressing the significance of the resurrection for the Christian understanding of Jesus: Jesus was "designated Son of God in power according to the Spirit of holiness by his resurrection from the dead." Until the resurrection, argues Pannenberg, Jesus was not considered to be the anointed one of God. Pannenberg's argumentation rests on his perception of a current majority opinion that the understanding of Jesus as God incarnate arose out of the resurrection of Jesus.[87] Pannenberg is arguing that the identification of Jesus with the eternal Son of God is to be made on the basis of the whole of his life. This whole is not available for any person until his or her death. In Jesus' case, however, the normal end of existence, death, is surpassed, is transcended. Jesus is resurrected.

This event, the post-Easter appearances, and the ascension combine to put the life and death of Jesus in a perspective, in a

Sinnganzheit (meaning-whole), that totally transforms what is known about Jesus and also what is known of the world. Particularly in the case of Jesus, his entire life, from conception to death, is reinterpreted by the disciples in the light of the resurrection and the events that followed.[88] The whole of Jesus' life comes to be understood as the appearance of the eternal Son of God in the history of Israel. Later experience pushes the early church to acknowledge that the meaning of Jesus' life, death, resurrection, and ascension goes far beyond the boundaries of any one people. The entire world and all its peoples are included in what is understood as nothing less than a "new creation." Pannenberg reinterprets this in the context of a process understanding of creation. The new creation here signifies the appearance of the ultimate goal of the process of creation, and all reality is reinterpreted in this light. After the resurrection of Jesus it becomes possible to perceive that the goal of creation is the unity of creation, in this newly understood and achieved form, with the Creator. No longer is death the final word on any individual's existence. No longer is it possible to ignore the dependence on and unity with God.

That the resurrection of Jesus is an event in our history, in the history of this world, forces a revision of the conception of reality. Pannenberg states that this has been and should remain foundational to Christian thinking.[89] The fact of the resurrection and the promise it holds for all creatures mean that participation in the unity of all reality with the Creator is not an empty unity. It is here and now a participation in the eternal life beyond death that is the destiny of the creation.[90]

The idea of resurrection values the individual in the face of his or her questionableness. Evil, suffering, and death negate the individual and radically call into question the value of individual existence. They call into question the power and/or goodness of God. Pannenberg maintains that the resurrection to new and eternal life is the ultimate and incontrovertible answer to the problem of theodicy.[91] He argues that only a resurrection to new life can fully address the value of the individual and promise to make good the wrongs endured.

The revelation of the image of God in the person of Jesus Christ—for Pannenberg this is focused especially in Jesus' resurrection—does more than affirm the unassailable value of each individual. As in the doctrine of creation, Christology brings to light the ultimate unity of all reality (universal history). God is the *one Other*, who is the sole source and end of history, and each individual is embraced by the love of God. The resurrection is God's eternal valuation of individual persons, but it is also the ultimate realization of the image of God in human life. It is life fulfilled.

> This eternal affirmation of the individual existence of created beings, found in eschatology, makes its appearance as the final aim of the divine creative will. Even the distinctively Christian idea that God seeks a relationship with every one of his creatures with eternal love . . . is tied closely with the affirmation that finite creatures will continue to exist beyond death and throughout eternity, an affirmation that is central to Christian eschatology.[92]

The resurrection of Christ is a divine affirmation of the eternal value of individual human existence, and ultimately, it is an anticipation of the goal of creaturely existence, of the eschatological fulfillment of creaturely being. The destiny of the creation is most fully expressed in the resurrection of Jesus. Creation is proleptically completed in Jesus' resurrection.[93] This destiny can be spoken of as the specific destiny of humans, even of individuals. However, it is not human destiny apart from the rest of the creation. It is the destiny of all creation, and when this destiny is attributed especially to humans it is intended as a representative determination.

The specific, concrete, and personal nature of this hope, however, opens it to various historical distortions. Lest this concept be mistaken for the justification of individualistic anthropocentrism, as in modern Western style, it must be added that resurrection is a fundamentally social concept.[94] It is a metaphor that is embedded in the notion of the Kingdom of God.[95] The Kingdom is itself a metaphor that points to a new creation, a world of creatures united in an eternal covenant of love with God and with each other.[96] The concepts of justice and righteousness are fundamental to this eschatological hope.[97] And these are fundamentally social concepts that depend on both the old covenant and the eschatological hopes of the Jewish community. The significance of the neighbor in the context of the love of God expresses the social character of the Kingdom.

The resurrection does not imply a special mystical view of reality. As the self-revelation of God in history it has universal character.[98] But is there not a mysterious aspect, a hiddenness to the activity of God in history? Has Pannenberg taken seriously the obscure and humiliating death of Christ, the stumbling-block character of this revelation? Indeed, Pannenberg acknowledges that the cross radically brought into question the claims of Jesus, but he points out that the resurrection vindicated these claims. He argues that individual events taken in their true context—history—speak in the language of historical facts, and taken together they speak of God. That many are blind to this does not mean that reason is not capable of understanding revelation or that something supernatural must be added to reason, but rather that people must be brought to reason.[99] The way to bring people to reason is to present the Christian claim to truth in its historical context and to interpret it in the context of modern perceptions of reality. In other words, the Christian claims are treated as hypotheses that need to be tested for their truth.[100] Pannenberg does not regard these claims as absolutely true. He admits that the truth will ultimately be known only when history has reached its goal. In this sense the truth remains hidden until the whole is available to all.

Prolepsis and the Determining Power of the Future

Both in creating the world and in sending the Son as the divine representative, God, the eternally loving parent, becomes the one

who is absent. The Creator is not present in the world. Pannenberg points out that this contributes to the "feeling of life in
secular culture."[101] This absence of God is experienced as the
truth of the judgment of death. And death is the inescapable end
of all creatures that emancipate themselves from God in order to
be independent. On the other hand, says Pannenberg, the death
of sinners also represents the powerlessness of God. For God
intends the life and well-being of creatures. It is in this context
that the presence of the Kingdom in the destiny of Jesus of
Nazareth represents the power and love of God.[102]

But this power and love, or at least their ultimate realization in
the Kingdom, remain questionable. At best they are the objects
of human (and sometimes explicitly Christian) hope and expectation, which at the same time exercise transforming power in the
lives of individuals and communities of believers. Pannenberg
also regards the future realization of the Kingdom as the future of
God. God is in the process of realizing divine kingship over the
creation. On the other hand, God is in eternity Father and King.
God will become what God always has been. Pannenberg
affirms both that God always has been what God is and will be,
and that God is becoming King.[103] From the point of view of the
economic Trinity, God is becoming the Lord and Father that God
always has been in the immanent Trinity.[104] And in this process
the whole creation is drawn into the inner-Trinitarian love. It is a
process that, having determined the independent existence of
creatures, continues to work toward the realization of that
determination.

Human sin, the refusal to acknowledge God as God, frustrates
this realization, for in not acknowledging God creatures are subject to death. The independence of the creature is only possible
inasmuch as its dependence on God is recognized. In other
words, apart from the source of its life the creature must die.
But God sends the Son in creaturely form to overcome this sinful
separation and death. Participation in the obedience of the Son
implies participation in the resurrection of the Son. The individ-

ual creature's realization of this participation remains essentially future, although its impact can be experienced in present reality—through trust and love.

The Kingdom of God already is present in history through Jesus' resurrection and determines history toward the complete appearance of the Kingdom in history. This appearance also provides rational insight regarding the source, character, goal, and truth of history. This is so because it is an anticipation of the whole of reality, of reality from the point of view of its completion. It is an anticipation of the unity that encompasses all the oppositions and pluralities within history.

Jesus' resurrection is understood by Pannenberg to represent the unsurpassable revelation of the ultimate end of reality. It is the presence within history of the end of history. There is only a quantitative, no longer a qualitative, difference between the anticipation of the end represented in Jesus' resurrection and the ultimate appearance of the Kingdom of God.[105]

Furthermore, the proleptic appearance of the end of history has a causal function in the process of history toward its ultimate goal. The ultimate unity of history in God and the ultimate realization of the image of God in humans is a future reality. But according to Pannenberg's metaphysics, it is already operative within unfinished history. The future reaches into history to draw history toward itself as history's goal. Pannenberg uses the idea of causality to describe this action of the future on all present moments of history. "If the future is the source of the possible wholeness of existence (*das Dasein*) then its essence and thus its being what it is (*Wassein*) is determined by its future."[106] All being is determined by the possibility of its wholeness, which is future. The future of each creature, as revealed in the resurrection of Jesus, already determines what it is in nature and essence within the historical process toward the ultimate perfection of its Being.

The nearness of the coming Kingdom means, for Pannenberg, the proleptic presence of the Kingdom. He claims that this is different from other attempts to deal with a supposed contradiction between the presence of the Kingdom in Jesus and the fact that it is announced by Jesus as yet to come.[107] The Kingdom of God breaks into the present from the future. The message is grounded in the unity of God and in his exclusive claim on the present life of the creature.[108] The future Kingdom of God is the one God's perfect rule over all creation. All competing considerations for loyalty and power are excluded by God's future rule. Creatures that already acknowledge God now participate in the unity of this future rule; they participate in the exclusion of all competing powers. In this sense the future is present to them now.[109]

Participation in the rule of God is made possible by Jesus through forgiveness of sin, that is, through the overcoming of the separation of humans from God.[110] "Individuals are caught up and snatched away in the process of their history; but Jesus, in bringing close to them the meaning that is tied up with their wholeness, discloses to them their salvation within a history that is not yet complete."[111] The wholeness of individuals is only available at the end of all history, in the context of the wholeness of all reality. But Jesus reveals that God is the "unifying unity" who is now already overcoming all evil with the unifying power of the love of the Son for the Father through the power of the Spirit.[112]

Pannenberg points out that there is no dualism of future and present reality in this understanding of the relationship of God to world. The future is an immanent reality. It has appeared in the message of Jesus. It is a motivational drive to reach out, at social and individual levels, toward the wholeness of the Kingdom. It stands as the relativization of all historical realizations of utopian social orders. Pannenberg argues that the eschatological nature of the Kingdom becomes the new foundation for the law of God.[113] The message of the Kingdom is fundamentally moral. Jesus calls humans into an ethical community of love whose aim is to live "that form of life which is appropriate to the impending Lordship of God."[114] This community includes both humans and the world.[115]   Although Pannenberg does not point it out, the argument implies that the coming Kingdom also should provide motivation for humans to live in a just relationship with the non-human world and should provide a standard of judgment on all historical realizations of justice in these relationships.

The proleptic appearance of the ultimate destination of humans makes that destination concrete within the still unfinished and universal history of the world.   Eschatological hopes are not incidentally related to the question of the meaning of human existence.   In a world in which human existence is best seen as a striving to achieve its purpose, a realistic hope for the achievement of this purpose is central.   Within an understanding of reality determined by the notion of God and of creation as a still unfinished process, the goal of the process also must play a fundamental role and must be determined by God: and so it does in the eschatological nature of Jesus' message and destiny.[116]

> It is possible to find in the history of Jesus an answer to the question of how "the whole" of reality and its meaning can be conceived without compromising the provisionality and historical relativity of all thought, as well as openness to the future on the part of the thinker who knows himself to be only on the way and not yet at the goal.[117]

The question is that of the historical relativism in which modern philosophical, theological, and ethical thought have found themselves and appear to remain bound to this day.   Pannenberg's answer to the problem is taken from the proleptic presence of the Kingdom.   In a manner similar to the Kingdom, the ultimate truth regarding the nature of reality is only available at the end of history.   But the truth, along with the Kingdom, is already present in our systematic and historical anticipations.   On the basis of such anticipations it is possible to know what our moral obligations are as humans.

The task of theology is to deal not only with God and eternity but also with this-worldly things.   The incarnation is the expression of the relationship of the physical creation to the Creator. The Apostle Paul wrote that in Jesus "are hid all the treasures of wisdom and knowledge."[118] According to Pannenberg, Augustine understood wisdom to refer to transcendent matters, what some would label metaphysics, and knowledge to refer to mundane realities, to the sciences generally.[119] Jesus encompasses all realms. Not only is the opposition of history and matter overcome, but the opposition of the eternal Creator and the time-bound material universe is overcome, as well. Dualism is not an option for anyone who takes the incarnation seriously. It would be false, however, to think that the unity of divine and creaturely reality means uniformity. The divine and human realms are separate, and Pannenberg continues to understand each in distinction from the other but still within the overall unity of the Creator and the Redeemer.[120]

The Unity of Creation and Redemption

The Image of God in Creation

It is significant for this study that Pannenberg's Christology includes the entire creation in the relationship of the second of the divine persons to the other persons of the Trinity. Pannenberg understands the fact of creation to be rooted in the self-differentiation of the eternal Son from the Father. In the context of Christology the relationship of the creation to the Son is further elaborated.

> The Son of God is still considered the second person of the Trinity, but while the Son became incarnate only in Jesus of Nazareth, he is conceived at the same time as being at work in the whole creation and especially in the life of human beings created in the image of God.[121]

Pannenberg draws this conclusion on the basis of (1) the Bible's connection of the act of creation with the Son, (2) the creation of humans in the image of God, and (3) the foreshadowing of the incarnate Son in both the Davidic king and in the people of the covenant.[122] The ideas of creation and redemption together give expression to the unified nature of the process of reality toward the realization of the incarnation of the eternal Son. "The incarnation of the Son is now seen as the completion of the creation of humanity in the image of God."[123] It is the Trinitarian focus of Pannenberg's theology that has unified the notions of creation and incarnation and has simultaneously given expression to the unity of all reality in the Creator God, as revealed in the incarnate Son.[124]

It is significant to note that all reality is grounded in the nature of the relationship of the Father and the Son. Humans can be differentiated by degree from other creatures, but they are fundamentally different neither in nature nor in ultimate destiny. This also holds for Jesus as the incarnation of the eternal Son. In Jesus the relationship of Son and Father is realized fully. But this is not an isolated occurrence. The incarnation is intended to draw all creatures into the fullness of this divine love.[125] In Jesus the unity of creature and the Creator is realized. In Jesus God has drawn near to the world. Thus, the incarnation is understood by Pannenberg as an essential act in the process of creating a world of creatures that are together determined to participate in the Kingdom of God.[126]

> It is the destiny of all creation that in the relationship of the creatures to God the eternal Son becomes manifest. That means that the creatures accept themselves in their finite existence as different from God and in voluntary subordination to him. In an explicit form, this can occur only in the human creature, because it is a peculiarly human ability to discern oneself from anything else and everything in its finite particularities from the infinite God. But in accepting themselves and anything finite in distinction from the infinite God and therefore in subordination to him, human beings do not only realize their particularly human destiny, but they also act in the place of every creature.[127]

This means that Pannenberg understands humans as fundamentally determined to differentiate themselves from the Father. The everyday human action of distinguishing oneself from others is here seen as a form of the self-differentiation of the Son from the Father. And the goal of all creaturely existence is to realize, or to make manifest, this humble self-differentiation of the Son. The unity of all reality becomes manifest in this conception of the message and destiny of Jesus. In Jesus' subordination to God is found the unity of all creatures with each other and with the Creator. The reflections of Paul in Rom. 1:18-32 appear to form part of the context for Pannenberg's thinking here. Especially vv. 21, 25, and 28, which state that the central problem of human existence is the refusal to "honor," "serve," and "acknowledge" God, seem to inform Pannenberg's interpretation of the fundamental character of Jesus' relationship to the Father, as well as the fundamental problem of human existence.

Just as the self-differentiation of the Son from the Father is regarded by Pannenberg as the ground of the possibility of the creation of independent creatures, so this self-differentiation is the ground of the appearance of the Son within history as a creature.[128]

> This self-distinction of the eternal Son from the Father may be understood as the basis of all creaturely existence in its distinction from God, and therefore as the basis of the human existence of Jesus, which gave adequate embodiment in its course to the self-emptying of the eternal Son in service of the rule of the Father.[129]

It is in Jesus' complete subjection of himself, in all his acts, to the Father that Jesus acknowledges and honors the Father as God. This is the mark of the divine Sonship of Jesus of Nazareth.[130] But it is the confirmation of this Sonship by God himself through the resurrection of Jesus that makes it possible for the disciples and all Christians thereafter to recognize Jesus as the Son.[131] Another side of this conception of the relationship of Jesus and the eternal Son is that theologically it is not possible to discuss the eternal and preexistent Son in isolation from Jesus of Nazareth.[132] It is in Jesus of Nazareth that the eternal Son has been revealed in the creation. Jesus reveals the humble self-differentiation of the Son from the Father and the connection of this self-differentiation with the independent existence of creatures. He reveals the honor and perfect obedience that the Son gives the Father as God. He reveals that the heart of the relationship of the Son to the Father is in self-giving love. The perfection of this love is the foundation of both the creation of the world and of its redemption and is the unity of creation and redemption.

In other words, apart from the realization of God's perfect rule in the world, which is mediated through the incarnation, death, and resurrection of the Son in the person of Jesus of Nazareth, God cannot truly be named Creator.[133] God has determined that the divine rule (*Basileia*) be realized in the world through the Son. To Pannenberg this means that the Godhood of the Father depends upon the success of the Son: "The rejection that the Son experiences puts the kingship of the Father in question too."[134]

Pannenberg uses the idea of the *Logos* to talk about the structural and generative character of the Son's part in the creation of the world. The Logos is defined by Pannenberg as the generative principle within the self-differentiation of the eternal Son from the Father. It is the generative principle of all finite reality. It is the principle that generates ever new forms of others. At the same time the Logos is the generative principle of relationships between everything finite, as well as between these and their eternal source.[135] Because the Logos is at the same time the *Logos ensarkos* (Jesus Christ) and the *Logos asarkos* (the eternal Son), it is the concrete ordering of the world.[136] This means that each creature has its being and structure or form (*logos*) through the creative work of the Son's love. In other words, the unity of each creature with all other creatures and with the Trinity is neither external to its existence nor is it anything other than a received unity.

The unity of creation and redemption, as well as the ultimate fulfillment of the process of history, is based on the unity of the Trinitarian persons. Ultimately God is one, and all three persons of the Trinity participate in the three aspects of the creative process.[137] The inner-Trinitarian unity, according to Pannenberg, is discovered through an examination of the qualities of God, especially those qualities that all three persons of the Trinity share. "In the identity of these attributes the God who acts in creation, redemption and fulfillment will be recognizable as [one and the] same."[138] Pannenberg argues that love is the one quality that lies at the root of all the divine attributes (eternity, omniscience, omnipotence, omnipresence, wisdom, justice, holiness, and mercy). Love, furthermore, is not merely a divine attribute but is identical to the divine essence. "Thus the sentence 'God is love' is to be understood as the summary expression of the Trinitarian communion of Father, Son and Spirit."[139]

When Pannenberg argues that history is the self-revelation of God, he means that it is the process aimed at the incarnation of the eternal Son. He means that all creation is the process toward the unity of creature with Creator. The appearance of the Son in the person of Jesus of Nazareth is the proleptic realization of this goal. As such, it reveals the ultimate unity that is the goal of creation.[140] It is the prior relationship of God, as well as each individual, to the whole of reality that makes it possible to speak of a manifestation of the one almighty and triune God in the context of such individual events.[141]

The Significance of Humans

History is the process that gives the opportunity to overcome the conflicts that result from the tendency of creatures to attempt to gain independence.[142] Jesus Christ is the goal of creation because in him the communion of creature and Creator was realized. This is so because in Jesus the second person of the Trinity appeared in the form of a human being. This means that humans can be regarded as the goal of creation. In other words, the entire history of the universe can be regarded as preparation for the appearance of humans.

Pannenberg regards the anthropic principle as showing significant coherence with this Judeo-Christian view of humans.[143]

The idea that the eventual discovery of other intelligent life in the universe would threaten the centrality of the incarnation of the Son in Jesus is discounted by Pannenberg. He observes that such a possibility is vague and speculative and that the Bible itself speaks of other intelligent life besides humans. Some of these require no salvation (angels), and others cannot be saved (fallen angels). He argues that there is no ground here for questioning the Christian understanding that "in Jesus of Nazareth the Logos who works throughout the universe became human and therein a crucial function for the [realization of the] unity and meaning of the entire creation has passed to humanity and its history."[144]

Pannenberg does differentiate between humans and the rest of creation, but he does so only in the context of a vision of unity and wholeness. The entire creation is included in the redemptive work of the second person of the Trinity, just as it was included in the creative work of the Father. The incarnation of the Son as a human is determinative for the meaning and end of the entire creation. In both creation and redemption humans are given a central function, but that function is in both instances directed toward the good of the entire creation.[145]

The Problem of Evil

Does Pannenberg's theology account for the possibility of the final defeat of God's love in persons such as Stalin and Hitler or in more ordinary persons who turn their backs to goodness and love, who fail to trust God and rely instead on their self-interested manipulations of created reality to stave off personal emptiness and death?[146] Pannenberg's arguments regarding the unity of reality under God attempt to make sense of the world in a manner that overcomes ontological dualism, at least. However, the consideration of radical evil seems to raise again the possibility of a dualist opposition of evil and God. Certainly, in Pannenberg's conception of reality, dualism is overcome at the ultimate level, and at the end of history. But radical evil works in opposition to the creative process that supposedly leads to the Kingdom of God. Evil at this level appears to be connected with a kind of dualism.

There are at least two dangers to be avoided here. One is to regard this dualism as ultimate. To regard evil as infinite is wrong. Good versus evil (God versus the devil) is not the final truth regarding reality. The subordination of Jesus to the Father and the resurrection of Jesus show, proleptically, that this dualism is not ultimate. Pannenberg is correct in arguing that in the Christian tradition the ideas of creation, incarnation, and resurrection are the answers to the question regarding the challenge of evil to God's kingship. Reality is ultimately created by God for communion with God. The incarnation, life, death, and resurrection of the eternal Son in the person of Jesus of Nazareth serves to overcome the opposition of sin and evil to God's intentions for creation. However, not until the resurrection is generally realized in all creation will the answer to evil be definitively given.

The second danger is to ignore the reality of evil's radical character. Evil and sin are indeed opposed to the Kingdom. And Pannenberg does acknowledge that sin and death are opposed to the intention of God. To ignore this opposition would not do justice to reality as we know it. If the Kingdom is not opposed to the corruption and destruction of reality then the Kingdom cannot be of God. Perhaps the dialectical "NO!" of God to the human "no" to life does reveal some truth about the radical neediness of the human situation. Evil must be opposed and cannot be taken into the ultimate synthesis that the Kingdom of God is.

Pannenberg acknowledges that the problem of existence is not only its finitude. Sin is not merely a result of the anxiety of death. Sin is the turning of a self away from the divine source of its existence.[147] Radical evil seeks its pleasure and good, if the terms can be so used, in the suffering, pain, and destruction of creatures and in the thwarting of God's goal, quite apart from pragmatic considerations of the one doing the evil.

E. Frank Tupper suggests that Pannenberg has not taken seriously enough the implications of radical evil. He states that "Pannenberg's theology all too frequently reflects an unqualified optimism that lends credibility to the charges of Christianized idealism of historical monism."[148] Does the emphasis on the unity of all reality in God, when emphasized as thoroughly as Pannenberg does, allow one to take evil seriously in its radical destructiveness? My concern is specifically with Pannenberg's understanding of the relationship of the Kingdom to the world as we experience it.

In his postscript to Tupper's book, Pannenberg contends that he has indeed taken evil seriously.[149] Pannenberg points to his anthropological study *What is Man?* To this can be added the later major monograph on anthropology and the appropriate sections of the *Systematic Theology*.[150] He notes specifically that he has identified sin as inescapably belonging to the self-centered character of human existence and admits that he feared he would be charged with Flacianism (identifying sin with human nature).[151] He further points out that he has defined freedom as a gift, not as self-constituted, and that this view of human nature has had a practical result in his reservations about the potential for political systems to overcome evil. Perhaps the best way to approach this problem, then, is to ask how Pannenberg connects his concept of the whole with his view of human sinfulness. These matters will be taken up in the next chapter.

The evil of Antiochus, for example, is turned by God to the ultimate good of the people—but not to the good of the oppressor. Entailed in the death of Jesus is a message of ultimate condemnation and separation from God of those who hate the Creator and oppress creatures. It is central to the message of the cross that Jesus has borne the condemnation that falls upon those who fail to acknowledge God. Does Jesus' death also atone for those who not only fail to acknowledge God but also hate God? It remains true that the Son has borne the condemnation of those who receive the grace of the cross. But there also remains the possibility of continued rejection of God's love. The life of a

Hitler exemplifies such rejection, but more than that it also represents a radical hatred of both God and creation.

Within Pannenberg's understanding of the overall unity of God's economy, there remains the freedom of creatures not only to turn from God but also to turn radically against the Kingdom. The exercise of this freedom introduces oppositions between creatures, among which is the opposition of humans to the natural world. The very possibility of speaking of history and nature in opposition to each other, as a dualism, is rooted in the refusal of humans to acknowledge God. The experienced duality of history and nature, of spirit and matter, is real and is connected with sin. Pannenberg does not deny this argument, but he does not make it explicit in his theology.

However, this duality is no more than the implication of evil within the context of God's unifying love. This duality presupposes the more fundamental unity of creation with its Creator. The power of the eschatological hope is that all such oppositions are regarded as overcome by God. Evil will be annihilated. Only the justified will participate in the ultimate Kingdom. But those who turn to the Kingdom of God are called to practice its love and unity within history. If the Kingdom is the determining power of the future, then it must show itself, albeit in provisional form, in the life of the community that joyfully anticipates the Kingdom.[152]

Through the fate of Jesus, his death and resurrection, the Kingdom of God appears in history and is present for each creature. Its presence enables persons to open themselves to the future and to transcend their own self-centeredness. In this way the Kingdom comes to them with forgiveness of sin and opens the imaginations of self-centered individuals to others, through the creative power of God's love. In other words, the power of the Kingdom is the manifestation in Jesus of the future perfection of love's rule of the universe. Openness to this future is based on trust in the power of God as revealed in the resurrection and hence justification of Jesus.

Redeeming Love

Pannenberg finds in the connection of God's creative goodness and redemptive love the grounding of the twofold motion of love.[153]

> [T]hose who open themselves to the summons of God's rule, who accept its imminence [Nähe or nearness] and thus receive present salvation, must also let themselves be drawn into the movement of the love of God as it aims beyond individual recipients to the world as a whole. We can have fellowship with God and his dominion only as we share in the movement of his love.[154]

Participation in God's Kingdom means participation in divine love, and this means love for God as well as love for the entire creation. Love of God and love of world are united. The Kingdom of God is the destiny of the entire creation. Although Pannenberg focuses on human creatures, he does include all creation in his conception of the creative, redemptive, and fulfilling activity of the Trinity. This is true even if he does not always make it explicit. The love of the Kingdom does not allow for human disregard of the nonhuman members of the world.

Pannenberg argues that the connection of the love of God and the love of others is given concrete expression in the parable of the unforgiving servant, which teaches the necessity of forgiving others in order that one may receive forgiveness of one's own sin.[155] And love of one's enemies is connected with the goodness of the Creator.[156]

Pannenberg argues that while there is an important agreement between Jesus and the Jewish leaders regarding the summation of the law in the double command of love (love God and love your neighbor), in Jesus' teaching this double command is not merely the law's summation. To the rabbinic interpreters this command continues to presuppose the authority of the entire legal tradition of Israel. But in Jesus' teaching this command stands independently over against the tradition as its critical principle.

The decisive point is that the authority of tradition no longer functions as the criterion, since in his eschatological message with its revelation of the love of God in the inbreaking of his rule, Jesus found a new basis for interpreting the law of God.[157]

Jesus himself is the mediator of the dawning of the ultimate reign of God, and he announces that forgiving love is the basic truth of this future reign. Pannenberg argues that this provides the theological foundation of ethics. For Pannenberg ethics is grounded on the basis of "the claim of the future of God on people, and from its dawn in Jesus'" appearance.[158]

"In him it has become manifest how the creature can relate to the eternal God in such a way as to enjoy communion with him in eternity, beyond this earthly life, but already in each present moment."[159] In the context of the concept of the two aspects of love this can only mean that communion with God can already be enjoyed through a total trust in the love of God. According to Pannenberg, the double command of love is not actually a law. It is the motion of the love of the Father and the Son for each other. This love is the active power of the Spirit of God, at work in creaturely life.[160] Love is not a law that is external or opposed to human reason. Love is the destiny from which reasonable creatures have their existence.[161] According to Pannenberg, love is the redemptive power that frees humans and enables them to love God and world.

In participating in the love of God, one's love is also directed to one's neighbors and enemies. Love takes the concrete form of forgiving both neighbors and enemies and seeking their good. Love is creative solidarity. It "contributes to individual and social integration, unity, and peace."[162] Love contributes to the freedom of the loved. It does not establish or entrench dependencies but overlooks vast social and personal differences to progress toward the realization of the fundamental creaturely equality of persons.[163] In other words, those who are less equal in practice are given opportunities to improve their lots.

Unlike law, the "imagination of love is capable of creating new codes of conduct" that reflect the needs of the situations that have come to prevail.[164] Laws are specific to concrete situations, and as cultures and needs change laws must be renewed. Pannenberg argues that the imaginative power of love, which is best understood as the heart of the future Kingdom of God, is the most fundamental creative source for both the formation of just laws and their renewal.[165] Furthermore, according to Pannenberg, the future of love (i.e., the Kingdom of God) also grounds the notions of justice, equality, and freedom, which are intermediary concepts between love and law. Justice, equality, and freedom are not regarded by Pannenberg as fundamental anthropological notions. He argues that in history humans are neither equal nor free but that they are destined by love for both freedom and equality.[166]

"Love is a power that goes forth from God. It is not primarily an act of humans. But it grips humans in a manner that allows them to become active."[167] According to Pannenberg, human love that is not concerned for the self is a gift that comes from the Kingdom. It is received in faith and trust that are oriented completely toward God's rule. Thus, love exists in the hope of perfect participation in the love of the Father and Son for each other.[168] "Genuine Christian hope means a fascinating vision of a new life for all mankind, even for the natural world. . . . It is only this comprehensive humanistic vision which opens up the universal perspective for the creative activity of Christian love."[169] The fascinating vision of a new life for all creation is founded on the forgiving love of God, who both creates and redeems. It is founded on the mediator of the Kingdom, Jesus of Nazareth, because he not only has taught that forgiving love is the basis of the Kingdom but also has brought it to complete concrete expression in his life, teaching, death, and resurrection. Pannenberg sums up the dual movement of love as follows:

> In love for God, as the answer to the received love of God—an answer made possible by the Holy Spirit—humans take part in the inner-Trinitarian life of God, in the reciprocity of communion between Father, Son, and Spirit. Through the love of the neighbor they take

part in the movement of the Trinitarian God in the creation, redemption, and completion of the world.[170]

These are two aspects of human participation in the love of God that the Spirit pours into creatures who turn to God.[171]

According to Pannenberg, it is in this way that the church is "called to continue Jesus' ministry and to further the Kingdom of God among all human beings so that the eternal Son may become apparent in their relations to God the Father and make them brothers and sisters in their relations with each other."[172] Pannenberg does not explicitly include the rest of creaturely reality here, but he does include all reality when speaking especially about humans.[173]

Pannenberg specifies that participation in the future Kingdom is made concrete through anticipatory experiences of "peace, spirit, love, and life" and that these are imperfect participations of creatures in eschatological life.[174] Pannenberg's argument for Christian ecumenicity can be generalized and made relevant in this context. He argues that unity among Christians cannot be based on either doctrinal unity or the authority of a single highest office; although the latter may need to be a manifestation of the spiritual unity Pannenberg feels has already begun to form among the laity.[175] Because unity with Christ is bound up with "the purposes of God concerning all mankind," that is, with the Kingdom of God, it is never a merely private relationship.[176] The unity of the Spirit goes beyond the bounds of the church; it involves "concern for the human situation in general," and this concern "belongs to the logic of catholicity."[177] Catholicity is defined by Pannenberg as excluding all claims to uniformity. "The unity it invokes is the unity of the spirit in the midst of pluriformity, and the unity of the spirit can emerge only when every attempt is avoided to impose uniformity."[178]

In other words, neither authoritative structures nor anthropology, but the coming Kingdom is the source of the unity.[179] This pluriformity grows out of the provisional character of all present knowledge and realizations of the ultimate goal of existence. The recognition of the difference between the final realization of the Kingdom and its historical approximations makes Christian freedom possible. It leaves room for the acknowledgment of doctrinal and institutional variety.[180] Variety in expression and doctrine does not negate the presence of the unifying love and peace of God. Again, this argument applies more broadly to human experience. It is not necessary to the experience of unity and love that all nations unite under one political and legal system. It is necessary, however, for political and legal systems to recognize the fundamental unity of humans, despite cultural differences.[181] Beyond this it is also necessary for institutions and individuals to recognize the fundamental unity of humans with the nonhuman world.

The catholicity of the Christian community is the heart of love and joy from which a Christian view of reality can make an impact on the thought and morality of the modern age. The power of the Christian faith is found in the proleptic presence in history of the ultimate hopes of creatures for harmony, love, and ecstasy. The Kingdom of God is not merely a vision, it is a present reality. Pannenberg's concern for Christian unity is rooted in his understanding that the church is to be a sign of the coming Kingdom of God. The disunity of the churches indicates not only the distance of the church from the goal of history but also its inability to witness to the truth of the Christian claim regarding the ultimate unity of reality under God. The role of the church in history is bound up with the truth of the Christian claim about the eschatological Kingdom.

> The church is called before the world to witness to the truth of the Gospel. This witness is connected with the notion that the church is itself in this world a sign of the destiny of humans, which is to be renewed to a communion of freedom, justice and peace in the future of the Kingdom of God.[182]

Pannenberg explains that the success of this task is directly related to the question of Christian unity.[183]

Conclusion

The promise of the Kingdom moves beyond strictly human concerns to include all of reality. It gives ultimate meaning to human life within the context of the destiny of mediating God's love in the world. Thus, it amounts to the rejection of the opposition of the history of human progress and untamed nature that has characterized much of modern technoscientific thought and practice. Capricious manipulation and consumption of the non-human world is opposed to the love of God—just as such abuse of humans is opposed to God's love. But the promise of the Kingdom also transcends merely human possibilities of achieving love, peace, and justice. Thus, it also demands the recognition of the provisional character of all historical realizations of peace and justice.[184] In this way the ossification of particular historical realizations of the peace of the Kingdom is prevented. The principle of love, in other words, is also the critical principle by which every political achievement of peace and justice is seen as less than ultimate.

The eschatology of Christian faith does not amount to a forsaking of present reality for the sake of the future and otherworldly Kingdom. Rather, in the context of a community it provides for a hope that overcomes the fear of death and condemnation, as well as the fear of the conflicts that threaten our existence. It opens imaginations to horizons beyond self-centered gratifications. The heart of the message and experience of reality from the Christian point of view is forgiving love. This love empowers and frees individuals to form communities of hope. It conquers cynicism and despair and fear. It thus enables persons both to value and to relativize all reality in the light of the ultimate good. Because this redemption is intimately connected with the creation of all reality, with its existence and ultimate end, this new life, in turning persons to God, turns them also to the whole of created reality.[185]

In the context of Christology, the unity of nature and history means the reconciliation of the oppositions introduced by sin and evil. This unity is the reconciliation of the opposition of divine and human, of human and nonhuman nature, and of humans between each other. In Christ all history is taken into that goal from which God has created all that has being. Love is at the core of this understanding of reality. Divine love creates, redeems, and completes the creaturely world. Love determines the very structure of creaturely existence. Love is its goal. And this divine love is the foundation and essence of all morality. Inasmuch as it structures existence, it structures its moral character as well. Finally, the creative and redeeming character of love means that love is neither external to existence nor opposed to the freedom of creaturely existence.

NOTES

1. My translation. "Im Prozeß der Überlieferung seiner eschatologischen Offenbarung ist Gott der Geschichte immanent, bestimmt er ihre Ganzheit nun von innen, von dem innergeschichtlichen Ereignis der Geschichte Jesus her, und erwiest sich so als Gott, als die alles bestimmende Wirklichkeit." Pannenberg, "Über historische und theologische Hermeneutik," in *GF* 1:139; *BQ* 1:158.

2. *IST*, 55.

3. Moltmann points out that Barth relies on ancient hierarchical conceptions of reality. According to Moltmann, Barth understands orders of domination to progress from heaven to soul, from soul to body, from man to earth, and from man to woman. This contributes to the opposition of humans and nature (Moltmann, *God in Creation,* 252-55). It should also be noted that Pannenberg's understanding of revelation, despite his differences from Barth, is deeply informed by Barth's notions that revelation is one and is the self-revelation of God. Carl E. Braaten suggests that the difference between Pannenberg and Barth is focused on methodology rather than dogmatic content. Braaten suggests that the primary difference lies in Pannenberg's complaint that Barth ultimately relies on the subjective assertion that God's self-revelation in Jesus has nothing to do with a general anthropological expression such as religion ("The Place of Christianity Among the World Religions: Wolfhart Pannenberg's Theology of Religion and the History of Religions," in *Theology of Pannenberg: American Critiques*, 299). It is integral to Pannenberg's thought to argue the truth of the divine revelation in Jesus in the context of the modern sciences generally. Pannenberg, in other words, wishes to overcome the epistemological gulf between theology and the other sciences. This is based on a revision of the ideas of God and revelation (see chapter 1).

4. Pannenberg states that in "Barth's systematics the key concept is that of the Son's eternal predestination and abandonment. The creation comes into the picture only secondarily." (*IST*, 68).

5. Löwith, *Meaning in History* (Chicago: University of Chicago, 1949), 1-20.

6. *CW*, 12. Löwith, *Meaning of History*, 1-20, 188-200.

7. Blumenberg, *The Legitimacy of the Modern Age*, trans. Robert M. Wallace (Cambridge: MIT, 1985), 27-32, 72. See also Pannenberg's criticism of Blumenberg in "Christianity as the Legitimacy of the Modern Age," in *IGHF*, 178-91.

8. *CSW*, 7; *CW*, 14.

9. Löwith, "Hans Blumenberg: *Die Legitimität der Neuzeit*," *Philosophische Rundschau* 15 (1968): 198.

10. Löwith, *Meaning in History*, 190-95.

11. My translation. The question Pannenberg asks is "ob die Wirklichkeit selbst in ihren fundamentalen Aspekten als geschichtlich und die Geschichte der Natur und des Menschen in ihrer Einheit als Geschichte Gottes zu verstehen ist" (*GF* 1:19; *BQ* 1:11).

12. *GF* 1:19; *BQ* 1:11.

13. See especially two essays in *GF* 1: "Hermeneutik und Universalgeschichte" and "Über historische und theologische Hermeneutik" (esp. 142-51; *BQ* 1:162-74). Cf. Ted Peters, "Truth in History," 36-56. Also see my comments in the previous chapter (93n84) regarding Pannenberg's argument that universal history is the final horizon presupposed by the notion of fusion of horizons.

14. *GF* 1:149; *BQ* 1:171.

15. *GF* 1:153; *BQ* 1:176.

16. My translation. "Durch jüdische Apokalyptik und christliche Geschichtstheologie ist das universalgeschichtliche Thema der neuzeitlichen Geschichtsphilosophie vererbt worden, und es ist fraglich, ob die Universalgeschichte ohne den biblischen Gottesgedanken überhaupt als eine Einheit verstanden werden kann" (*GF* 1:19; *BQ* 1:12).

17. *GF* 1:19; *BQ* 1:12.

18. Helmut G. Harder and W. Taylor Stevenson, "The Continuity of History and Faith in the Theology of Wolfhart Pannenberg: Toward an Erotics of Faith," *Journal of Religion* 51 (1971): 34f., 47f. Harder and Stevenson point out that Pannenberg attempts to overcome the separation of event and meaning and associate this with reconciling the opposition of human and natural worlds.

19. The translated phrase is: "Abschattungen eines mythischen Urgeschehens" (*GF* 1:24; *BQ* 1:17).

20. *BQ* 1:17. "Demgegenüber ist es spezifisch für Israel, daß es . . . immer entschiedener gerade im geschichtlichen Wandel selbst die Wirklichkeit seines Gottes erfuhr" (*GF* 1:24).

21. *GF* 1:24f.; *BQ* 1:17-19.

22. This essay first appeared as "Späthorizonte des Mythos in biblischer und christlicher Überlieferung," in *Terror und Spiel, Probleme der Mythenrezeption* (*Poetik und Hermeneutik IV*), ed. H. Fuhrmann (1971), 473-525. It then appeared separately under the title *Christentum und Mythos* (1973). The page references here are to its most recent publication in Pannenberg's *GF* 2:13-65.

23. Myth functions as "*gründender*, fundierender Geschichte" (*GF* 2:14). Emphasis is Pannenberg's. He refers to B. Malinowski, *Myth in Primitive Psychology* (1926).

24. *GF* 2:17.

25. Pannenberg quotes Bultmann's phrase that myth speaks "vom Unweltlichen weltlich, von den Göttern menschlich" (*GF* 2:17f). The phrase is found in Bultmann's *Kerygma und Mythos*, vol. 1 (Hamburg, 1948), 23.

26. "Die stereotypen Gegenüberstellungen der Struktur angeblich 'mythischer' Vorstellungen zur Erkenntnis der wahren Ursachen, Kräfte und Gesetze der Natur von Heyne bis Bultmann lassen erkennen, daß es sich hier um einen Gegenbegriff zum Weltverständnis der modernen, durch Galilei und Newton begründeten und heute als 'klassisch' bezeichneten Naturwissenschaft handelt. Dieser Gegenbegriff einer mythischen Bewußtseinsverfassung sollte allerdings ursprünglich keine polemische, sondern hermeneutische Funktion haben" (*GF* 2:21).

27. *GF* 2:60-65.

28. "Der Mythos wurde . . . herabgesetzt zum Interpretament der Geschichte." (*GF* 2:65).

29. My translation. "Innerhalb der durch immer neues Wirken Gottes gekennzeichneten Wirklichkeit entsteht Geschichte dadurch, daß Gott Verheißungen ergehen läßt und diese Verheißungen erfüllt. Geschichte ist das zwischen Verheißung und Erfüllung hineingespannte Geschehen, indem es durch die Verheißung eine unumkehrbare Zielrichtung auf künftige Erfüllung hin erhält" (*GF* 1:25; *BQ* 1:18).

30. Pannenberg, *Jesus--God and Man*, 2d ed, trans. Lewis L. Wilkins and Duane A. Priebe (Philadelphia: Westminster, 1977), 208. Hereafter *JGM*.

31. *OG*, vii.

32. Ibid.

33. Pannenberg argues that Israel's faith did not so much develop on the basis of an original and natural knowledge of God as on the basis of Jahweh's acts, which overcame the estrangement of God from the world. Israel comes to know God "not as much through acceptance of an originally general knowledge of God in the sense of natural theology, as in the overcoming of the absence of God from the world through the acts of God in history." (Israel came to know God "weniger in der Annahme eines anfänglich-allgemeinen Wissens von Gott im Sinne natürlicher Theologie als in der Überwindung der Gottferne der Welt durch das Geschichtshandelns Gottes") (*OG*, viii).

34. "The development of the Israelitic writing of history is distinguished by

the fact that the horizon of this historical consciousness becomes ever wider, the length of time spanned by promise and fulfillment ever more extensive" (*BQ* 1:19). ("Die Entwicklung der israelitischen Geschichtsschreibung aber ist dadurch gekennzeichnet, daß der Horizont des geschichtlichen Bewußtseins immer weiter, der von Verheißung und Erfüllung umspannte Verlauf immer umfassender wurde") (*GF* 1:25).

35. The following are the phrases I have translated: "die Wirklichkeit des Menschen und seiner Welt . . . als unumkehrbare Abfolge je neuer Ereignisse;" "das Handeln Gottes in der Kontingenz der Ereignisse;" "konstitutiv für Zusamenhang und Sinn der Ereignisfolge;" and "Entgegensetzung von Natur und Geschichte, wie sie sich im abendländischen Denken der Neuzeit herausgebildet hat" (*ST* 2:86; *STe* 2:67f.).

36. *ST* 2:87; *STe* 2:68 (Bromiley's translation does not mark the citation). The quotation is from Gerhard von Rad, "Aspekte alttestamentlichen Weltverständnisses," *Evangelische Theologie* 24 (1964): 65. The article is pages 57-98. On page 64 von Rad contrasts ancient Israel's concept of nature with that of the modern West.

37. *ST* 2:87; *STe* 2:68f.

38. *OG*, vii.

39. *GF* 1:152-53; *BQ* 1:174-76.

40. Joel 2:10, for example, includes the sun, moon, and stars in the events of the "Day of the Lord."

41. *JGM*, 32.

42. Pannenberg, "Response to the Discussion," in Robinson, et al., eds., 246.

43. "Für den Apokalyptiker kann darum die Geschichte auch keinen Offenbarungscharakter annehmen; das Eschaton kann nicht das Ziel, sondern nur das Ende der Geschichte bedeuten. Er ist einem völligen metaphysischen Dualismus nur dadurch entgangen daß er Gott als den versteht, der dem gegenwärtigen bösen Äon bald für immer ein Ende zu setzen die Macht hat" (Betz, "Apokalyptik in der Theologie der Pannenberg-Gruppe," *Zeitschrift für Theologie und Kirche* 65 [1968]: 265).

44. Ibid., 269f.

45. Cf. Polk, *On the Way to God*, 151-82 for a detailed analysis of the criticism of Pannenberg's theological interpretation of Jewish apocalypticism. I agree with Polk that aspects of apocalyptic thought appear not to support or even to contradict Pannenberg's understanding of history. It is also quite true, as Polk argues, that we do not yet know enough about apocalyptic and its relationship to both the Hebrew Bible and Christian origins. However, in my judgment none of the arguments against Pannenberg's position are a threat to his admittedly Christian evaluation of the significance of Jewish apocalyptic for the rise of Christianity. Pannenberg's *überlieferungsgeschichtliche* perspective defines itself as a transmission that quite legitimately transforms the traditions it receives. This methodological issue appears to have been passed

over by Pannenberg's critics. Polk himself points out that Pannenberg regards Jesus as significantly different from his apocalyptic predecessors (188f.).

46. *ST* 2:366f., 371; *STe* 2:326f., 331.

47. *ST* 2:367; *STe* 2:327.

48. Luke 7:37-50; 19:2-10

49. *ST* 2:372; *STe* 2:332

50. *IST*, 58.

51. *ST* 2:370; *STe* 2:330. See Deut. 6:4f.

52. Matt. 5:45.

53. "Zur *rettenden* Liebe wird diese Schöpfergüte in der Sendung Jesu zur *Ankündigung* der nahen Gottesherrschaft" (*ST* 2:371; *STe* 2:331). Bromiley's translation does not include Pannenberg's emphases of "rettenden" and "Ankündigung." It also translates "nahen" with "imminent," which sacrifices the spacial aspect of nearness (of God's rule) that is primary in the word "nahe" without excluding the temporal aspect.

54. "Jesus did not teach participation in salvation without repentance. But his message did not begin with a demand for repentance. It began with the nearness of the kingdom, in the receiving of which salvation is present and repentance is included." ("Eine Teilhabe am Heil ohne Umkehr hat Jesus nicht gelehrt. Aber seine Botschaft begann nicht mit der Umkehrforderung, sondern mit der Nähe der Gottesherrschaft, in deren Annahme das Heil gegenwärtig ist, das die Umkehr einschließt") (*ST* 2:372n.22). My translation benefits from Bromiley's (*STe* 2:331n22) but differs slightly. Pannenberg argues that the point of Jesus' message is the salvation of the lost (*Rettung des Verlorenen*). It is in the joy of participating in the Kingdom that the message of forgiving love finds its mark: "In dieser Freude findet die an ihr Ziel gelangte, vergebende Liebe ihren Ausdruck" (*ST* 2:372).

55. *IST*, 59.

56. *ST* 2:370; *STe* 2:330.

57. *IST*, 59.

58. *ST* 2:370; *STe* 2:331.

59. *ST* 3:535-38.

60. Pannenberg refers to Mark 2:19 and parallels: "Can the wedding guests fast while the bridegroom is with them?" (*ST* 2:371; *STe* 2:331).

61. *ST* 3:577-88.

62. Pannenberg acknowledges the role of Barth in reintroducing the positive role of eschatology in theology. However, he argues that both Barth and Bultmann limited this to a metaphorical role in depicting the judgment of God against the world. He points out that when Barth turned to concentrate on divine grace (in the *Church Dogmatics*), the eschatology of the early work disappeared (*ST* 3:579 and cf. *CS*, 90-92).

63. *ST* 3:656-59.

64. See below the section on resurrection. Also see Helmut Harder, "Continuity Between Method and Content in Contemporary Theology: The

Achievement of Wolfhart Pannenberg," Th.D., Toronto School of Theology, 1971, 130f. Harder argues that Pannenberg understands history as resurrection. There is no discontinuity, in other words, between the Kingdom of God (in which the general resurrection will be realized) and history.

65. Pannenberg, "Response to Discussion," in Robinson, et al., eds., 262n72.

66. Matt. 21:23-27.

67. Matt. 11:16-24.

68. Matt. 23.

69. *JGM*, 61-63.

70. *IST*, 59.

71. *IST*, 60.

72. *Ibid.*

73. *TKG*, 83f.

74. *STe* 2:375. "Die Gottesferne des Kreuzes Jesu war die äußerste Zuspitzung seiner Selbstunterscheidung vom Vater. Insofern ist der Kreuzestod Jesu mit Recht als das 'Integral seiner irdischen Existenz' bezeichnet worden" (*ST* 2:418). The phrase is quoted from Eberhard Jüngel, *Entsprechungen: Gott—Wahrheit—Mensch* (1980), 283.

75. *STe* 2:379. "Gerade dadurch ist der Weg des Sohnes auch Ausdruck der Liebe Gottes zu den Menschen" (*ST* 2:422).

76. Matt. 27:40-43.

77. *ST* 2:417; *STe* 2:374.

78. *ST* 2:385; *STe* 2:344.

79. *ST* 2:387f.; *STe* 2:346f.

80. *ST* 2:390f.; *STe* 2:349.

81. *ST* 2:392f.; *STe* 2:350f.

82. *STe* 2:351. "Dem proleptischen Grundzug der Geschichte Jesu entspricht die christliche Osterbotschaft, indem sie als Verkündigung eines besonderen Geschehens in geschichtlicher Vergangenheit doch immer schon die Allgemeinheit einer noch in der Zukunft liegenden Veränderung und Vollendung der Wirklichket des Menschen und seiner Welt voraussetzt" (*ST* 2:393).

83. *GF* 1:222.

84. *STe* 2:360. "'Historizität' muß nicht bedeuten, daß das als historisch Behauptete analog oder gleichartig mit sonst bekanntem Geschehen sei" (*ST* 2:403, and see "Heilsgeschehen und Geschichte," in *GF* 1:49ff.; *BQ* 1:43ff.). See Pannenberg's "Response to the Debate" in Gary R. Habermas and Antony G. N. Flew, *Did Jesus Rise From the Dead?: The Resurrection Debate*, ed. Terry L. Miethe (San Francisco: Harper & Row, 1987), 125-35. Habermas is somewhat more optimistic than Pannenberg regarding the historical verifiability of the resurrection of Jesus. Habermas bases his conclusion on what he perceives to be a consensus of critical scholarship regarding the Gospel accounts of the resurrection. He provides a good bibliography.

85. *ST* 2:404f.; *STe* 2:361f.

86. *JGM*, 391.

87. *IST*, 56.

88. *ST* 2:341-44, 352-54; *STe* 2:301-4, 312-14.

89. *OG*, xiv; 1 Cor. 15:17.

90. *IST*, 61.

91. *ST* 2:389; *STe* 2:347.

92. *MIG*, 65f. "Diese ewige Bejahung des individuellen Daseins der Geschöpfe in der Eschatologie erscheint als die Vollendung des göttlichen Schöpfungswillens, und auch der eigentümlich christliche Gedanke, daß Gott jedes einzelne seiner Geschöpfe . . . mit ewiger Liebe sucht, steht in enger Verbindung zur Bejahung des endlichen Daseins der Geschöpfe über den Tod hinaus und in alle Ewigkeit, wie sie für die christliche Eschatologie charakteristisch ist" (*MG*, 49).

93. *JGM*, 205f., 206n13.

94. Rom. 8:29.

95. Rev. 21:22-22:5.

96. Cf. Isa. 11:1-10.

97. Cf. 1 Enoch 1:1-9.

98. *OG*, 98f.; *RH*, 135f.

99. *OG*, 100; *RH*, 136f.

100. Regarding Pannenberg's tests of truth see the subsection "Whole and Part" in chapter 1.

101. This is my translation. The absence of God "gehört nicht zufällig zum Lebensgefühl der säkularen Kultur" (*ST* 2:435; *STe* 2:391).

102. *ST* 2:435f.; *STe* 2:391f.

103. *ST* 2:437f.; *STe* 2:393f.

104. Cf. *OG*, 97; *RH*, 134. There Pannenberg states that God has a history—the history of his becoming the one God of all people. Cf. also "Probleme einer trinitarischen Gotteslehre," 333.

105. *GF* 1:155f.; *BQ* 1:178f.

106. Translation is mine. "Wenn die Zukunft der Ursprung möglicher Ganzheit des Daseins ist, dann heißt es, daß sein Wesen und also sein Wassein durch seine Zukunft bestimmt wird" (*MG*, 63; *MIG*, 87).

107. *ST* 2:371; *STe* 2:330f.

108. *ST* 2:370; *STe* 2:330.

109. *ST* 3:573.

110. "But there can be no doubt whatever that the presence of God's rule and participation in its salvation include remission of sins and the overcoming of that which separates us from God" (*STe* 2:332). ("Daß aber die Gegenwart der Gottesherrschaft und die Teilhabe an ihrem Heil ganz allgemein Vergebung der Sünden, Überwindung alles den Menschen von Gott Trennenden einschließt, kann nicht zweifelhaft sein.") (*ST* 2:372).

111. "Theology and Science," 381.

112. See Pannenberg, *Grundzüge der Christologie*, 5th ed. (Gütersloh: Gerd Mohn, 1975), 240f.

113. *ST* 2:372; *STe* 2:331f.

114. *JGM*, 194.

115. Cf. *GF* 1:155n31; *BQ* 1:178n43.

116. *GF* 1:154; *BQ* 1:177.

117. *BQ* 1:181. "An der Geschichte Jesu ließe sich eine Antwort gewinnen auf die Frage, wie 'das Ganze' der Wirklichkeit und ihrer Bedeutung gedacht werden kann unbeschadet der Vorläufigkeit und geschichtlichen Relativität alles Denkens, sowie der Offenheit der Zukunft für den Denkenden, der sich erst auf dem Wege und noch nicht am Ziele weiß" (*GF* 1:158).

118. Col. 2:3.

119. *WT*, 14; *TPS*, 10.

120. *WT*, 15; *TPS*, 11.

121. *IST*, 65.

122. *IST*, 65f.

123. *IST*, 66.

124. *IST*, 67; *OG*, xi.

125. *ST* 2:433; *STe* 2:389.

126. Stanley Grenz, *Reason for Hope*, 114, sees the significance of the incarnation to be relevant only for understanding human nature. I here argue that while Pannenberg's focus is clearly on humanity, he gives explicit indication that his intention is to include all reality in the determination toward the realization of the incarnation of the image of God.

127. *IST*, 61.

128. *ST* 2:360; *STe* 2:319.

129. *STe* 2:377. "Diese Selbstunterscheidung des ewigen Sohnes vom Vater läßt sich als Grund alles geschöpflichen Daseins in seiner Andersheit gegenüber Gott und so auch als Grund der menschlichen Existenz Jesu verstehen, die in ihrer eigenen Lebensbewegung die Selbstentäußerung des Sohnes im Dienst an der Herrschaft des Vaters adäquat verkörpert" (*ST* 2:420).

130. *ST* 2:406f.; *STe* 2:363.

131. *ST* 2:408f.; *STe* 2:365.

132. *ST* 2:411; *STe* 2:368.

133. *ST* 2:434; *STe* 2:389f.; *ST* 3:583.

134. *STe* 2:391. "Die Ablehnung, die dem Sohn widerfährt, stellt auch das Königtum des Vaters in Frage" (*ST* 2:435).

135. *ST* 2:80; *STe* 2:62; John 1:3.

136. *ST* 2:81; *STe* 2:63.

137. Pannenberg, "Probleme einer trinitarischen Gotteslehre," 339.

138. "An der Identität dieser Eigenschaften wird der in Schöpfung, Versöhnung und Vollendung handelnde Gott als *derselbe* erkennbar" (Ibid.).

139. "So ist der Satz 'Gott ist Liebe' als zusammenfassender Ausdruck der trinitarischen Gemeinschaft von Vater, Sohn und Geist zu verstehen" (Ibid.,

341, and cf. 339-41).

140. Cf. *OG*, xiif.

141. *OG*, xiiif. Also see the section "Whole and Part" in chapter 1.

142. *ST* 2:83; *STe* 2:65.

143. Chapter 1 and cf. *ST* 2:93f.; *STe* 2:74f.

144. My translation of the following: "in Jesus von Nazareth der das ganze Universum durchwirkende Logos Mensch geworden und dadurch der Menschheit und ihrer Geschichte eine Schlüsselfunktion für einheit und Bestimmung der gesamten Schöpfung zugefallen ist" (*ST* 2:96; *STe* 2:76).

145. See Harder and Stevenson, "Continuity of History and Faith," 47. They agree that Pannenberg regards humans as instrumental to the divine plan for the entire creation.

146. Polk in *On the Way to God*, 219-24, 293, argues that Pannenberg's conception of the ultimate unity of reality in the Kingdom of God includes evil. In other words, the most horrible criminals are thought to be united in and through God with their victims. My interpretation of Pannenberg does not come to this conclusion. I am in agreement with Stanley Grenz's conclusion (*Reason for Hope*, 200f.).

147. *ST* 2:304-14; *STe* 2:265-75.

148. Tupper, *The Theology of Wolfhart Pannenberg*, 301.

149. Pannenberg, "Postscript," in Tupper, *The Theology of Pannenberg*, 304.

150. The relevant texts are as follows: *Was ist der Mensch?* (Göttingen: Vandenhoeck & Ruprecht, 1962), 40-49; *What is Man? Contemporary Anthropology in Theological Perspective*, trans. Duane A. Priebe (Philadelphia: Fortress, 1970), 54-67; *ATP* 80-153, 265-312; *ST* 2:266-314; *STe* 2:231-75.

151. Cf. Pannenberg's "Probleme einer trinitarischen Gotteslehre," 338. Here, Pannenberg, in connecting sin with the self-differentiation of creatures from God, is very close to identifying sin with the possibility of independent creaturely existence (Cf. also *ST* 2:288f., 296-303; *STe* 2:251f., 258-65).

152. *ST* 3:204, 573, 583.

153. *ST* 2:372-74; *STe* 2:331-34.

154. *STe* 2:332. "Wer sich dem Ruf in die Gottesherrschaft öffnet, sich ganz auf ihre Nähe einstellt und darin die Gegenwart des Heils empfängt, der muß sich auch selber hineinziehen lassen in die Bewegung der Liebe Gottes, die über den einzelnen Empfänger hinaus auf die Welt gerichtet ist. Man kann mit Gott und seiner Herrschaft nur so Gemeinschaft haben, daß man an der Bewegung seiner Liebe teilnimmt" (*ST* 2:372f.).

155. Matt. 18:22-35

156. Matt. 5:45f.; *ST* 2:373; *STe* 2:333.

157. *STe* 2:334. "Entscheidend ist, daß als Kriterium nicht mehr die Autorität der Tradition fungiert, weil Jesus in seiner eschatologischen Botschaft mit der Offenbarung der Liebe Gottes im Anbruch seiner Herrschaft

eine neue Basis für die Interpretation des Gottesrechts gefunden hat" (*ST* 2:374).

158. *ST* 3:73.

159. *IST*, 55.

160. *ST* 3:87.

161. *ST* 3:104-13.

162. *TKG*, 118.

163. *TKG*, 118-21.

164. *ST* 3:91.

165. *ST* 3:89-93, 108-11.

166. *ST* 3:89f.

167. "Die Liebe ist eine Kraft, die von Gott ausgeht. Sie ist nicht primär ein Akt des Menschen. Aber sie ergreift den Menschen so, daß sie ihn selber aktiv werden läßt" (*ST* 3:207). Pannenberg refers to 1 John 4:10.

168. *ST* 3:206.

169. Pannenberg, "The Working of the Spirit in the Creation and in the People of God," in *Spirit, Faith, and Church*, Pannenberg, Avery Dulles, Carl E. Braaten (Philadelphia: Westminster, 1970), 28.

170. "In der Liebe zu Gott als durch den Heiligen Geist ermöglichter Antwort auf die von Gott empfangene Liebe nimmt der Mensch teil am innertrinitarischen Leben Gottes, an der Gegenseitigkeit der Gemeinschaft zwischen Vater, Sohn und Geist. Durch die Nächstenliebe nimmt er teil an der Bewegung des trinitarischen Gottes zur Schöpfung, Versöhnung und Vollendung der Welt" (*ST* 3:218).

171. Rom. 5:5.

172. *IST*, 64.

173. Cf. *IST*, 60f.

174. "Response to Discussion," in Robinson, et al., eds., 263.

175. "The Working of the Spirit in the Creation," 29f.

176. Pannenberg, "The Church and the Eschatological Kingdom," in *Spirit, Faith, and Church*, 110.

177. Ibid., 116.

178. Ibid., 117.

179. Ibid., 114f.

180. Pannenberg, *Die Bestimmung des Menschen: Menschsein, Erwählung und Geschichte* (Göttingen: Vandenhoeck & Ruprecht, 1978), 39.

181. *TKG*, 125.

182. "Der Welt die Wahrheit des Evangeliums zu bezeugen, ist die Kirche berufen. Deises Zeugnis ist damit verbunden, daß die Kirche selbst in dieser Welt Vorzeichen der Bestimmung der Menschheit ist, zu einer Gemeinschaft in Freiheit, Gerechtigkeit und Frieden in der Zukunft des Reiches Gottes erneuert zu werden" (*ST* 3:11 and cf. 48-51).

183. *ST* 3:10f.

184. *TKG*, 126.

185. This analysis of Pannenberg's understanding of the relationship of love for the Kingdom and love for the world is in basic agreement with Ted Peters, "Pannenberg's Eschatological Ethics," 242-44. Peters, however, does not include all creation in his analysis of Pannenberg's understanding of unity.

CHAPTER 3

THE UNITY OF CREATION AND GOD

The claim that humans are the epitome of all created reality is a dangerous and discredited one in an age in which the human endeavors of science and technology threaten the continued existence of organic life on the planet Earth.[1] Furthermore, some people might consider such anthropocentrism as a naive notion connected with a geocentric conception of the universe.[2] Nonetheless, Wolfhart Pannenberg states that humans are at the center of concern in the universe.[3] This, he argues, is grounded in the creation of all reality toward the end of manifesting the eternal Son's acknowledgement of the Father. In the Christian understanding of creation, humans have a special place as representatives of God. The notion of the incarnation of the Son in the person of Jesus of Nazareth implies that the creation most fully realizes its relationship to the Creator through humankind.[4]

In his account of the priority of humanity Pannenberg emphasizes the unity of humans with the entire created world. In their destiny to oneness with God humans are not set completely apart from the nonhuman creation. Rather, through humans the entire creation is destined to oneness with its Creator. That the notion of the special place of humans in creation has been abused, and has been interpreted as a separation and elevation of human beings from and above nonhuman existence, reveals not the fault of the notion but a particular sin of modern humanity—a sin in which much modern Christian thought and practice participate. Although one may very well regard this as a character-istically modern sin, it is necessary to point out that the opposition between human and nonhuman reality goes back into our prehistory and is, perhaps, always connected with sin. How then is this universal opposition of human and nonhuman reality taken up in Pannenberg's notion of wholeness? How is the particular sin of the modern age against the nonhuman world addressed? How, in other words, does the unity of nature and history in Pannenberg's theology fare in the face of human experience?

Pannenberg regards the idea of the creation of humans toward the image of God and the human sin of turning away from God as the two fundamental statements of a Christian anthropology.[5] They are presupposed in the notions of incarnation and salvation, which provide the most complete picture of the human situation. The notions of creation, sin, and incarnation indicate the origin, the situation, and the destiny of existence. This chapter is focused on the situation of life in the world: on sin, misery, and the solution of the problems of existence. Pannenberg's theological concentration on anthropology is an attempt to understand humans in the context of the creative and redeeming love of God for the entire universe.

Finally, it must be stated that the questions regarding anthropology and the idea of unity in history are here asked in the context of the quest for a theological ethic that at its foundation also addresses the questionable character of the relationship of humans to the nonhuman world.

The Idea of Human Dominion

The idea that humans rightfully exercise dominion over the nonhuman world has come under severe criticism.[6] It is at times regarded as the ultimate religious root of the ecological crisis. Pannenberg admits that some theologians have appealed to the biblical idea of dominion with apologetic motives. They have wanted to show the legitimacy of Christianity in the context of the hegemony of modern science and technology.[7] This fact not only implicates these theologians as possibly contributing to the wanton exploitation of nature but also coincidentally and ironically shows the fallacious character of attempts to blame the Judeo-Christian tradition for a uniquely modern problem. That is to say, biblical statements regarding human dominion did not themselves lead to the exploitation of nature but were misused in apologetic form by theologians who wished to show the correspondence of Christianity to a dominant facet (i.e., the scientific and technological exploitation of nature for purely human ends) of emancipated modern culture.

It is true, says Pannenberg, that Judaism and Christianity resulted in the desacralization of the world of nature.[8] The gods of wood, sky, and water were shown to be empty notions. Yet it is also true that primitive cultures used the gods of nature to make themselves masters of nature.[9] The biblical understanding of God, humanity, and world brought the human-world relationship into a new and explicit focus: everything is created by God, and human creatures are specially commissioned as regents of the Creator. The world continues to belong to the Creator, and the will of God for creation continues to be the measure for human activity in the world. Thus, according to Pannenberg, the desacralization of nature that is entailed in Judeo-Christian faith submits the relationship of humans with nature to their prior relationship to God. Furthermore, it is important to note that nature is here seen as sharing in this prior relationship to God.

Pannenberg argues that an interpretation of the role of humans in the world that is grounded in Genesis and the Psalms results in the rejection of certain modern criticisms of these texts and the traditions that are dependent on them. He rejects the argument that the biblical notion of humanity is responsible for the "limitless exploitation of the natural world by modern technology and industrial society."[10] Rather, the ecological crisis needs to be seen as the consequence of modernity's (*Neuzeit*) emancipation.

> Emancipation from religious commitments and considerations and from
> the general guidelines of social life was one of the presuppositions for
> the autonomous development of the economic life of modernity.
> Modern secularism cannot simultaneously pride itself in its emancipa-
> tion from religious ties and load the responsibility for the consequences
> of its absolutization of earthly acquisitiveness on those religious origins
> from whose restrictions it has freed itself.[11]

In the modern age humans have made themselves the ultimate
goal of their actions and have thereby usurped the throne of God.
The creature has declared itself to be the absolute monarch over
all reality. Pannenberg suggests, moreover, that it has been
proven that nature is guaranteed far less protection by human
autonomy than by a Christian conception of reality—a conception
that regards humans as creatures alongside all other creatures and
in submission to God.

> This is especially the case when the idea of autonomy is connected not
> with a concept of reason to which the individual is subordinate, but
> with the modern understanding of individual freedom as an unlimited
> power of self-disposition which is subject to factual limitations only by
> the demands of society.[12]

Any attempt to solve the environmental crisis that does not
also deal with the fundamental issues raised by Pannenberg's
theological enterprise is unlikely to penetrate to the root of the
problem. To seek the cause of a modern problematic in ancient
notions that long have been rejected is symptomatic of shallow
thinking. This practice can only further hinder the recognition of
the true problem. It can only delay the fundamental change in
thinking that is required if we are to deal effectively with our
problem. The responses of various governments to the current
economic difficulties are also particularly telling. The nonhuman
world continues to be treated simply as a resource and as an
environment for the task of generating wealth. The current disposition appears to continue unabated by any significant shift in
understanding of the problems that have led to the destructive
impact of our culture upon the world. Canadian and U.S. bills of

rights have entrenched notions of individual rights and freedoms that are not readily open to correction by biblical notions of human responsibility. The Cartesian and Baconian dualism of mind versus matter and human versus nonhuman nature appears to continue to inform the character of Western culture.

Pannenberg's Christian anthropology attempts to cut away the foundation of such extreme oppositions. He recognizes the special place of humans in the world without losing sight of the ultimate unity of reality. This makes it possible to ground a fundamentally different approach to understanding the relationship of humans to the world. Humanity cannot renounce its rule over nature, but it needs to accept its destiny to rule lovingly within the created world. Pannenberg calls for a "responsible exercise of dominion."[13]

He argues that humanity is intended to participate in God's rule of creation.[14] "As the image of God, we are God's vicars preparing the way for his own dominion in the world."[15] Human rule of the world is to be similar to God's rule and follows from the likeness of humans to God. Human dominion over creation and human likeness to God are not, however, reducible to each other.[16] Pannenberg suggests that the statement in Gen. 1:26f. is intended to ground the place of humans as rulers of the world. The commission to rule is regarded by the biblical text as the immediate consequence of the image of God in humans.

Pannenberg notes the connection of the idea of the "image of God" with notions of kingship in the ancient Near East.

> For in the ancient Near East the king was regarded as the earthly representative of God and of the divine rule over the world. By making the statement about the image of God in the human being the Priestly document is thus assigning the human being as such the role of king in the context of the creation.[17]

In the ancient Near East the king is regarded as God's son. The Israelite conception of the role of the king is, however, more akin to the notion of regency than to other ancient notions of kingship, some of which appear to have almost literally regarded the king as the son of a god.[18]

This implies that God does not rule the world directly and is not directly manifest in the world. It is particularly through humans that the rule and presence of God in the world are to be manifest—to human and nonhuman creation alike. But humans have denied this destiny to represent the rule of God as first among creatures and thus have failed to make the rule of God manifest. It is only with the appearance of the Christ that the rule of God and the divine intention for humans become manifest. It is worth adding that Pannenberg locates this manifestation especially in the crucifixion of Jesus, whereby all "customary notions of sovereignty among human beings are turned upside down."[19] Pannenberg quotes Mark 10:43f., where Jesus explicitly makes the demand that rulers and leaders must be the servants of all.

No right to arbitrary exploitation is handed to humans.[20] The intent of the commission to rule the world is compared to a type of affirmation and protection of nature that is most perfectly described as gardening.[21] While Pannenberg does not do so, it is in concert with his theological program to characterize this responsible dominion as a loving rule; Pannenberg connects both the loving self-differentiation of the Son from the Father and Christ's death for the sake of the world with the image of God and, thus, with the divine determination of humans to represent God's dominion in the world.

It is true that Pannenberg draws a significant distinction between God and the world and that the biblical notion of creation coupled with that of human regency "locates human beings on the side of God and thus sets them too over against the world."[22] But this does not contradict Pannenberg's intentions to overcome dualism. This distinction must be understood in the context of an overarching and pervasive unity of reality in God, who is Creator, Redeemer, and Perfecter of reality.

Pannenberg does not so distinguish humans from the rest of the world that the world's creatures can be regarded as objects

whose sole purpose is to serve human ends. The creatures participate in the determination of existence toward communion with
God. Their use by humans should be guided by the goal of this
communion. The nonhuman world should never be used to serve
merely pragmatic human interests.

The notions of evolution and differentiation of species confirm
that human life can legitimately be viewed as the highest achievement of the evolution of complex and conscious life.[23] If this is
combined with the idea that the intention of creation is the communion of creatures with the Creator, and that this is fully realized in the incarnation of the Son as the person Jesus of Nazareth,
then the rise of human history is at the center of the creative
processes of nature. The meaning of nature is then bound up
with human history, and the meaning of human existence does
not belong to humans in isolation from the rest of reality but is
the meaning of all creation. If this is so then the meaning of
human existence cannot be determined apart from the incorporation of the beauty and purpose of nonhuman existence. This
beauty and purpose exist quite apart from any immediately evident benefit to human interest that is not completely subject to the
end of communion with God.

The existence of most, if not all, creatures allows of no total
reduction of purposefulness to merely human interest. The nonhuman world is not merely the environment or stage of human
history. The meaningfulness of nonhuman existence is to be
found in relationship to God in concert with the human relationship with God. In the context of Pannenberg's conception of
creation, this means that the relationship of creatures to God is
ultimately a unified relationship that finds its perfect expression
in the destiny of Jesus. It also means that no individual can
achieve this relationship in complete independence of others or
apart from nonhuman life.

In spite of the self-serving abuse of human power over nature
the world continues to be God's—if Pannenberg's idea of creation is true. Pannenberg recognizes in the self-centeredness of
human domination a destructiveness that will fall and indeed

already has begun to fall on humans themselves. The ecological crisis can in part be understood as a consequence of the emancipation of modern culture from its Judeo-Christian heritage. "In this sense we may view the ecological crisis at the end of the modern age of emancipation as a reminder that God is still the Lord of creation and that human arbitrariness in dealing with it is not without limits or consequences."[24]

The understanding that the image of God is not a possession but a task that must be achieved in history also accounts for the possibility of brokenness and corruption in the exercise of the commission to rule the world. In this world there are approximations to God's creative love just as there are examples of the most destructive forms of hatred. That the maltreatment of nature rebounds onto humans reflects not only the continued Lordship of God, as Pannenberg argues, but also the participation of nature in the history of the formation of the image of God in humans. Stated plainly, the ecological crisis, among other things, is nature's condemnation of modernity. If Pannenberg is correct regarding the relationship of the crisis to the emancipation of the modern West from its religious origins, then the ecological crisis is also a call to repentance. It is a summons from nature to humans to again acknowledge God as Creator and as Lord of creation and to leave off the tyrannic usurpation of this kingship. Positively, it is a call to take up our destined regency and to determine our actions in the world by the creative love of God.

The following discussion of Pannenberg's theological anthropology focuses on the relationship of humans to the nonhuman world and how this is ultimately grounded in the relationship of all reality to God.

Theological Anthropology

According to Pannenberg, the tendency in the modern age has been to develop the concept of "person" in contrast to "the objectified world of technology," as well as in contrast to the formation of social structures by technology. The attempt is made, in other words, to develop a humanized anthropology in the face of a culture that frequently exercises its technological powers in dehumanizing ways.[25] In contrast to such approaches Pannenberg begins with the Christian ideas of creation and redemption. He regards the story of human existence as the history of realizing the incarnation of the image of God, toward which God creates all reality, and which has been proleptically realized in the life and destiny of Jesus.[26] It is in this context that he critically appropriates the insights of philosophical anthropology.

The Image of God

The intention of this section is to show how the image of God is operative within history. As was pointed out in chapter 2, Pannenberg argues that humans do not possess the image of God. Rather, its realization is the goal toward which they are created. Nonetheless, this goal is present as an openness that is constitutive of human existence. It is an openness that reaches beyond the self to others, beyond the others of the immediate environment to the world, and beyond the world to what is without limit. Through this openness the image of God is present as the determinative power of the eschatological future.[27] The image of God is understood by Pannenberg as the goal of perfect communion with God.

Pannenberg's understanding of the image of God moves away from the notion of intelligence as providing the fundamental distinguishing factor that makes human existence unique among creatures. He focuses rather on the notion of the relationship of the Father and the Son as determinative regarding the destiny and meaning of human life. He understands the image of God in terms of the communion of the eternal Son with the Father. Each person is of inviolable worth through the determination of his or her existence toward perfect communion with the Father.[28]

Pannenberg argues that the biblical documents have not specified clearly what the image of God is and that this open-endedness may be intentional.[29] He contends that the image of God is nowhere realized by humans except in the person of Jesus of Nazareth. All other humans approximate the image to a greater or lesser degree. In other words, the image of God is something that must yet be achieved by humans. It is a future reality, but it has determinative power throughout the history of creation. "Its full realization is the *destiny* of humans that opened forth in history with Jesus Christ and in which the rest of humanity is to participate through transformation into the image of Christ."[30]

Pannenberg understands the image of God to be centered on the determining of humans to communion with God.[31] Present existence is to be understood from the point of view of this future communion. Pannenberg argues that it is especially in human personality that the future communion with God (the image of God) is already present in humans.[32] It is what we are becoming but do not yet see clearly.[33] These concerns come together in Pannenberg's understanding of the person of Jesus and in the conception of creation.

> If the creation of humans toward the likeness of God implies their destining toward communion with the eternal God, then the incarnation of God in Jesus of Nazareth can be regarded as the fulfillment of this determination. The unity of God and humanity in the life of one human is obviously unsurpassable by any other form of communion between God and humans.[34]

The acceptability of this depends ultimately on the verity of the claim that Jesus has risen from the dead and that the resurrection of Jesus has implications for all creatures.[35] The final proof of these claims depends on the future general realization of the promises entailed in the message of Jesus. For the present Pannenberg offers historical evidence backed by arguments to show the coherence and correspondence of Christian faith and hope.[36]

But the determination to communion with God, or the image of God in humans, cannot be a merely future hope if it is to function as the foundation of a Christian anthropology that itself is to be the foundation of morality. Pannenberg suggests that there is a disposition (*Anlage*) of humans toward the goal of communion with God. He argues that this goal is present not as a consciously chosen task but "in the indefinite trust that opens up the horizon world experience and intersubjectivity, and also in a restless thrust toward overcoming the finite."[37] He argues that this is not merely a failure of humans to come to terms with the finitude of existence, but that it also is connected with the development of the notion of world and with the differentiation of finite objects. In both instances Pannenberg argues that an openness beyond the world, a dim awareness of the infinite, is necessary for humans to reason about finite objects and about their unity in a concept like world.[38]

This disposition does not imply that humans have a capacity to reach the goal of their existence through their own work or thought alone. Rather, humans are dependent on "the working of divine providence through tradition and teaching, reason and experience."[39] Neither God nor the determination of humans to communion with God are directly present to consciousness. Only in the process of history, in reflection on concrete experiences of God, is the relationship of humans to the Creator manifest. Thus, the religious theme of existence is an ambiguous reality, open to misinterpretation. It is just as possible for humans to deny its reality as to claim its unambiguous presence falsely. When the distinction between God and creatures is recognized and honored, the likeness of humans to God is most open to realization.[40]

This amounts to accepting one's finitude while at the same time transcending the finitude of existence. This is essential to self-differentiation from God, and Pannenberg suggests that it is only possible when the Spirit of God lifts humans beyond their finitude, thereby enabling them to accept their finitude.[41]

Humans must be "fashioned into the image of the Son, of his *self-distinction* from the Father. We participate thus in the *fellowship* of the Son with the Father."[42]

For it is in acknowledging God as God and themselves as finite creatures that humans most fully correspond to their calling and most nearly anticipate the ultimate communion with God that is the destiny of creation. Pannenberg explicitly states that it is in this context that the human commission to rule over the earth must receive its character. All creation is to be united with the Creator.[43] Human recognition and acceptance of the finitude of existence "must also mean giving to all other creatures the respect that is their due within the limits of their finitude."[44] Each creature has a place in the order of God's creation. "*Only in this way can humans unite the whole creation in praise to the Creator, and together with the gratitude for their own existence offer the gratitude of all his creatures.*"[45] This text clearly indicates that Pannenberg understands humans, in their special role with regard to the image of God, to be representatives of the whole creation. All creatures are included in the destiny to praise the Creator.

Pannenberg points to relationships with others, specifically as relationships find their fulfillment in love, as the heart of personal existence.[46] In this, human existence can be seen to reflect the self-differentiating love of the Son for the Father. In other words, the communion with God that defines the image of God toward which creatures are created also finds expression in the day-to-day relationships among creatures. Relationships with others are destined to be taken into the divine love that is manifest in Jesus. The foundation of life is the divine love that reaches out to all creation. Human destiny is to participate in this operation of love. In the course of history it means to love God, other humans, and all creation. This is the character of the image of God, and it entails a fundamentally religious conception of life. Here it is seen to be the immediate source of the moral character of life.

Openness to the World

In his theological anthropology Pannenberg attempts to show the correlation of his Judeo-Christian understanding of humans with that of secular modern anthropology. It should be noted that certain traditional notions are modified and even rejected in the process. The critical interaction of these two perspectives cuts both ways. Rather than attempt to evaluate this dialogue, this section will simply round out the theoretical aspects of the discussion of the unity of nature and history, and move toward their practical implications.

At the root of uniquely human existence are qualities that are variously described by notions such as exocentricity, openness to the world, freedom from the environment, and lack of instincts.[47] Pannenberg argues that rather than speaking of the lack of instincts as a deficiency at birth we should think of humans as incomplete, as creatures who experience "a hiatus, a gap, between perceptions and impulses."[48] This "incompleteness" is really a freedom from the limitations of instincts. "Openness to the world" is a common anthropological phrase used in describing this aspect of human existence. Instincts determine within a narrow range responses to stimuli. The absence of instincts is an opening up of the range of relational possibilities, but it is also a need within human existence to develop successful means of relating to the world.

Openness to the world makes it possible for humans to develop languages, rational processes, cultures, and technical skills; indeed, it drives them to do so. Thus, humans "convert the disadvantages of their initial biological condition into advantages."[49] The development of individual selves is here seen as a sociocultural process that is rooted in the peculiar biology of humans. Individuals and entire cultures must learn particular sets of responses that correspond to particular stimuli within particular ecological and sociocultural systems. In light of this discussion one could describe the ecological crisis as a radical failure of modern culture to be adequate to this need. This failure is especially visible in its sciences, technologies, and industries. Pannenberg's thought provides a way to understand the deeper cause and possible solution to this problem.

The concept of openness to the world describes the free space for interpretation and decision over against the tyranny of the content of perception.[50] Pannenberg maintains that this free space could also be described as the differentiation of the individual from the environment. In animals the instincts determine responses that are appropriate to particular situations. This incorporates the animal and the environment into one process. Varying gradations of incorporation are reflected in various species. In no species other than humans, however, is the free space so great as to amount to an openness to develop complex languages, cultures, sciences, and technologies and beyond that to allow for the yearning to transcend the limitations of finite existence on the finite planet Earth. Here there is a definite distinction of humans from all other creatures. Yet it is a distinction rooted in the evolutionary processes of natural history. What sets Pannenberg's theological view of this fundamental human openness apart from a secular anthropological one is that he regards it as reaching beyond the limits of the world to the eternal and infinite.

The Open Image

Pannenberg argues that this phenomenon that modern anthropology has called "openness to the world" is connected with both the image of God in humans and the commission to rule the world.

> Only because in their exocentric self-transcendence they reach beyond the immediately given to the broadest possible horizon of meaning that embraces all finite things—only because of this is it possible for them to grasp an individual object in its determinateness that distinguishes it from other objects. . . . We are dealing here with the action of reason

which conceives the individual in the light of the universal as it stands out in its particularity against the background of the universal. This process of defining the individuality of things has become the basis for all human mastery of nature.[51]

Pannenberg notes that the naming of the animals is analogous to having dominion over the world.[52] Naming the animals is part of the differentiating activity of human reason. This ability to differentiate the objects of the world from each other in the context of their interrelationship within the whole of reality is what enables humans to rule the world.

According to Pannenberg, a significant aspect of this openness is the capability of humans to develop the tools and machines that manifest the power humans exercise over the rest of the world. This power is rooted in the freedom of humans vis-à-vis their perceptions, which enables them to discern and direct themselves to objects as *other* from themselves. It enables them to distance themselves from the perception of one object in favor of another object. This capability to distance oneself from objects is the basis for distinguishing the self from its environment. The individual moves in thought beyond the self and then from the object back to the self. In the process the self is perceived as one object among other objects.[53] It is in this exocentricity (being outside of oneself) that the self becomes aware of itself as a self.

Pannenberg argues that neither individually nor corporately can humans realize their own destiny. He agrees with J. G. Herder that "as instinct guides the behavior of animals, so the image of God guides human beings."[54] Herder has understood the image of God as that which must be achieved through "tradition and learning, reason and experience."[55] But Herder understands this process in the context of faith in divine providence. The image of God, while remaining the destiny that will be achieved eschatologically, is "already present in outline form and thereby gives human life a direction."[56]

But the connection between this present anticipation and the future fulfillment of human destiny has its basis in the plan of divine providence, which coordinates the influences coming from other human beings with the impulses of the person's own reason and experience and thereby turns these into means contributing to a single result, the formation of human beings.[57]

As Pannenberg points out Herder has changed the Enlightenment idea of human-driven progress toward perfection into human participation in the realization of a destiny that depends ultimately on the continued work of divine providence.

Pannenberg also notes that regarding the development of the image of God as the task of history, Herder removed "the restriction of the problems of human life to a moral task."[58]   In other words, human freedom and destiny are not first of all moral, nor is the problematic of existence epitomized by moral issues. Most basically human existence is here described as the history of the realization of the image of God.   The moral character of existence is entailed in this process.

This basic anthropological openness and exocentricity is described by Pannenberg as historicity.   But he does not intend that persons should on this basis be understood only as "autonomous subjects of historical action."[59]   History is the tale of what people have done, but it is also true that persons themselves are the products of their histories.   Human beings are directed beyond themselves and to the future, to the fulfillment of their destination.   They are not yet complete, not even in the unity of their subjectivity.   It is the end of their history that brings them to completion and the end of all history that brings the story of the entire human race and of all nature to its completion.   Each event along the way is not fully understood until the one goal of all history is attained.   This is true whether it is the history of an individual or of the whole of creation.[60]

Openness to God

Pannenberg regards humans as created with the image of God as their ultimate destination.   He transforms the notion of openness to the world in this context. He argues that although humans are finite, they have an orientation toward infinite self-transcendence.

In the reflexive, exocentric process of existence the unlimited character of basic openness becomes apparent. There are no limitations in the process of perceiving ever greater wholes. The self eventually arrives at the notion of a world and the eternal and "divine reality that is the ground of the world."[61] According to Pannenberg, openness to the world is therefore better described as an unlimited openness, one that transcends the world and can best be understood as an openness to God.[62] The discernment of objects "also includes a discernment of their finitude, and therefore it includes an awareness of what is other than finite."[63] Pannenberg contends that the awareness of the whole of reality and the infinite that encompasses it is presupposed by all discernment of individual finite objects. This is the case even though such awareness is often vague or not even present to consciousness. The Judeo-Christian tradition identifies this infinite source of the world with the creating and redeeming God.

Thus, he argues that the capacity to discern objects is grounded in the explicitly religious nature of existence. Pannenberg contends that "humans are essentially directed to the infinite, but are never in themselves already infinite."[64] In other words, humans are in large degree oriented to the infinite transcendence of finite existence. Even in the simple perception of objects of the world humans experience dependence on something that "surpasses and sustains everything finite."[65] Pannenberg maintains that if humans are fundamentally directed beyond the finite to the infinite then religion is never merely a mistaking of human essence for an infinite and divine Other, then religion is an expression of the innate drive of humans toward an infinite Other. Moreover, this openness to the infinite makes possible the perception of a unity that encompasses all the diversities and conflicts of finite existence. This unity transcends the limits of finitude and gives rise to the idea of a world. In this divine way specifically individual human existence becomes possible.[66]

In other words, God is the goal toward which human openness reaches out.[67] God alone is infinite. God is the goal as well as the source (Creator) of human existence (including freedom), and human existence is incomplete, still on the way to its fulfillment. This is true for both individuals and the human race as a whole. Thus, in Pannenberg's understanding, human openness (exocentricity) is fundamentally oriented to the future and "to an Other beyond all the objects of their world, an Other that at the same time embraces this entire world and thus ensures the possible unification of the life of human beings in the world, despite the multiplicity and heterogeneity of the world's actions on them."[68] Pannenberg has elaborated an anthropology that is in essence also a philosophy/theology of history, that includes the entire world in this process toward God.[69]

Pannenberg also draws a formative link between Christ's self-subordination, which is part of his self-differentiation from the Father, and human self-discernment. He notes that exocentricity involves self-effacement.[70] The individual must forget himself or herself in order to focus on other objects, to understand them as they are in themselves. The human creatures of God's world reflect the self-differentiation of the eternal Son. It is noteworthy that this eternal self-differentiation is also regarded as the source of all finite existence. The principle of otherness that is the source of creation also is reflected both in the fundamental structure of human existence and in its destiny.

Human self-differentiation is regarded by Pannenberg as an act of self-denial. This disregard of the self makes possible both the differentiation of finite objects from each other and human power over these objects. In the case of the Son and the Father the self-differentiation is a humble act of love and recognition. By contrast, arrogant self-assertion rather than love seems to characterize the goal of much of human self-differentiation. It may be true that modern technology often has this character, but it is important to note that the cause for the arrogance and abusive application of the technology lies elsewhere than in the connection with the action of the eternal Son. It lies in human perversion of the power gained through self-differentiation. And as Pannenberg suggests, the problem lies in the dualistic separation of discernment of finite objects from discernment of the infinite power that creates them.

Pannenberg argues that the self-effacing power of discernment is most fundamentally related to the self-differentiation of the Son from the Father. Human self-differentiation from God is the source of human freedom and is essential to participation in the inner-Trinitarian communion. It is in this context that the earthly dominion of humans is considered by Pannenberg. The rule of humans over the rest of creation is more fundamentally connected with the determination of humans to communion with God than with the intelligence of humans.[71]

In this way Pannenberg attempts to understand God as the source and destiny of human freedom. Pannenberg thus describes the fundamental structure of human existence as religious. It is of crucial importance, according to Pannenberg, that the power of domination gained by the discernment of finite objects in the creaturely world be subordinated to the discernment of what is not finite. Pannenberg is not arguing that religious and/or magical belief should control the sciences. Rather, he is arguing that subordination to the triune Creator is fundamental to independent creaturely existence. The separation of these two types of discernment, he argues, is the source of ecological disaster. It is also the loss of human freedom. Paradoxically, freedom for the creature comes in subordination to the Creator, which takes perfect form only in the self-differentiation of Jesus.

The Unity of the Self

Each person is unique in the context of her or his relationships with other creatures and things. But each person also transcends these relationships and the transitions between various finite contexts of life. Ultimately it is in the relationship to God, who is the source of the identity of the self, that the individual is a unique person. Out of this identity it is possible for the individual to integrate the various moments of life, which would otherwise fall apart. Pannenberg argues that action presupposes an acting subject who already has an identity that bridges the flow of time from intention to achievement. "The unity and integrity of human life are constituted in another sphere that precedes all action."[72]

Nonetheless, the identity of a person is in a process of becoming throughout the history of the individual.[73] Only at the end of history in the context of the completed whole of reality will it be apparent what each person is becoming during the course of history. The individual, though still in becoming, is the unity that makes possible the appearance of an acting subject (*Handlungssubjekt*). The identity of the person cannot be reduced to the actions she or he undertakes.[74]

Pannenberg attempts to show that the self is neither the source of its own unity nor the source of the unity that is discovered in the world.[75] Rather, he states that the self becomes aware of an overarching wholeness in a process of disciplined and discriminating reflection on perceptions (*Anschauungen*) that come to one's feelings (*das Gefühl*) through the receptive imagination (*Phantasie*).[76] Perceptions arise as the imagination moves between the unfathomableness of feeling and the finite realities that have been distinguished by the activities of consciousness.[77] But it is only in the process of submitting these perceptions to differentiating reflection that the unity of all the diverse objects becomes visible. The perceptions must be connected with the appropriate objects in their diversity, as well as with the unity within which the diversity appears.[78] The following lengthy quotation shows the relation of unity to consciousness:

> Grasping the unity in distinction is a function of the ability to keep ones distance in an awareness of otherness [here the other is the unity of all the distinct entities in the universe]. The unity of what is distinct is thus a different thing from the consciousness. It is not owed to the

unity of the ego. This unity [the ego's], as the basis of all experience that underlies the unity of its contents subjectively and gives them unity in the course of life, is correlative to the objective unity of the "concept" that comprehends in its unity what is objectively distinct.[79]

The unity of the self develops in response to the reflectively perceived unity of reality.

By means of this process the concept of a world comes to be formed in consciousness. The concept of a world includes all the multifarious and finite objects of reality. Pannenberg notes that in a further step of reflection, the notion of the eternal or infinite is conceived over against the concept of a world (which epitomizes all finite existence). However, an additional step of reflection is required to recognize that the eternal cannot be thought of as limited by an external other—the world, or everything that is not eternal.[80] For this other would set a limit to the eternal. Rather, the eternal is seen to encompass the finite world within itself.

In this notion of eternal oneness becomes thematic that which is always already present to consciousness as indeterminate eternity and which forms the spiritual-mental (*geistig*) space in which the distancing of the self from others and all determination of otherness and relationship are exercised. And in this exercise it [the notion of eternal oneness] is disclosed to consciousness.[81]

This argument, as well as Pannenberg's discussions of the categories part and whole and the openness beyond the world to an eternity only vaguely perceived, reflects parallels to Anselm's argument for the existence of God. In each case one is led to think of ever greater or more encompassing realities until one reaches toward that which thought and experience can neither surpass nor fathom.[82] Pannenberg, unlike Anselm, does not intend to prove that God exists. His intention is to point out the innate and inescapably religious structure of human existence. His argument intends to show that the basic unity of personal existence, as understood by anthropologists, lends itself to a religious construal of reality.

In this passage the unity in diversity is taken as a fundamental aspect of both human consciousness and the world. Furthermore, the experience of unity is shown to be rooted in the eternal, which itself pervades all reality and is the ground of the exercise of the faculties that form human consciousness. There is no dualistic opposition of mind-body, world-human, or eternal-finite. Pannenberg provides an interpretation of mind, body, world, finitude, and eternity that transcends facile oppositions. He makes a strong case for the fundamentally spiritual and religious character of existence. The relationship of humans to the divine is neither external nor secondary to human existence. On the other hand, neither is the relationship of humans to the natural and social worlds secondary. All reality is intertwined and brought into oneness in the relationship of the individual to God. It is this character of reality that Pannenberg argues is the root of the unity of the self. It is important to note that Pannenberg sees this as perhaps the most fundamental fact of human subjectivity. Not the self, but the divine Spirit is the ground of unity.

As might be expected, the development of a unified consciousness in individuals is connected by Pannenberg with the self-differentiation of the Son from the Father.

> In spite of all the perversion due to sin . . . human intelligence, in its perception of the otherness of the other participates in the self-distinction of the eternal Son from the Father by which he is not merely united to the Father but is also the principle of all creaturely existence in its individuality. Human reason, of course, can generate only thoughts and not directly the reality of finite things. But these thoughts do not simply represent finite objects in their distinction from one another. They can also form a basis for the constructs of human technology.[83]

The development of a self is dependent on the differentiation of finite objects from each other. One of these objects is the human whose self is developing. Pannenberg states that just as the Son differentiates himself from and is united with the Father through the Spirit, so humans are dependent on receiving from the Spirit (through the *Phantasie*) the capacity to apply reason to the naming (differentiation) of each actuality and to perceiving the unity in the differences. Human reason is not itself filled with the Spirit, but it is dependent on the Spirit to be lifted beyond its finitude to perceive also the presence of truth and wholeness amid all creaturely limitations.[84]

All life is given by the Spirit, but among creatures human life is most fully awake. Pannenberg suggests that to understand the role of reason in life, it is best to consider it from the point of view of the connectedness of all individual creaturely existence with its environment (*Umweltbezogenheit*).

> The higher that consciousness is evolved the more the individual life-form in its consciousness will exist outside of itself and simultaneously, the more its reference to the world (*Weltbezug*) will be internal, present within itself. . . . To our knowledge human self-consciousness forms the highest level of this intermeshing of the ecstatic and inwardness.[85]

Pannenberg defines the "ecstatic" of consciousness as intensified participation in the life-giving Spirit, as increased inwardness of life. This is not a withdrawal from the world but a taking of the perceived objects of the world into the consciousness of the self. This complex process—moving outward, differentiating and objectifying things in the world, perceiving the unity of these objects (the concept of world), and internalizing them—makes it possible for persons as members of the world to regard themselves as objects in the world.[86] It also makes possible the dualistic opposition of self and other, be it other persons or creatures or inanimate objects. But most significant, it makes possible the recognition of the promised wholeness of life. It is possible to perceive this promise in the anticipations of wholeness that we encounter in the process of history. This ultimate step, however, is what has been rejected by modern culture, and this rejection is connected with the abuses of modern culture in its self-interested objectification of the world and the objects within it.[87]

The Self and Culture

In this interpretation of Pannenberg, human openness can be understood to be a space in which humans both need and are enabled to receive and construct cultures, which in this context appear to be sophisticated patterns and methods of relating to the environment. Culture replaces instinct. The environment includes not only the nonhuman world but also other humans and the self as well. It also includes the vague infinity within which the world of finite objects takes shape. Individuals receive their culture but have the ability to transform these traditions at every stage: reception, practice, and transmission.

The development of rapid means of transportation—of marine vessels, of aircraft, and of spacecraft—appears as a particularly transparent and successful example of the striving to transcend the limitations that are "normal" to creaturely existence in time and space. The striving to reach beyond the bounds of finitude also is evident in the scientific imagination of time travel, cloning, space travel beyond the speed of light, ad infinitum. These human activities are no doubt also connected with the special human awareness of death, but here it appears as quite reasonable to connect them with the fundamental openness that is seen to reach beyond the finite world.

Pannenberg connects openness to the world with the need of humans to realize their destiny. Human openness is ultimately openness to communion with God. It is openness to the love of the Son and the Father. It is openness to the life-giving Spirit. Humans are not in a position to achieve this destiny apart from the life-giving Spirit. They are needy creatures.

Cultures provide ways of attempting to address this neediness. They provide means of achieving the common goals of human existence. They are also experienced as rigid structures that seek to restrict human openness. They function not only to educate but also to set limits upon individuals. Sociocultural rules (set patterns of responses to stimuli) are often used in the interests of powerful groups and individuals. Less insidiously, every human culture is limited in the options and tools that it provides to its members. Individuals ultimately are driven beyond the limits of their cultures. Culture can as easily cut humans off from their destiny as help them to achieve it.

In this context it becomes possible to argue that when a particular culture's practices have a widespread and massively negative impact on the world (which includes humans), then the entire tradition can be regarded as having become questionable and in need of revision. This applies to its scientific achievements as well as to its morality. The successes of the natural sciences and their application in technology and industry are in need of criticism. The sciences have failed to take account of the complexity of the relationships that unite the objects of the world with each other. We have especially failed to note the wider contexts of these relationships. If Pannenberg is correct then this failure is directly linked to the mechanistic and atheistic assumptions of an emancipated age. Here one can regard positively the attack of Lynn White on the Judeo-Christian tradition as a wake-up call; although otherwise it must be regarded as an expression of the hypocrisy of emancipated modernity.[88] It is emancipated modernity that is in need of critical revision, and Pannenberg attempts this by looking to its religious roots.

Sin and Human Destiny

Separation from God

Pannenberg points out that the self-chosen independence of modern Western culture from its religious roots has only served to heighten the problem of evil.[89] Modern societies have committed some of the worst atrocities in history. Aside from the outrages against humans they threaten the continued existence of organic life on Earth. And having turned away from its religious traditions, Western culture has only itself to look to for responsibility for this mass destructiveness.

It is incredible that having rejected God and thereupon having committed such atrocities against humans, while continuing to ravage the Earth, modern humans would point the finger of blame for these evils at others.[90] There is a tendency to blame social, economic, religious, and political structures. There is a temptation to look to the past and find the source of evil in the premodern traditions and concepts that were rejected in the eighteenth-century Enlightenment. It appears that modern society is not able to come to terms with its own evil. Pannenberg argues that the Christian tradition very clearly points out that the source of evil is in the universality of individual sin.[91] While modern culture has had limited success in separating itself from the religious character of human existence (at least in public life), try as they might humans cannot distance themselves from evil.[92]

We know that cultural constraints have with some success attempted to restrict the objectification of other humans. To some extent animals also have been drawn into the protective umbrella of social mores. The existence of laws prohibiting the mistreatment of animals restrict the unlimited objectification of these creatures through the attempts of the self to gratify its capricious cravings. However, these restrictions and others that apply more widely to wildlife have only recently come into effect as the destructive consequences of human whim and greed have become evident. Modern society has been unable to address the moral causes of such destructiveness. It has merely responded to the appearances of evil with new external restrictions. Thus, society becomes increasingly legalized. In this process society has become increasingly dependent on experts to recognize, define, and prescribe treatments for its individual and corporate destructiveness. Specialization and professionalization have accompanied the legalization of modern culture. These trends do not appear capable of providing holistic solutions.[93] They tend, rather, to introduce new difficulties, such as an increase in the experience of alienation, violence, and oppression. Modern pluralistic culture appears to be unable to address the root cause of its evils.

The Enlightenment notion of the autonomy and reasonableness of the individual appears to continue to inform society in this process. Unfortunately, this has not made it possible for modern culture to penetrate to the idea that reason itself is distorted by the sinful character of cravings that are warped in upon the self. The professionally trained specialist is also a self driven by desires and cravings that are perverted by the failure to recognize, acknowledge, and love God above self and the world on par with the self.

Tragically, all relationships, all others, and even one's self are sometimes sacrificed in this pursuit of power. The individual vaguely recognizes his or her determination to eternal life and either seeks to flee from this destiny or attempts to achieve it on the basis of finite existence. This attempt is doomed to failure, and the individual who makes the self the objective of existence will live in frustration, anxiety, and dread.[94] Anxiety and anger are already the result of sin, but they motivate further evils that range from self-deception to consumptive attempts to allay the dread of death and meaninglessness.

Pannenberg argues that a failure to trust God underlies the turning of humans away from God.[95] Lack of trust that God will bring to completion the destination toward which the world is created leads humans to trust in themselves and their manipulations of others. Nonetheless, says Pannenberg, that this lack of trust in God is the root of sin and evil becomes evident only in the context of the historical self-revelation of God. Similarly, the hubris of wanting to be as God is evident only through an awareness of the God of history.[96]

The notions of misery (*Elend*) and alienation (*Entfremdung*) serve Pannenberg in describing the separation of humans from God. The misery of humanity exemplifies its sinful lostness in its separation from God.

> The term "misery" sums up our detachment from God, our autonomy, and all the resultant consequences. . . . Alienated from God, we live in the misery of separation from God, far away from the home of our own identity.[97]

That independence and separation from God is discussed in terms of estrangement, misery, and sin presupposes that humans (and through humans all creatures) are created and destined to communion with God.[98] Pannenberg argues that this misery is at its worst in situations where people live in the midst of wealth and luxury but know nothing of their separation from God, who is their true good.[99] It should perhaps be countered that this misery is yet worse where people live in physical misery, still know nothing of their separation from God, and seek only to obtain power and wealth.

Sin

With regard to individual actions Pannenberg states that "[r]esponsibility and guilt arise only when there is a valid norm that we should follow or should have followed."[100] When the individual has incorporated a norm into her or his self-identity then failure to follow the norm leads to the experience of guilt. Pannenberg connects this experience with the idea of sin. Both are experiences of a condition in which the self is separated from its identity and destiny.[101]

But sin precedes all individual acts as a power that indwells subjectivity and overpowers it. "It is a state of alienation from God."[102] Estrangement is the result of attempting to achieve true life apart from the source of life—the Creator. Eternal life is the eschatological destiny of humans, and it is to be realized in a historical process that is most fundamentally the history of God's creative love. Pannenberg argues that this is the basic fact of human existence and that sin is the failure to trust and love God as the one who will bring creation to completion. The power of sin lies in its ability to deceive us into believing that this fullness is possible apart from trust in God.[103]

Pannenberg notes that the first eleven chapters of Genesis point to a series of actions—from Adam's and Eve's disobedience, to Cain's murder of Abel, and to the evil conditions that led to the Flood, to which one might add the Babel story—that are presented as a steady increase of the power of evil among humans. God is depicted as countering this process and as protecting creation from the full consequences of evil.[104] This destructive process and God's creative counterinitiative are presented as descriptive of the fundamental character of individual and social existence in all history. It is not primarily an account of the origin of evil and provides no ground for metaphysical dualism. It is an account of reality as the history of God creating and then redeeming his creation from evil. God is not surprised by evil but has foreseen it as a danger inherent in the process of creating independent creatures.[105] According to Pannenberg evil must be seen as anticipated by God and as relativized by the anticipated future salvation and fulfillment of creation.[106]

> As creatures that have attained to full independence, we humans must develop and become what we are and ought to be. In the process we can all too easily give our independence the form of an autonomy in which we put ourselves in the place of God and his dominion over creation. But without creaturely independence the relation of the Son to the Father cannot manifest itself in the medium of creaturely existence.[107]

In other words, the possibility of evil is risked and its reality is endured and overcome to achieve the appearance of the Son's relationship to the Father. This appearance does not refer merely to the incarnation of the Son in the person of Jesus of Nazareth. All creation is determined to participate in the relationship of the Son with the Father. Apart from creaturely independence creatures could not come to participate in the eternal love of the Son and the Father through the Spirit.

Pannenberg also considers the possibility that sin and evil are rooted in the finitude of creaturely existence. Because they are creatures humans are limited in certain ways. They cannot know and accomplish everything. Therefore, they are liable to deceive themselves and engage in other wrong actions.[108] However, Pannenberg argues that this does not account for the source of evil. Both the notions of creaturely independence and limitation contribute toward understanding evil. But according to Pannenberg, they are not themselves already evils: "We are to seek the root of evil, rather, in revolt against the limit of finitude, in the refusal to accept one's own finitude, and in the related illusion of being like God (Gen. 3:5)."[109] The attempt of creatures to achieve fulfillment independent of God plays the central role in Pannenberg's understanding of the origin of evil.[110]

In Pannenberg's understanding of freedom and sin the focus is not on the ability of the will to select between good and evil actions. He suggests that a will that can choose to do evil is already less free than one that cannot choose evil. For in the ability to choose evil the corruption of the will is already evident. The will is entrapped in evil. The will that is able to choose evil cannot choose good that is unqualified by evil.[111] From the perspective of the two aspects of love, we could say that the self is never able so to love God and others that it does not also in seeking its own advantage alienate itself from God and others.[112]

The self-centeredness of personal existence is inescapable. Pannenberg, however, does not identify this fundamental self-centeredness with sin. This personal centeredness is essential to the nature of human existence as creatures with a high degree of independence from and control over their environment.[113] He argues that when the self shuts itself in by absolutizing the self, a decision that entails the refusal to acknowledge God and others, then self-centeredness has become sin. The will to self-realization is rightly exercised in the context of trusting self-differentiation from God.[114] The sin of turning from God already underlies the choices made regarding individual actions.

The biblical idea of sin addresses human existence at the level of the fundamental attitudes and convictions of individuals. The longings and desires of persons are the manifestations of these attitudes.[115] If a person's desires are turned away from God and against the love of God this is a reflection of the refusal of the person to acknowledge God as God. Humans turn to themselves. The individual chooses to love the self and to honor the self as god rather than to love and acknowledge the Creator as God. The implication of this for the relationship of the individual to God is that he or she comes to hate God.[116] The individual regards herself or himself as the center of reality and uses everything else as a means to achieve the ends of the self. God can only be recognized as a hindrance to such self-realization. Needless to say, other creatures can then only be viewed either as objects of self-gratification or as hindrances to these desires.

The structure of the craving that is so turned to the self is described by Augustine as concupiscence. Pannenberg argues that it is a mistake to think that Augustine thought of concupiscence as only or even primarily associated with sexual desires. All desires that are ultimately centered on the self are concupiscent desires.[117] The implication of such a focus on the self and the realization of its desires is that everything else in the world tends to be reduced to its value for the ends of the self and the reduced world within which it lives.

Consequences of Sin

According to Pannenberg, it "does not follow from finitude, that death belongs to the nature of human" existence.[118] Pannenberg states, rather, that

> Death is the result of the break with God, who is the source of life. It is to be seen in concert with the other results of sin. Being in opposition to the Creator, we are also in opposition to our fellow creatures, to the earth, to animals, and to other people.[119]

God does not intervene in history to punish sin. The consequences of sin follow naturally quite apart from any special activity of God. "The conflict of sinners with creation, with other people and even with themselves follows from the nature of sin as a breaking of the relationship with God."[120] Just as God the Creator is the source of life so is God the source of wholeness and unity. Thus, when humans fail to acknowledge God they are separated not only from God but also from the source of wholeness within which good relationships with all creatures are possible. This separation signifies an inability to fully acknowledge other creatures as existing independent of the aims of the self.

The whole of one's identity is not available until beyond the end of life. As long as existence is within time both past and future are lost from the possibilities of the present moment. Neither is wholeness present at death, as Heidegger argued. Death is the dissolution of the individual and is not the individual's source of wholeness. Wholeness is given only in the Christian idea of resurrection to communion with the Creator, who sees beginning and end, to whom nothing is lost in the passage of time.[121] What remains true of Heidegger's connection of death and wholeness is the unity of these two fundamental realities: "the future and the possible wholeness of existence."[122] The Christian hope of resurrection to communion with God does not imply a unity that subsumes creaturely existence in God but the renewal and consolidation of creaturely life. Pannenberg argues that *Endlichkeit* (finitude) will continue to be a mark of participation in God's eternal life.[123] However, as long as finite existence is in time it continues to be subject to death. During its finite existence in time the self is separated from its true identity.

Death remains as the final threat to self-realization. It is the unbridgeable gulf between existence in the process of time and the realization of human destiny in eternity. Death is connected with sin. It belongs to the separation of human existence from the Creator, who gives not only wholeness but also life itself. Death is the consequence of humans turning from God and placing themselves in God's position. It is not, however, thereby to be understood that God created death. God's actions in history are of the character of limiting evil and the consequences of sin.[124] That humans at times do remarkable things and reach great heights of "cultural flowering" is regarded by Pannenberg as a sign not of the continued operation of human capacity to do good (freedom of the will) but of the creative and renewing activity of the "Divine Spirit in the life of humanity." This occurs where the "image of the Son takes form" in history.[125]

Pannenberg nowhere restricts this activity of the divine Spirit to the church. Quite the contrary, he attempts to show that this activity of God is open to perception even in natural processes. For example, he connects death and evil with entropy, the second law of thermodynamics, which states that more highly organized forms of energy will tend to change to warmth, a less highly organized form of energy. While this inexorable process implies the death of individual organisms, it is a necessary process for the evolution of higher life forms. It can be regarded as a precondition for the development of order out of chaos.[126] Pannenberg agrees with the possibility of connecting entropy with the notion of demonic opposition to the creative purposes of God. However, he also notes the greater power of God to turn the power of dissipation to serving the goal of creating various forms of independent creatures.[127] Here Pannenberg envisions the promise of God to work for good in everything as defining the structure of reality.[128]

This example makes plain that Pannenberg regards all reality from the point of view of the process of God's creative activity, which is aimed at the establishment of independent creatures. This is the unity of nature and history. All reality is regarded as history. And if we also take into account that the goal toward which God determines these creatures is participation in the love of the Son and the Father for each other as mediated through the Spirit, then it becomes clear that all reality is also regarded as the history of God's self-revelation in creation. Furthermore, in the context of sin and death all reality is the history of God's redemptive activity. God overcomes the separation of creatures from their destiny.

The Future and Morality

The Crisis in Ethics

The moral character of existence is rooted in the creative love of the Father and the Son. Pannenberg states that "our destiny is not primarily ethical but eschatological" and that "it will be achieved in salvation history."[129]   That the realization of the destiny of human existence is thought of in terms of the action and image of God, does not, according to Pannenberg, undercut the moral implications of his theological anthropology.[130]   Rather Pannenberg seeks to ground ethics in the religious character of existence, thereby reversing Kant's derivation of God from practical reason.

Pannenberg points out that one significant difference between Plato and Kant lies in the more fundamentally anthropological nature of Kant's position.   For "Kant not only is the link between material nature and the soul broken down, but he has also no further reason for supposing that all phenomena have as it were a soul within them.   Something like a soul is only to be found in man, in so far as man is a subject."[131]   For Plato the stars and the soul were phenomena that led the lover of wisdom to the divine. For Kant the stars no longer provide a way to God.   Instead, God is conceived as a requirement of moral experience in human relationships.[132]   Pannenberg points out that with Kant anthropology has become the battleground regarding the truth of the idea of God.   What is further evident here, as Pannenberg also points out, is that Kant grounds religion in the moral character of existence.   Pannenberg rejects Kant's moral conception of religion, as well as the idealistic separation of soul (with the notions of spirit and mind that are associated with it) and body (with the notions of physical reality associated with it).   Pannenberg's work aims to reverse this order by convincingly pointing out that humans are fundamentally religious creatures, that soul and body belong together. He argues this by returning to a biblical conception of humanity.[133]

Pannenberg understands Hegel as completing the Kantian anthropological interpretation of reality. He points out that for Hegel the connection of the absolute with the human spirit expresses "the relationship of man to nature, man's elevation above the finitude of natural phenomena to the idea of the infinite."[134] In the context of the ontological proof, which begins with the assumption of God, it is the religious elevation of the human mind above all finite reality "to the idea of the infinite and absolute" that must be shown both to be true to human existence and to lead to a divine being.[135] Pannenberg's essential disagreement with both Kant and Hegel regarding the soul involves a fundamental difference in the understanding of the relationship of both God and humans to the natural world. The disagreement starts from a different understanding of soul, body, and spirit and their unity.

Pannenberg argues that a notion of the independence of the soul from the body entered Christian thought in the second century. He suggests that this neo-Platonic conception of the soul is not in agreement with the Hebrew notion of the unity of human existence as body and soul. He also states that Plato's notion of the undying soul does not place the same worth on the individual as does the biblical notion of one life (with no reincarnation) followed by a bodily resurrection.[136] Jesus presented God as the one who eternally loves each individual person and thus gives each person measureless value.

Along with introducing a notion of the soul that has proved unacceptable in the modern period, according to Pannenberg, neo-Platonism introduced an unnecessary and unfortunate dualism of soul and body.[137] Pannenberg argues that the Hebrew understanding of the soul is of a living but needy being. "In Gen. 2:7 the soul is not merely the vital principle of the body but the ensouled body itself, the living being as a whole."[138] Nevertheless, humans are beings who are in need of receiving the life-giving Spirit.[139] Humans do not exist of themselves and on their own power. They require the gift of life from the Spirit. Only thus does the soul live.[140] And the animals also share this nature with humans. They too as a result of the life-giving Spirit are living creatures, are ensouled bodies.[141]

Pannenberg's disagreement with Gerhard Ebeling's attempt to ground Christian theology in the moral character of human experience is relevant in this context.[142] Ebeling claims that the theme of morality is the universal problematic that Christian faith addresses.[143] Pannenberg argues that modern historical consciousness has resulted in the relativizing of all ethical norms as cultural phenomena. They can no longer be grounded in a universal moral character, for this has no content that is not subject to historicality.[144] In the interest of ethics also, says Pannenberg, the theologian must seek to establish the truth of the Christian claims regarding God and divine self-revelation in the love of Christ.[145] Ebeling suggests that Pannenberg's attempt to ground ethics within the context of a Christian conception of reality results in an ethic that is valid only for those who first believe the Christian claim.[146] Pannenberg's response to this is that the claim of Christianity regards all reality and addresses all people. It addresses the fundamental questions of meaning and existence.[147] If it is not true for everyone, then it is true for no one.[148]

To this we could add that Ebeling's criticism would have more weight if Pannenberg sought to base his arguments on theological grounds only. As it is, however, Pannenberg also draws on arguments from philosophical anthropology and physics, to give only two examples. It is the development of his theological position in interaction with current scientific, historical, and philosophical views of reality that Pannenberg expects will lend additional credence to the argument that Christianity has a universal claim to truth regarding the nature of reality and hence has both critical and constructive roles in the realm of public morality.

Pannenberg notes that the problematic of morality presupposes a generally accepted notion of the good. He states that as Plato knew, the metaphysical and religious questions regarding the notion of the good underlie concrete forms of resistance to evil.[149] Pannenberg's aim is to argue convincingly at this foundational level that experience shows all reality to be consistent with the Christian claim that God creates and redeems, and that he does so toward an eschatological consummation in which sin and death are transcended. Ebeling counters that Pannenberg is attempting to undo the emancipation from religion achieved by the Enlightenment and to "re-theologize" the modern sciences.[150]

While these charges have an element of truth, it is not true that Pannenberg is attempting to reintroduce premodern Christendom. He is not attempting to reestablish the authority of the church over human reason. Rather, he is attempting to reestablish in the context of modern (scientific and secular) culture the validity of the Judeo-Christian conception of reality as grounded in the creative and redemptive activity of God's love. This is seen specifically in the context of Pannenberg's efforts to show how both "the connection of Christian faith with the historical form of [revelation in] Jesus" and "the special relationship of the biblical God with the experience of reality as history" through the history of their transmission (*Überlieferungsgeschichte*) have led to the development of modern notions of reality and history and also serve to correct the atheistic assumptions of emancipated modern culture.[151]

In other words, on the basis of the Judeo-Christian tradition and the history of its transmission, Pannenberg develops a critique of the post-Enlightenment West and its understanding of reality.[152] He argues that the opposition of soul and body on the one hand and the pluralism of values that has resulted from the emancipation and autonomy of reason on the other hand fail to acknowledge the inescapably religious character of reality. Therefore, modern culture and its sciences have fallen short of understanding the most basic characteristic of all existence.

Modern dualism is linked with the modern crisis in ethics, one aspect of which is seen in the problematic relationship of materialist culture to nonhuman reality.

In short, Pannenberg's thought can be seen as an attempt to overcome the destructive character of reason's autonomy in modern culture. He does so by seeking to establish a theological/metaphysical foundation for reason. In other words, according to Pannenberg, both theoretical and practical reason are grounded in a transcendent good (God).[153]

Eschatology and Ethics

Pannenberg employs the image of God rather than a notion of autonomous human reason as the true ground of social mores. He argues that purely rational attempts to ground the worth of individual human life have long fallen in ruins, due to individualistic arbitrariness and the pluralism that grows in its seedbed. Modern notions of equality and reciprocity also fail to provide grounds for the absolute valuation of individual existence. Only the notion of worth given in the ideas of creation and redemption (incarnation, salvation, resurrection) provides a durable ground for the ineradicable value of individual human existence.[154] The worth of the individual person's existence goes beyond the person's place in nature and in her or his social world.[155] Disease, poverty, oppression, suffering, misery, and death cannot rob an individual of this worth. Only one's own action in contradiction to this worth can so set one against God that one is condemned by the worth toward which all are destined.[156]

In addition to God's creative and redeeming love, Pannenberg connects the image of God especially with two further characteristics of God—eternal life and righteousness. Especially moral determination (*moralische Bestimmung*) is grounded in the expectation of humans to be united in an eternal communion with God, which means a participation in God's eternal life and righteousness. This moral determination not only aims at the relationship of humans with God but also intends the perfection of interhuman relationships.[157] The communion of individuals with God forms the foundation of communion with each other. "Only in the relation to God, and therefore in terms of the eschatological future of our destiny, does our moral self-determination or ethical autonomy, find a firm and solid basis."[158] In other words, social existence is intended by God to be fundamentally shaped by love. And love is defined by its future perfection in communion with God.[159]

We have seen that Pannenberg argues that humans are fundamentally oriented toward the future realization of the image of God. He argues that the future is real and that "it already determines the present."[160] The Kingdom of God as proclaimed by Jesus is already operative in history. It is most fundamentally connected with human exocentricity or openness. The Spirit of God providentially guides (determines) history through the human imagination, through education, through the transmission of religious traditions, through rational reflection, and through experience generally. Love, righteousness, and eternal life are divine categories. They define the Kingdom of God. Therefore our experiences of them are fleeting and imperfect. Our experiences and our knowledge of history confirm this. These qualities are at home in the promised future (eschatological) realization of perfect communion with God and others. But Pannenberg's argument is that this future realization is already operative. It has ontological priority. It is on its foundation that the world exists. It is toward its creaturely realization that the process of history moves. And it is on the basis of its creative, providential, and redemptive power that there is this process.[161]

Both Plato and Jesus taught that human life needs to find its focus outside of itself.[162] The one pointed to the Good and the other to the Father. "The pursuit of happiness for its own sake is egocentric and leads astray. Only those who seek the good for its own sake will thereby find happiness and identity."[163] Pannenberg continues with a quotation of Matt. 16:25: "For whoever would save his life will lose it, and whoever loses his life for my sake will find it." Pannenberg combines this with the Platonic notion that happiness follows from goodness. Only when God is honored as the highest Good of the self will the self achieve its own identity.[164] The individual receives life through recognizing and praising God in Jesus. This recognition involves the ordering of personal existence in accord with Jesus' love for the Father and his love for the creation as it is entailed in his love for the Father.[165] This is summed up by Jesus in the admonition to "seek first his Kingdom and his righteousness, and all these things shall be yours as well."[166] Blessedness follows goodness.

The other aspect of this goodness is expressed by the dual character of the movement of love: "You shall love the Lord your God with all your heart, and with all your strength, and with all your mind; and your neighbor as yourself."[167] Proper recognition and love of others is unfailingly implied by love of God (the Good).[168] The moral quality of existence is fundamental and inescapable. It characterizes all existence from beginning to end. It is the structure of existence. "God is the ultimate good of the ethical quest, not when he is conceived in splendid self-isolation, but when he is understood as relating himself to our world in the coming of his rule."[169] Thus, all moral concern is set within this understanding of God as the concrete future realization of our good.

The Kingdom of God is deeply concerned with the world and is emphatically not a merely otherworldly goal, disengaged from history. This means that human "striving for God as the ultimate good beyond the world is turned into concern for the world."[170] Pannenberg is not suggesting that human activity will gradually, or suddenly through some revolution, progress until the Kingdom is realized in the world. Jesus already represents the concrete, but preliminary, appearance of the Kingdom in history. In Jesus is revealed the right human relationship of love for and participation in ultimate reality, and within this divine love is included the self-giving love for all creation. In Jesus' resurrection is revealed the power of God to realize the Kingdom as the ultimate goal of history. Faith in God and devotion to Jesus results in the conversion of the individual to the coming Kingdom and to the world.[171]

Taken together—the unfinished and future-oriented character of human existence, the capacity of humans to respond freely to experience, the determinative and moral character of the future fulfillment of human life (the image of God) in the coming Kingdom of God, and the inclusion of nonhuman reality in a theology of history—these aspects of Pannenberg's anthropology and theology of history provide an understanding of human life as intrinsically moral in character and fundamentally concerned with all aspects of the world. Furthermore, his taking nature into a unified philosophy of nature and history shows the intimate connection of humans with the natural world.

Participation in the love of God means to participate in the giving of oneself for others as Jesus has done. To obey the command of love is to serve others and to be willing to give one's life for them. To those who lose their lives now is given the promise of eternal life.[172] This future reality is the source of existence, and it is the source of love. It gives human existence its peculiar exocentric and self-differentiating form. It is also the answer to the deepest longings and hopes of human existence. Therefore the command of love is not external to the self but resonates with the exocentric character of human being. The image of God that is the source of the command of love is no heteronomous authority. It is the source and goal of all reality.

The Ethics of Dominion

It is important to note the positive and central role Pannenberg gives to the human activity of differentiating the various finite things of the world. The sciences of the modern world are here seen as rooted in a theological view of human nature. This amounts to a basically positive evaluation of a *wissenschaftliches* point of view. A scientific approach to knowledge of the world is quite appropriate for humans. However, it must be clearly noted that this scientific approach to the world is grounded in a religious conception of existence.

Furthermore, Pannenberg conceives of humans as coexistent with all creatures and fundamentally belonging to the world. All reality is determined by God to be united with the Father. It is true that Pannenberg regards humans as having a special role in the creaturely expression of this future unity, but neither as isolated from nor as opposed to other creatures. The innate curiosity of humans is rightly structured by logical methods. But these methods are secondary to both the differentiating curiosity of humans and the unifying work of God, a work that makes a world of the multifarious things that exist. This means that all the differentiating activities of humans are subject to this work of God. And since the character of God's unifying action is best described as love, the human activity that corresponds to the self-differentiation of the Son from the Father also needs to conform to the love of the Father and Son for each other and of the Trinity for the world. In other words, the differentiating activities of humans—which include the sciences—must be structured by love for every creature in the context of love for God.

The notion that the human drive for knowledge is rooted in the self-differentiating love of the Son for the Father can provide a critical principle by which to guide and evaluate human activities, including modern science and technology.[173] It certainly provides a theological rooting for morality. All creaturely activity is here seen to be destined to participate in the inner-Trinitarian love. The ultimate destiny determines the very character of human subjectivity and is also the ground of all morality. But it so determines humans that each individual must either codetermine his or her personhood in accord with this end or determine it in some other way. The character of love is that it must be given and received freely. Otherwise it is not love. Therefore, in every thought and action a person must love or not love.

In relation to the God of the power of the future, man is free: free for a truly personal life, free to accept the provisionality of everything, free with regard to nature and society, free for that creative love that changes the world without destroying it. This creative love proceeds from freedom and is directed toward affirming and creating freedom in the world. If the unity of mankind, which is the purpose of history, one day becomes reality, it will be achieved by this love.[174]

This applies as much to relationships with the nonhuman world as to those with other humans. All relationships are grounded in the relationship of each creature to the Creator.

Let God be God. This is the fundamental task of humans. It is to recognize their own status as creatures in submission to the Creator. To do so is to honor God as God. It is to trust in the eschatological realization of God's rule. And it is to achieve the freedom of creatures under the Father.[175] It might be helpful to rephrase the above charge: Let the Creator be Lord. In other words, in the exercise of our dominion we must acknowledge that the objects of the world are not at our disposal apart from the freedom and authority granted us by the Creator. Each has its own prior relationship to the Creator and is part of the history of the revelation of the image of God.

To Pannenberg's analysis we must add that we live in virtual isolation from the Earth and its wild creatures. We are surrounded by objects that we have created, objects that appear to be completely at our disposal. Yet these *products* are formed out of the earth, plants, and creatures. Our production of books, tools, machines, and so on, is dependent upon the world. We have come to regard these naturally occurring objects as raw materials. Most of us have only occasional concourse with the raw world. We have grown very accustomed to having considerable powers of disposal over the objects (*products*) we generally perceive. Only social and legal considerations interfere with this power. Except for our relations to other humans, we are generally removed from immediate interaction with the world of divinely created things.[176] It perhaps has become all too easy to extend the character of our authority over our products to our relationship to the nonhuman world and increasingly to humans as well. But in this subworld of cultural artifacts, too, love can be accepted as the foundation of morality. Love for God, for humans, and for the whole of divinely created reality is the foundation for guiding our relationship to our culture and its accoutrements. This foundation also provides a critical principle for judging these relationships and products.

Modernity's self-emancipation from religion has resulted in the loss of orientation toward the eternal future. This is ironically also a loss of freedom, since true freedom is rooted in trust in the power and love of God, which hold the promise of resurrection and fulfillment. Apart from this humans are left to their own resources to achieve their destiny, to make themselves persons. However, apart from the relationship to God, who is the source of unity, who makes it possible to conceive of a world, we become separated from ourselves. We no longer know how to direct the infinite openness of our being. Augustine might say that our self-assertion has cut off our restless hearts from the source and the goal of their infinite rest. In this situation modern culture has become enslaved to its economy of production and consumption. Materialist culture is anything but free. The attempt to sate our infinite openness with finite objects is doomed to failure.

This is but one sign of our loss of freedom. Another is seen in the changing character of our relationship to science and technology. Here we see how dependent we have become on the ability of our efforts to free us from the fears and threats of existence. As modern culture has become aware of the destructive consequences of science, technology, industry, and normal daily life it has turned to science and technology to save the situation. The economics of consumption, which is the driving engine of all these activities, continues to dominate us.[177]

Pannenberg attempts to show that secular views of reality do not adequately account for existence.[178] He argues that the religious character of existence needs to be recognized and allowed to shape the self and culture. He argues that humans have a fundamental openness

> to an Other beyond all the objects of their world, an Other that at the same time embraces this entire world and thus ensures the possible unification of the life of human beings in the world, despite the multiplicity and heterogeneity of the world's actions on them. A mere very general horizon containing all objects would have no inherent existence. In fact, when human beings reach out to a very general horizon embracing all the individual objects of actual or possible perception, they are relating themselves exocentrically to a *reality* prior to them; in this reaching out they are therefore implicitly affirming at the same time the divine reality, even though they have not yet grasped this thematically as such, much less in this or that particular form.[179]

This openness to the infinite does not entail an abandonment of the world of finite objects, but it entails the recognition that the objects can be neither accounted for of themselves nor used to satisfy the basic neediness of finite existence. It is a consciousness of the absolute contingence of all finite objects that leads to the idea of a transcendent ground of the world.[180] But every attempt to understand this infinite is itself finite and able to be transcended. According to Pannenberg, this means that the human relationship to the infinite is mediated through the finite world. Thus, "from the transcending of all finite realities" consciousness is always turned back to the reality of its finite self and environment. This line of reasoning leads Pannenberg to conclude that human experience reveals a dependence on something that "surpasses and sustains everything finite."[181] He claims that his argument serves as proof, not that God exists, but that the question of God cannot be separated from the question of the nature of existence.[182]

One of the significant implications of this argument is that the movement of the self beyond itself and toward the infinite goal of its existence is only and always achieved in and mediated by the finite natural and social worlds. To love God is to participate in

God's love for the world.[183]   The fundamental requirement of this self-transcending process is a basic trust in the world, as well as in the ultimate human destiny—the image of God.   This second type of trust is ultimately expressed in the hope of bodily resurrection.   Trust flourishes in the soil of love.

Creative and redeeming love is at the heart of Pannenberg's understanding of reality.   The eternal Son's self-differentiating love is the principle of otherness that is the source of the independent existence of creatures.   The redeeming love of the Son aims to draw alienated and dying creatures back to the eternal love that is the source of their existence.   Perfect communion with the faithful love of the eternal Father is the goal toward which the divine Spirit draws history.

Love is the formative ground upon which existence is based. The exocentricity of human existence is an essential capacity that enables humans to recognize others as other from themselves and to recognize their worth apart from any advantage to the self. This is fundamental to love.   In this way love shows its absolutely basic significance for responsible human existence. Love is the structure of our being.   It is not an external authority that bids us to love God and to love others.   This theological conception of reality is the foundation of Pannenberg's understanding of the moral character of existence.

The rule of humans over creation is to have the character of a servant priesthood and kingship, both of which are defined through the character of Jesus' self-giving love.   The image of Jesus, the king of kings and high priest who came in the form of the suffering servant, who submitted all notions of authority to the law of love, is the anticipation of the goal of existence.   As such it is also the root of the moral responsibility of existence.   In Pannenberg's conception of existence morality begins with an appropriate response to God and finitude, and this is achieved in relations with humans, the products of culture, and all creation.

NOTES

1. See Erazim Kohák, *The Embers and the Stars: A Philosophical Inquiry into the Moral Sense of Nature* (Chicago: University of Chicago Press, 1984), 90-93, and James Gustafson, *Ethics from a Theocentric Perspective*, vol. 1, *Theology and Ethics* (Chicago: University of Chicago Press, 1981), 95-99 and cf. 4-7, 82-84.

2. H. Paul Santmire, *The Travail of Nature: The Ambiguous Ecological Promise of Christian Theology* (Philadelphia: Fortress Press, 1985), 1-3. Santmire briefly surveys some of the ecologically motivated attacks against the Western heritage, especially against the Christian tradition. Stephen Hawking, *Brief History* 126, criticizes some forms of modern anthropocentrism by linking them with the Ptolemaic view of the cosmos.

3. In *Was ist der Mensch?* (1962), 44f., 60; *What is Man* 60, 85 Pannenberg almost appears to provide a theological foundation for the continued destructive domination of the natural world by humans. However, this is neither his intent nor the necessary outcome of that booklet. Nonetheless, he does appear to focus on humans to the exclusion of the nonhuman world. However, in *Anthropology in Theological Perspective* (74-79) Pannenberg claims that his theological anthropology provides for an understanding of humans that places them in a fundamentally moral relationship with the nonhuman world. Pannenberg is able to do this without altering the basic arguments of *Was ist der Mensch?*

4. "Only in the light of the incarnation of the eternal Son as a man [in the form of a human], however, can we say that the relation of creatures to the Creator finds its supreme and final realization in humanity" (*STe* 2:175). ("Daß im Menschen das Verhältnis des Geschöpfes zum Schöpfer überhaupt seine höchste und endgültige Realisierung findet, läßt sich allerdings erst angesichts der Inkarnation des ewigen Sohnes in der Gestalt eines Menschen behaupten") (*ST* 2:203). This implies that the idea of creation alone neither fully guarantees nor fully realizes the special place of humans in the world. Since this is only realized in the incarnation of the eternal Son its character must be sought in the life and destiny of Jesus. This character is especially marked by the servant and priestly character of his kingship.

5. *ST* 2:208; *STe* 2:179f.

6. See the surveys of these criticisms in Kurt Koch, "Der Mensch und seine Mit-Welt," 29-33 and Santmire, *Travail of Nature*, 1-3.

7. *ATP*, 77.

8. *ST* 2:234; *STe* 2:204f.

9. *ATP*, 77.

10. "In view of these findings [that the dominion of humans over the creation is to be 'like' that of the Creator's] the criticism of biblical anthropology that blames the giving of dominion in Gen. 1:28 for the unrestricted exploitation of nature by modern technology and industrial society, and for the

resultant ecological crisis, must be rejected as without merit" (*STe* 2:204). ("Angesichts dieses Befundes [daß die Herrschaft des Menschen über die Schöpfung der des Schöpfers selber 'ähnlich' sein soll] muß diejenige Kritik am biblischen Menschenbild, die die hemmungslose Ausbeutung der Naturwelt durch die moderne Technik und Industriegesellschaft mit der daraus folgenden ökologischen Krise dem biblischen Auftrag an den Menschen zur Herrschaft über die Schöpfung (Gen 1,28) zur Last legt, als unberechtigt zurückgewiesen werden.") (*ST* 2:234). Pannenberg refers specifically to Lynn White, "The Historical Roots of our Ecological Crisis," in *The Environmental Handbook* (New York, 1970), and Carl Amery, *Das Ende der Vorsehung. Die gnadenlosen Folgen des Christentums* (1972). Cf. *ATP*, 74-79.

11. "Die Emanzipation von religiösen Bindungen und Rücksichten und von den darin begründeten Rahmenbedingungen des gesellschaftlichen Lebens ist eine der Voraussetzungen für die eigengesetzliche Entwicklung des Wirtschaftslebens in der Neuzeit gewesen. Der neuzeitliche Säkularismus kann sich nicht gleichzeitig der Emanzipation von religiösen Bindungen rühmen und die Verantwortung für die Fogen seiner Verabsolutierung irdischen Besitzstrebens jenen religiösen Ursprüngen aufbürden, von deren Beschränkungen er sich gelöst hat" (*ST* 2:234; *STe* 2:204). I prefer my translation since Bromiley misses the negation in the second sentence. Cf. *ATP*, 77-79.

12. *ATP*, 79.

13. *ATP*, 79.

14. Ps. 8:6f.; Gen. 1:26f.

15. *STe* 2:203. "Als 'Bild Gottes' soll der Mensch Platzhalter und Wegbereiter der Gottesherrschaft in der Welt sein" (*ST* 2:233).

16. *ST* 2:233f.; *STe* 2:203f.

17. *ATP*, 75.

18. Gerhard von Rad, *Old Testament Theology*, vol. 1, 41.

19. *ATP*, 76.

20. *ST* 2:234f.; *STe* 2:204f.

21. Gen. 2:15; *ATP*, 79; *ST* 2:235; *STe* 2:205.

22. *ATP*, 76f.

23. The anthropic principle offers a possible further confirmation (cf. chapter 1).

24. *STe* 2:205. "In diesem Sinne läßt sich gerade die ökologische Krise am Ende der emanzipatorischen Neuzeit als Erinnerung daran verstehen, daß nach wie vor der Gott der Bibel Herr seiner Schöpfung bleibt und die Beliebigkeit menschlicher Willkür im Umgang mit ihr nicht ohne Schranken ausdehnbar und nicht folgenlos ist" (*ST* 2:235).

25. Pannenberg, "Das christologische Fundament christlicher Anthropologie," *Concilium* 9,6 (1973): 425.

26. Ibid., 426f.

27. Ibid., 427.

28. *ST* 2:204; *STe* 2:176.

29. *ST* 2:249, 251; *STe* 2:217, 2218f.
30. Translation is mine. "Ihre volle Realisierung ist die *Bestimmung* des Menschen, die mit Jesus Christus geschichtlich angebrochen ist und an der die übrigen Menschen teilnehmen sollen durch Verwandlung in das Bild Christi" (*ST* 2:249; *STe* 2:217).
31. *ST* 2:255-58; *STe* 2:222-24.
32. *ST* 2:258; *STe* 2:224.
33. Rom. 8:19-25.
34. The translation is mine. "Wenn die Erschaffung des Menschen zum Ebenbild Gottes seine Bestimmung zur Gemeinschaft mit dem ewigen Gott impliziert, dann wird die Menschwerdung Gottes in Jesus von Nazareth als Erfüllung dieser Bestimmung gelten dürfen. Dei Vereinigung Gottes und der Menschheit im Leben eines Menschen is offenbar durch keine andere Form der Gemeinschaft von Gott und Menschen überbietbar" (*ST* 2:259). Bromiley's translation (*STe* 2:225) appears to reduce the force of Pannenberg's argument that humans are not so much created in the image of God as created with that image as their destiny.
35. *ST* 2:259; *STe* 2:225.
36. See chapter 2 on Christology.
37. *STe* 2:228. "Das Ziel ist ihm primär unbestimmt gegenwärtig, nicht einmal *als* Ziel, sondern in dem unbestimmten Vertrauen, das den Horizont der Welterfahrung und der Intersubjectivität eröffnet, sowie andererseits im unruhigen Drang zur Überschreitung jeder endlichen Gegebenheit" (*ST* 2:263).
38. *ST* 2:263; *STe* 2:229.
39. *STe* 2:228. Pannenberg is relying on the Enlightenment figure J. G. Herder: "der Mensch könne das in ihm angelegte Gottesbild nicht selber aushauen und ausbilden . . ., sondern sei dazu angewiesen auf das Wirken der göttlichen Vorsehung durch Tradition und Lehre, Vernunft und Erfahrung" (*ST* 2:262). See the appropriate section in *ATP*, esp. 43-47. He appears willing to see this as the work of the divine Spirit and parallel to the work of the prophets of ancient Israel ("Das christologische Fundament christlicher Anthropologie," 428).
40. *ST* 2:264; *STe* 2:230.
41. *ST* 2:264f.; *STe* 2:230.
42. *STe* 2:230. I have added the emphasis of Pannenberg, which Bromiley omits. "Die Menschen müssen dem Bilde des Sohnes gleichgestaltet werden, seiner *Selbstunterscheidung* vom Vater. So werden sie auch an der *Gemeinschaft* des Sohnes mit dem Vater teilnehmen" (*ST* 2:265).
43. Rom. 8:19-23.
44. *STe* 2:231.
45. The translation and emphasis are mine. "Annahme der eigenen Endlichkeit muß auch einschließen, daß jedem anderen Geschöpf in den Grenzen seiner Endlichkeit die ihm gebührende Achtung erwiesen wird. Damit kommt die Vielheit der Geschöpfe als eine Ordnung in den Blick, in der jedes von

ihnen seinen Platz hat. Nur so kann der Mensch die ganze Schöpfung im Lobe ihres Schöpfers zusammenfassen und dem Schöpfer mit dem Dank für das eingene Dasein zugleich den Dank für alle seine Geschöpfe darbringen" (*ST* 2:266; *STe* 2:231).

46. *GF* 1:197; *BQ* 1:232f.

47. *ATP*, 34-42.

48. The term *hiatus* is taken from Arnold Gehlen, *Der Mensch* (1950) (*ATP*, 39).

49. *ATP*, 39.

50. *ATP*, 61f.

51. *ATP*, 76.

52. Gen. 2:19f.

53. *ATP*, 67.

54. *ATP*, 45. This is taken from Herder, *Outlines of a Philosophy of the History of Man*, trans. T. Churchill (London, 1800), xi, 5.

55. Ibid.

56. *ATP*, 46, cf. 60.

57. *ATP*, 47.

58. *ATP*, 53.

59. *ATP*, 491f.

60. *ATP*, 492-515.

61. *ATP*, 68.

62. *ATP*, 69.

63. *IST*, 51.

64. "Der Mensch ist auf Unendlichkeit wesentlich bezogen, aber er ist nie in sich selbst schon unendlich" (*GF* 1:353; *BQ* 2:191). In the context Pannenberg is arguing against the Hegelian roots of Feuerbach's atheism.

65. *IGHF*, 95.

66. Ibid.

67. Pannenberg, *Grundzüge der Christologie*, 197.

68. *ATP*, 69.

69. It should be remembered that he regards all creation as destined to the realization of the image of God. Cf. chapter 2.

70. The human capacity for domination "is rooted in the peculiarly human ability to discern—to discern between objects, but above all to discern between the objects themselves as self-centered entities, not simply as correlates to our own drives; that is to say: to discern them from ourselves and ourselves from everything else. Paradoxically, this ability of discernment empowers human beings to make themselves masters of the world" (*IST*, 50, cf. 51).

71. *ST* 2:219; *STe* 2:190.

72. *STe* 2:202. "Einheit und Integrität des Lebens werden in einer anderen Sphäre konstituiert, die allem Handeln vorausliegt" (*ST* 2:232).

73. *ST* 2:231; *STe* 2:201f.

74. *ST* 2:231f.; *STe* 2:202.

75. See *ST* 2:204-32, esp. 220f., 224-32; *STe* 2:176-202, esp. 191f., 194-202.

76. Pannenberg suggests that feeling (*Lebensgefühl*) is the expression of the creative life-giving presence of the divine Spirit (*ST* 2:225, cf. 220-22, esp. n58; *STe* 2:195f., cf. 191-93, esp. n58). Pannenberg appears to use the concept feeling in a less differentiated manner than Schleiermacher does in his discussion of the consciousness of dependence. Pannenberg defines feeling as rendering "us familiar with ourselves in the whole of our being, without our as yet having or needing an *idea* of our self" (*ATP*, 251). Feeling preceedes and embraces the differentiation of subject and object (cf. *ATP* 247-53 for Pannenberg's discussion of the agreement and difference between himself and Schleiermacher on this point).

The subsection "Whole and Part" in chapter 1 deals with notions that inform Pannenberg's means of conceiving the relationship of individuals to the world.

77. *ST* 2:224f.; *STe* 2:194f.

78. *ST* 2:224; *STe* 2:194f.

79. *STe* 2:195. "Insofern ist auch die Erfassung der Einheit im Unterschied noch eine Funktion der Fähigkeit zur Distanznahme im Bewußtsein der Andersheit. Die Einheit des Unterschiedenen ist somit selber dem Bewußtsein ein anderes. Sie verdankt sich nicht der Einheit des Ich. Die Einheit des Ich als Boden aller Erfahrung, der die Einheit ihrer Inhalte im subjektiven Erleben begründet und sie im individuellen Lebensvollzug zur Einheit integriert, bildet sich aus als Korrelat der objektiven Einheit des 'Begriffs,' der das gegenständlich Unterschiedene in seiner Einheit begreift" (*ST* 2:224).

80. *ST* 2:224f.; *STe* 2:195.

81. I have preferred to offer my own translation of this passage. Bromiley interprets, wrongly in my opinion, "der selber" as referring back to the "geistigen Raum." However, I believe the final phrase makes most sense if it is understood to refer back to the notion that is the subject of the sentence, namely, the idea of the eternal One. "In diesem Gedanken des unendlich Einen wird thematisch, was als unbestimmt Unendliches immer schon dem Bewußtsein präsent ist und den geistigen Raum bildet, in welchem das Distanznehmen vom anderen und alle Bestimmung der Andersheit und Bezogenheit sich bewegt und der selber durch diese Bewegung für das Bewußtsein erschlossen wird" (*ST* 2:225; *STe* 2:195).

82. As far as I know Pannenberg does not make this connection.

83. *STe* 2:196f. "Trotz aller infolge der Sünde eingetretenen Perversionen . . . hat die menschliche Intelligenz in der Wahrnehmung der Andersheit des Anderen teil an der Selbstunterscheidung des ewigen Sohnes vom Vater, durch die er nicht nur mit dem Vater vereint, sondern auch Prinzip alles geschöpflichen Daseins in seiner Besonderheit ist. Die menschliche Vernunft erzeugt freilich nur Gedanken, nicht unmittelbar die Wirklichkeit der endlichen Dinge. Doch diese Gedanken repräsentieren nicht nur die endlichen

Gegenstände in ihrer Unterschiedenheit von anderen, sondern können darüber hinaus auch zur Basis fur die Gebilde menschlicher Technik werden" (*ST* 2:226).

84. *ST* 2:226; *STe* 2:197.

85. My translation. "Je weiter entwickelt das Bewußtseinsleben, desto mehr ist das Lebewesen in seinem Bewußtsein außer sich und desto mehr ist ihm zugleich sein Weltbezug innerlich, in ihm selber präsent. . . . Das menschliche Selbstbewußtsein bildet die für under Wissen höchste Stufe dieses Ineinanders von Ekstatik und Innerlichkeit" (*ST* 2:227; *STe* 2:197).

86. *ST* 2:227; *STe* 2:197f. and 3:29.

87. See above the section in this chapter on "The Idea of Human Dominion."

88. Cf. Matt. 7:5.

89. *ST* 2:272; *STe* 2:236f.

90. *ST* 2:272; *STe* 2:237.

91. *ST* 2:272; *STe* 2:237f.

92. cf. *ST* 2:294; *STe* 2:256f.

93. Pannenberg points out that "laws cannot achieve the justice we seek precisely because they are abstract and general." He argues that only love that cares for the individual can achieve true justice and that such just love is the central characteristic of the Kingdom of God (*TKG*, 79).

94. *ST* 2:284-86; *STe* 2:247-49.

95. *ST* 2:288f.; *STe* 2:251f.

96. *ST* 2:289f.; *STe* 2:252.

97. *STe* 2:179. The term *isolation* would better translate "Absonderung." "Detachment" is too weak in this context. "Im Begriff des Elends ist die Absonderung und Verselbständigung des Menschen von Gott mit den daraus hervorgehenden Fogen zusammengefaßt. . . . Der Gott entfremdete Mensch lebt im Elend der Trennung von Gott, fern von der Heimat der eigenen Identität" (*ST* 2:207).

98. *ST* 2:208; *STe* 2:180.

99. *ST* 2:206f.; *STe* 2:178f.

100. *STe* 2:262. "Verantwortlichkeit und Schuld ergeben sich erst aus der Geltung einer Norm, der der Handelnde folgen soll oder hätte folgen sollen" (*ST* 2:300).

101. *ST* 2:300; *STe* 2:262.

102. *STe* 2:262. "Es ist ein Zustand der Entfremdung von Gott" (*ST* 2:301).

103. *ST* 2:303; *STe* 2:264.

104. *ST* 2:302; *STe* 2:263.

105. *ST* 2:194ff., 302f.; *STe* 2:166-68, 263-65.

106. *ST* 2:303; *STe* 2:264f.

107. *STe* 2:264f. "Der Mensch als das zu voller Selbständigkeit gelangte Geschöpf muß das, was es ist und sein soll, durch sich selber werden und aus-

bilden. Dabei liegt es nur allzu nahe, daß das in der Form einer Verselbständigung geschieht, in der der Mensch sich selber an die Stelle Gottes
und seiner Herrschaft über die Schöpfung setzt. Aber ohne geschöpfliche
Selbständigkeit kann auch das Verhältnis des Sohnes zum Vater nicht im
Medium geschöpflichen Daseins zur Erscheinung kommen" (*ST* 2:303).

108. Pannenberg refers to Leibniz, *Theodizee*, 20f., 156, 288 (*ST* 2:197;
STe 2:170).

109. *STe* 2:171. "Die Wurzel des Bösen ist eher im Aufstand gegen die
Schranke der Endlichkeit zu suchen in der Weigerung, die eigene Endlichkeit
anzunehmen, und in der damit verbundenen Illusion der Gottgleichheit (Gen
3,5)" (*ST* 2:199).

110. *ST* 2:199; *STe* 2:171f.

111. *ST* 2:296f.; *STe* 2:258f.

112. *ST* 2:298f.; *STe* 2:260f.

113. *ST* 2:298; *STe* 2:260.

114. *ST* 2:298f.; *STe* 2:260f.

115. *ST* 2:274f.; *STe* 2:239.

116. *ST* 2:280; *STe* 2:244.

117. *ST* 2:277-79; *STe* 2:241-44.

118. "Aus der Endlichkeit folgt nicht, daß der Tod zur Natur des Menschen gehört" (*GF* 2:153).

119. *STe* 2:270. "Der Tod ist die Folge des Abbruchs der Beziehung zu
Gott, der Quelle des Lebens, und er ist im Zusammenhang mit den übrigen
Sündenfolgen zu sehen, die darin bestehen, daß der Mensch durch seinen
Gegensatz zum Schöpfer auch in Gegensatz zu seinen Mitgeschöpfen, zur
Erde, zu den Tieren und zu den andern Menschen gerät (vgl. Gen 3,14-19)"
(*ST* 2:309).

120. *STe* 2:270. "Vielmehr folgt aus der Wesensart der Sünde als Bruch
des Gottesverhältnisses der Konflikt des Sünders mit der Schöpfung Gottes und
dem Mitmenschen und sogar mit sich selber" (*ST* 2:309).

121. *MG*, 62; *MIG*, 85f.

122. Translation is mine. "Bestehen bleibt aber die Zusammengehörigkeit
von Zukunft und möglicher Ganzheit des Daseins." (*MG*, 62; *MIG*, 86).

123. *ST* 2:310f.; *STe* 2:271f.

124. *ST* 2:313; *STe* 2:274f.

125. "We achieve liberation from sin and death only where the image of
the Son takes shape in human life through the operation of the Spirit of God"
(*STe* 2:275; *ST* 2:314).

126. Pannenberg (*ST* 2:118f.; *STe* 2:97) cites Carl F. v. Weizsäcker, *Die
Einheit der Natur* (1971), 172-82; C. F. v. Weizsäcker, *Zum Weltbild der
Physik* (1954), 224f.; A. M. K. Müller, *Die präparierte Zeit* (1972), 287f.; R.
J. Russell, "Entropy and Evil," *Zygon* 19 (1984): 449-68.

127. *ST* 2:131, 199f.; *STe* 2:108, 171-72.

128. Rom. 8:28.

129. *STe* 2:262n300. In regard to avoiding the "the danger of a moralization of evil" ("Gefahr einer Moralisierung des Bösen") as a failure to achieve the spiritual/historical goal of existence Pannenberg notes the significance of the eschatological character of existence: "daß der Gedanke der Bestimmung des Menschen nicht in erster Linie ethisch, sondern eschatologisch und hinsichtlich seiner Realisierung heilsgeschichtlich gedacht wird, was nicht ausschließt, daß daraus dann auch ethische Verbindlichkeiten folgen" (*ST* 2:300n300).

130. Ibid.

131. *IGHF*, 81.

132. *IGHF*, 84.

133. Pannenberg argues with both philosophical atheism and the methodological atheism of the modern sciences. See "Typen des Atheismus und ihre theologische Bedeutung" and "Die Frage nach Gott," both in *GF* 1; *BQ* 2: chapters 6 and 7. See also *IGHF*, esp. 80-177, and *WT*, pt. 1. Pannenberg treats the claims of the Christian tradition as rationally testable hypotheses about the nature of reality.

134. *IGHF*, 84.

135. *IGHF*, 86.

136. Pannenberg, *Bestimmung des Menschen*, 10. Pannenberg interprets the biblical understanding of life after death through the resurrection of Jesus. Other ancient Jewish notions of the afterlife are excluded by the New Testament.

137. *ST* 2:211; *STe* 2:182.

138. *STe* 2:185; *ST* 2:213.

139. *TKG*, 87.

140. *ST* 2:214f.; *STe* 2:186.

141. Gen. 1:30; 2:19; *ST* 2:218; *STe* 2:189.

142. The argument between Pannenberg and Ebeling focuses on Wilhelm Hermann's ethics, which Pannenberg regards as a continuation of Kant's moral anthropology (*EE*, 45-54; *Ethics*, 60-70). See Gerhard Ebeling, "Die Krise des Ethischen und die Theologie: Erwiderung auf W. Pannenbergs Kritik," in *Wort und Glaube*, vol. 2: *Beiträge zur Fundamentaltheologie und zur Lehre von Gott* (Tübingen: J. C. B. Mohr, 1969), 42-55 and Pannenberg, "Antwort an Gerhard Ebeling," in *EE*, 55-69; *Ethics*, 71-86.

143. Ebeling, "Die Kriese," 47.

144. *EE*, 47f.; *Ethics*, 62-64.

145. *EE*, 47, 53f.; *Ethics*, 63, 69f.

146. Ebeling, "Die Kriese," 50f.

147. *EE*, 66-68; *Ethics*, 83-86.

148. *ATP*, 15.

149. *EE*, 57f.; *Ethics*, 74.

150. Ebeling, "Die Kriese," 44.

151. *EE*, 66f.; *Ethics*, 83f.

152. Pannenberg also makes use of Plato's conception of the good. See "Christentum und Platonismus: Die kritische Platonrezeption Augustins in ihrer Bedeutung für das gegenwärtige christliche Denken," *Zeitschrift fur Kirchengeschichte* 96 (1985):esp. 151, 158f.

153. Pannenberg recognizes that the modern period has understood God to be the opponent of reason's autonomy. His arguments against the atheism of Feuerbach and others show his concern to conceive God as the ground of human freedom (cf. *GF* 1:347-86; *BQ* 2:184-233 and *IGHF*, 80-115). Also see Pannenberg, "Rezeptive Vernunft: Die antike Deutung der Erkenntnis als Hinnahme vorgegebener Wahrheit," in *Überlieferung und Aufgabe: Festschrift für Erich Heintel zum 70. Geburtstag*, ed. Herta Nagl Docekal (Wien: Wilhelm Braumüller, 1982), 273, 299f.; and Oswald Bayer, "Die Gegenwart der Güte Gottes," *Neue Seitschrift für systematische Theologie* 21 (1979): 266. Bayer points out Pannenberg's use of the Platonic notion of the good.

154. *ST* 2:205; *STe* 2:177.

155. *ST* 2:204; *STe* 2:176.

156. *ST* 2:206; *STe* 2:178. It appears that this provides a Christian foundation to criticize some modern forms of devaluation of individual life. While it is beyond the focus of this book, I believe that this would provide grounds for addressing issues such as abortion and euthanasia.

157. *ST* 2:258; *STe* 2:224f.

158. *STe* 2:224. "Nur in der Gottesbeziehung also und darum von der eschatologischen Zukunft seiner Bestimmung her findet auch die moralische Selbstbestimmung des Menschen, seine sittliche Autonomie, eine feste und tragfähige Basis" (*ST* 2:258).

159. Pannenberg argues that the Platonic notion of the good already recognized—on the basis of a structural analysis of existence—that the good was not a possession but had to be striven for. The good is "beyond the presently realized human condition" (*TKG*, 106).

160. *IGHF*, 110.

161. Pannenberg's theology addresses questions like those of physicist Stephen Hawking (*A Brief History of Time*, 174): 'Why is there a universe for us to describe with theoretical models?' In addressing this question, Pannenberg's theology also bridges the disciplines in a way that Hawking hopes for (*Ibid.*, 174f.).

162. See Ted Peters, "Pannenberg's Eschatological Ethics," 241f. Peters notes that Pannenberg connects a Platonic notion of the good with the future rule of God (see *TKG*, 111).

163. *STe* 2:249. "Das Streben nach dem Glück um seiner selbst willen ist egozentrisch und führt in die Irre. Nur wer nach dem Guten um seiner selbst willen strebt, wird dadurch auch das Glück und seine eigene Identität finden" (*ST* 2:286).

164. Pannenberg refers to Plato, *Gorgias*, 470e, 491bff. (*ST* 2:286; *STe* 2:249; and see *MG*, 46; *MIG*, 62).

165. Pannenberg argues that Plato did not adequately determine what the nature of the good was. This left the idea of the good open to association with happiness. It did not allow for a clear distinction of the good as being both prior to and the source of happiness (*TKG*, 106-8).

166. Matt. 6:33; *ST* 2:286; *STe* 2:249f.

167. Luke 10:27.

168. These are not two kinds of love (*TKG*, 112).

169. *TKG*, 111.

170. *TKG*, 111.

171. *TKG*, 126.

172. John 12:25.

173. Pannenberg notes the critical function of the Kingdom over against all political achievements. He also identifies the heart of the Kingdom as love (*TKG*, 80, 65f., 79).

174. *TKG*, 69f.

175. Cf. *IST*, 68.

176. Cf. *CS*, 73f.

177. C. S. Lewis, in *The Abolition of Man*, 42-44, argues that in the modern practice of science and technology, humans themselves are objectified and lose their humanity—including their freedom.

178. Cf. *CW*, 68; *CSW*, 52.

179. *ATP*, 69.

180. Pannenberg points out the affinity of these results with Hegel's view that the experience of finitude already implies its transcendence and the elevation of consciousness to the idea of the infinite (*ATP*, 70).

181. *ATP*, 70.

182. *ATP*, 73.

183. *TKG*, 111-13.

CONCLUSION

This study has focused on how Wolfhart Pannenberg's Trinitarian understanding of God, as Creator and Redeemer, and his theological anthropology provide for a conception of the unity of nature and history. I have attempted to show how this theological conception of reality and of the role of humans in it might ground moral thought. I have tested this by examining how Pannenberg's thought addresses the ecological problematique.

Pannenberg's eschatological notion of creation is conceived as the unified action of the Trinitarian God. The idea of creation encompasses the entire process of reality in its movement toward participation in the love of the Creator. Thus, creation is joined with the ideas of redemption, providence, and fulfillment. He also makes philosophical arguments regarding universal history, the notions of *whole* and *world* and he reflects philosophically on scientific notions such as *field* and *contingency*. On these and other grounds he argues that reality should be understood within the context of this unity. Human and nonhuman creatures are radically distinguished and even opposed only on the basis of the false modern dichotomization of reality and the subsequent reduction of nature to serving merely human interests.

I also attempted to show how Pannenberg's Christology and theological anthropology support and augment the arguments presented in the chapter on creation. Of central significance to the Christology of Pannenberg is the idea of the self-differentiating love of Jesus. This is seen especially in the self-effacing intimacy of Jesus' relationship to God, whom he regarded as his Father. The love of the eternal Father and Son for each other is manifested in Jesus' destiny. Jesus submitted his life to the will of God, and God raised Jesus from the dead. Pannenberg conceives of this divine love as encompassing the created world. In loving the Father, Jesus loves the world. In loving Jesus, the Father loves the world. Together, Father, Son, and Spirit create and redeem the world and bring it to the realization of its destiny.

The central role of humans in this process, according to Pannenberg, is based on the incarnation of the eternal Son in the person of Jesus of Nazareth. Jesus represents the proleptic realization of the image of God in history. The eschatological goal of history is the perfect realization of the image of God in creaturely reality. This image includes, through humans, all creatures. The content of the image is divine love. Humans are called, therefore, to participate most fully in divine love—as representatives of the entire creation.

Pannenberg thinks of all reality, nonhuman nature as well as the story of human cultures, as one process. It is a process that goes forth from the creative and powerful love of God. Pannenberg's philosophy of universal history is grounded in a theological system that unites nature and history on the basis of his interpretation of the ideas of creation, redemption, and fulfillment. The eschatological source and destiny of creation—the God whose future rule is love—is the "unifying unity" of reality.

Though creatures turn from God and from divine intentions, God responds with forgiving love. God enters redemptively into a history with creatures. Love seeks to save the creatures that have turned away from the divine source and goal of life. Pannenberg argues that the process of creation is providentially guided toward the perfect realization of God's Kingdom. Trust in this future is the appropriate attitude of humans as they live within the process of history. Trust is based on the ever faithful love of God, which is reflected also in those regularities of nature that allow description in the form of laws of science.

Pannenberg characterizes the relationship of God to creation in terms of faithfulness and love. The resurrection of Jesus especially reveals the eternal love and value that God has for individual creatures. Divine love aims to free and enable creatures to enter into the twofold motion of love. Love is not an authority that is external to creaturely existence. The transforming power of love comes to creatures through the ecstatic and open structure of their being. Love empowers their imaginations and makes them free. Participation in the eschatological Kingdom of God is the central expression of the hope of the Christian faith. On this understanding of love and the unity of the process of creation Pannenberg would ground ethics.

Human life is to be guided by the love of God, which includes all creation in its movement. The good of humans is not opposed to that of other creatures. The good of humans is the perfection of the image of God, which is realized in Jesus' self-giving love of God and creation. This is the ground of moral responsibility. It is not the authority of law but the response of the spirit of love. All life is to be lived in the Spirit, which originates in God and is directed back to God and therein is directed to others.

I have tried to show that Pannenberg's thought aims to overcome both the dualism of nature and history and the isolation of religion from public and scientific life. I have argued that Pannenberg's thought seeks to provide a universal ground for moral thought in the idea of the twofold movement of God's love. Taken together, these aspects of Pannenberg's thought provide both a critique of the relationship of the modern West to the nonhuman world and a foundation for a positive ecological ethic.

Although Pannenberg attempts to undercut Cartesian dualism with the idea of a universal history that is grounded in the love of God, his thought focuses on human life. He includes all creation in the goal of the realization of the image of God, but he does not consistently make this explicit. He has connected the idea of dominion with an understanding of the image of God that does address ecological concerns. However, I have extended his thought to include more consistently and explicitly the nonhuman world in the process of love. I have attempted to show that his thought can ground an ecologically conscious theological ethic. Pannenberg has not consistently made this application but it appears to be consistent with his theology. It may be worth recalling that Pannenberg has decided in favor of addressing fundamental theological issues rather than developing a theory of justice and a full-fledged ethic.

That the process of reality is the work of God's love and that creatures are destined to participate in this love indicates, for Pannenberg, that love is to function as the motivation for and guiding principle of creaturely communication and action. This also indicates that the movement of love that has its origin in the end of the process, if one accepts Pannenberg's arguments regarding the goal of history, can serve as (1) the creative force for the development of just forms of life and (2) the critical principle by which to judge all human achievements. It is important to note that the justice of particular relational structures needs to be informed by the love that includes the entire creation in its redemptive force. For example, loving the natural world would mean losing our fear of it and losing the drive to so transform it as to reduce it to serving human ends only. Loving nature may mean granting it freedom to express its own relationship to God, apart from merely human ends. Human action must be guided by a love that values the independence of others, human and nonhuman, each in its relationship to God and other creatures.

Pannenberg's argument regarding the theological unity of nature and history is coherent and shows significant correspondence with reality. Pannenberg is also able to show some significant agreement of his conception of reality with other scientific views of the world. Several of his claims, however, are controversial. For example, his claim regarding the ontological priority of the future has come under critical scrutiny and requires further examination.

His theology regards divine love as the source and goal of existence. Divine love, as Pannenberg has presented it, appears capable of providing a theological ground for the unity of nature and history. It also appears to be capable of supporting and even facilitating the development of an ecologically concerned public morality. His argument claims to take account of the pluralistic character of modern culture. Other aspects of his argument for the unity of reality show promise for overcoming the isolation of theology from public life. This, however, requires further testing. Whether the Christian idea of love can contribute a guiding critical principle and a creative force to public moral issues needs to be tested in the process of developing both a theory of justice and concrete ethical guidelines.

Fifteen years ago David McKenzie applied a paraphrase of John 21:25 to Pannenberg: "But there are also many other things which he has written . . . ."[1] McKenzie adds that, in addition to the number of Pannenberg's publications, one must also consider the vast scope of subjects to which he has applied his attention. I, like McKenzie before me, have of necessity chosen a strand of Pannenberg's work and have attempted to present it somewhat systematically. There is no pretense here to presenting an epitome of his work. There is no claim to have done justice to the whole of Pannenberg's corpus and the numerous critical inter-,changes in which he has been involved. I can only hope that my work can contribute to the challenge that Pannenberg has taken up, that of bringing theology into a more meaningful role in public life. My hope is that this work can make a contribution to the critical task of rethinking the relationship of modern techno-scientific culture both to its religious roots and to the natural world.

NOTES

1. David McKenzie, *Wolfhart Pannenberg and Religious Philosophy*, 143.

SELECT BIBLIOGRAPHY

Selected Works of Wolfhart Pannenberg:

Anthropology in Theological Perspective. Trans. Matthew J. O'Connell. Philadelphia: Westminster, 1985.

"Atom, Duration, Form: Difficulties with Process Philosophy." Trans. John C. Robertson, Jr., and Gérard Vallée. *Process Studies* 14 (Spring 1984): 21-30.

Die Bestimmung des Menschen: Menschsein, Erwählung und Geschichte. Göttingen: Vandenhoeck & Ruprecht, 1978.

"Bewußtsein und Geist." *Zeitschrift für Theologie und Kirche* 80/3 (1983): 332-51.

Christentum in einer säkularisierten Welt. Freiburg: Herder, 1988. *Christianity in a Secularized World.* Trans. John Bowden. New York: Crossroad, 1989.

"Christentum und Platonismus: Die kritische Platonrezeption Augustins in ihrer Bedeutung für das gegenwärtige christliche Denken." *Zeitschrift fur Kirchengeschichte* 96 (1985): 147-61.

Christian Spirituality. Philadelphia: Westminster, 1983.

"Christianity, Marxism, and Liberation Theology." *Christian Scholar's Review* 18/3 (1989): 215-26.

"Christliche Rechtsbegründung." In *Handbuch der christlichen Ethik*, vol. 2. ed. A. Hertz, et al. Freiburg: Herder & Gütersloh: Gerd Mohn, 1978.

"Christlicher Glaube und Naturverständnis." In *Gott—Geist—Materie: Theologie und Naturwissenschaft in Geschpräch*, ed. Hermann Dietzfelbinger und Lutz Mohaupt. Hamburg: Lutherisches Verlagshaus, 1980.

"Das christologische Fundament christlicher Anthropologie." *Concilium* 6 (1973): 425-34.

"The Doctrine of Creation and Modern Science." *Zygon: Journal of Science and Religion* 23 (March 1988): 3-21.

"Erfahrung der Wirklichkeit: Fragen an Carl Friedrich von Weizsäcker." *Evangelische Kommentar* 4 (1971): 468-70.

Ethik und Ekklesiologie. Göttingen: Vandenhoeck & Ruprecht, 1977. *Ethics.* Trans. Keith Crim. Philadelphia: Westminster, 1983.

"Fluch und Segen der Arbeit." In *Der Mensch und seine Arbeit*, ed. Venanz Schubert. Sankt Ottilien: EOS Verlag, 1986.

"Geist und Energie: Zur Phänomenologie Teilhard de Chardin." *Acta Teilhardiana* 8 (1971): 5-12.

"Geschichtstatsachen und christliche Ethik." In *Möglichkeit und Grenze politischer Wirksamkeit*, ed. W. Boehme. *Radius Projekte* 32 (1970): 72-89.

"Gott und die Natur: Zur Geschichte der Auseinanderseztung zwischen Theologie und Naturwissenschaft." *Theologie und Philosophie* 58, 4 (1983): 481-500.

Grundfragen systematischer Theologie. Vols. 1 & 2. Göttingen: Vandenhoeck & Ruprecht, 1967, 1980. *Basic Questions in Theology.* Vols. 1 & 2. Trans. George U. Kehm. Philadelphia: Fortress, 1970, 1972.

Grundzüge der Christologie. 5th ed. Gütersloh: Gerd Mohn, 1975. *Jesus—God and Man.* 2d ed. Trans. Lewis L. Wilkins and Duane A. Priebe. Philadelphia: Westminster, 1977.

"History and Meaning in Lonergan's Approach to Theological Method." *Irish Quarterly Review* 40 (1973): 103-14.

The Idea of God and Human Freedom. Philadelphia: Westminster, 1973.

An Introduction to Systematic Theology. Grand Rapids: Eerdmans, 1991.

"Der Mensch als Person." In *Das Verhältnis der Psychiatrie zu ihren Nachbardisziplinen*, ed. H. Heimann and H. J. Gaertner. Berlin: Springer-Verlag, 1986.

Metaphysik und Gottesgedanke. Göttingen: Vandenhoeck & Ruprecht, 1988. *Metaphysics and the Idea of God.* Trans. Philip Clayton. Grand Rapids: Eerdmans, 1990.

"Person." In *Religion Geschicht und Gegenwart.* 3rd. ed., vol. 5. Tübingen: Mohr, 1961.

"Eine philosophisch-historische Hermeneutik des Christentums." *Theologie und Philosophie* 66 (1991): 481-92.

"Probleme einer trinitarischen Gotteslehre." In *Weisheit Gottes—Weisheit der Welt*, ed. W. Baier. St. Ottilien: EOS Verlag, 1987.

"Response to the Debate." In Gary R. Habermas and Antony G. N. Flew. *Did Jesus Rise From the Dead?: The Resurrection Debate*, ed. Terry L. Miethe. San Francisco: Harper & Row, 1987.

"Rezeptive Vernunft: Die antike Deutung der Erkenntnis als Hinnahme vorgegebener Wahrheit." In *Überlieferung und Aufgabe: Festschrift für Erich Heintel zum 70. Geburtstag*, ed. Herta Nagl Docekal. Wien: Wilhelm Braumüller, 1982.

"Schöpfungstheologie und moderne Naturwissenschaft." In *Gottes Zukunft—Zukunft der Welt*, ed. H. Deuser, et al. Munich: Christian Kaiser Verlag, 1986.

"Signale der Transzendenz: Religionssoziologie zwischen Atheismus und religiöser Wirklichkeit." *Evangelische Kommentar* 7 (1974): 151-54.

"The Significance of the Categories 'Part' and 'Whole' for the Epistemology of Theology." *The Journal of Religion* 66/4 (October 1986): 369-385.

Systematische Theologie. 3 Vols. Göttingen: Vandenhoeck & Ruprecht, 1988, 1991, 1993. *Systematic Theology*. Vols. 1 & 2. Trans. Geoffrey W. Bromiley. Grand Rapids: Eerdmans, 1991, 1994.

"Theological Appropriation of Scientific Understandings: Response to Hefner, Wicken, Eaves, and Tipler." *Zygon* 24 (June 1989): 255-71.

"Theological Questions to Scientists." *Zygon* 16 (March 1981): 65-77.

"Theologische Motive im Denken Immanuel Kants." *Theologische Literaturzeitung* 89, 12 (1964): 897-906.

"Theology and Science." *Princeton Seminary Bulletin* 13,3 (November 1992): 299-310.

Theology and the Kingdom of God. Philadelphia: Westminster, 1969.

Toward a Theology of Nature: Essays on Science and Faith. Ed. Ted Peters. Louisville: Westminster/John Knox, 1993.

"Unity of the Church—Unity of Humankind: A Critical Appraisal of a Shift in Ecumenical Direction." *Mid-Stream: An Ecumenical Journal* 21 (October 1982), 485-90.

"Vom Nutzen der Eschatologie für die christliche Theologie." *Kerygma und Dogma* 25 (April-June 1979): 88-105.

Was ist der Mensch? Die Anthropologie der Gegenwart im Lichte der Theologie. Göttingen: Vandenhoeck & Ruprecht, 1962. *What is Man? Contemporary Anthropology in Theological Perspective*. Trans. Duane A. Priebe. Philadelphia: Fortress, 1970.

"Weltgeschichte und Heilsgeschichte." In *Probleme biblischer Theologie*, ed. H. Wolff. Munich: Christian Kaiser Verlag, 1971.

Wissenschaftstheorie und Theologie. Frankfurt: Suhrkamp, 1973. *Theology and the Philosophy of Science*. Trans. Francis McDonagh. London: Darton, Longman & Todd, 1976.

Pannenberg, Wolfhart, ed. *Die Erfahrung der Abwesenheit Gottes in der modernen Kultur*. Göttingen: Vandenhoeck & Ruprecht, 1984.

Pannenberg, Wolfhart, ed. *Offenbarung als Geschichte*. Göttingen, 1961. *Revelation as History*. Trans. David Granskou. New York: Macmillan, 1968.

Pannenberg, Wolfhart, Avery Dulles, and Carl E. Braaten. *Spirit, Faith, and Church*. Philadelphia: Westminster, 1970.

Pannenberg, Wolfhart, and Gerhard Ebeling. "Ein Brief Wechsel." *Zeitschrift für Theologie und Kirche* 70 (1973): 448-75.

Pannenberg, Wolfhart, and Lewis S. Ford. "Dialogue About Process Philosophy." *Encounter* 38 (Autumn 1977): 318-24.

Pannenberg, Wolfhart, and Richard John Neuhaus. "The Christian West?" *First Things* 7 (November 1990): 24-31.

Pannenberg, Wolfhart, and A. M. Klaus Müller. *Erwägungen zu einer Theologie der Natur*. Gütersloh: Gerd Mohn, 1970.

Selected Secondary Works

Bayer, Oswald. "Die Gegenwart der Güte Gottes." *Neue Zeitschrift für systematische Theologie* 21 (1979): 253-71.

Beam, Jerry Norris. "A Critical Assessment of Wolfhart Pannenberg's Relation to Process Thought." Ph.D., Baylor University, 1985.

Betz, Hans Dieter. "Das Verständnis der Apokalyptik in der Theologie der Pannenberg-Gruppe." *Zeitschrift für Theologie und Kirche* 65 (1968): 257-70.

Braaten, Carl E. "Wolfhart Pannenberg." In *A Handbook of Christian Theologians*, enlarged ed., ed. Dean G. Peerman and Martin E. Marty. Nashville: Abingdon, 1984.

Braaten, Carl E., Philip Clayton, eds. *The Theology of Wolfhart Pannenberg: Twelve American Critiques. With an Autobiographical Essay and Response*. Minneapolis: Augsburg Publishing House, 1988.

Bridges, James Terrell, Jr. *Human Destiny and Resurrection in Pannenberg and Rahner*. New York: Peter Lang, 1987.

Deuser, Hermann. "Kritische Notizen zur theologischen Wissenschaftstheorie." *Evangelische Theologie* 36 (1976): 216-25.

Ebeling, Gerhard. "Die Krise des Ethischen und die Theologie: Erwiderung auf W. Pannenbergs Kritik." In *Wort und Glaube*. Vol. 2, *Beiträge zur Fundamentaltheologie und zur Lehre von Gott*. Tübingen: J. C. B. Mohr, 1969.

Eicher, Peter. "Geschichte und Wort Gottes: Ein Protokoll der Pannenberg-diskussion von 1961-1972." *Catholica* 32 (1978): 321-54.

Ford, Lewis S. "God as the Subjectivity of the Future." *Encounter* 41 (1980), 287-92.

_____. "Whiteheadian Basis for Pannenberg's Theology." *Encounter* 38 (Autumn 1977), 307-17.

Galloway, Allen D. *Wolfhart Pannenberg*. London: George Allen & Unwin, 1973.

Gózdz, Krzyszof. *Jesus Christus als Sinn der Geschichte bei Wolfhart Pannenberg*. Regensburg: Pustet, 1988.

Grenz, Stanley J. *Reason for Hope: The Systematic Theology of Wolfhart Pan-nenberg.* New York: Oxford University, 1990.

Grenz, Stanley J., Roger E. Olson. *20th Century Theology: God and the World in a Transitional Age.* Downers Grove: InterVarsity, 1992.

Habermas, Gary R., Antony G. N. Flew. *Did Jesus Rise From the Dead?: The Resurrection Debate.* Ed. Terry L. Miethe. San Francisco: Harper & Row, 1987.

Harder, Helmut G. "Continuity Between Method and Content in Contemporary Theology: The Achievement of Wolfhart Pannenberg." Th.D., Toronto School of Theology, 1971

Harder, Helmut G., W. Taylor Stevenson. "The Continuity of History and Faith in the Theology of Wolfhart Pannenberg: Toward an Erotics of Faith." *Journal of Religion* 51 (1971): 34-56.

Holwerda, D. "Faith, Reason, and the Resurrection in the Theology of Wolfhart Pannenberg." *Faith and Rationality,* ed. Alvin Plantinga and Nicholas Wolterstorff. Notre Dame: University of Notre Dame, 1983.

Hubbeling, H. G. "Einige kritische Fragen an Pannenberg." *Kerk en Theologie* 21 (1970): 346-59.

Joseph, Ipe. "The Hermeneutic of Human Openness." Th.D., Lutheran School of Theology, 1987.

Kim, Kyuun-Jin. "Offenbarung Gottes und die Geschichte bei W. Pannenberg und J. Moltmann." In *Gottes Zukunft—Zukunft der Welt,* ed. H. Deuser, et al. Chr. Kaiser Verlag, 1986.

Koch, Kurt. "Der Mensch und seine Mit-Welt als Schöpfungsebenbild Gottes: Schöpfungstheologische Aspekte der menschlichen Verantwortung für die Natur." *Catholica: Vierteljahresschrift für Kontroverstheologie* 42/1 (1988): 28-55.

_____. "Gottes Handeln in der Geschichte und die Bestimmung des Menschen." *Catholica: Vierteljahresschrift für Kontroverstheologie* 33/3 (1979): 220-39.

Koch, Traugott. "Das Böse als theologisches Problem." *Kerygma und Dogma* 24 (1978): 285-319.

Kuhn, Helmut. "Die Theologie vor dem Tribunal der Wissenschaftstheorie. Wolfhart Pannenberg: *Wissenschaftstheorie und Theologie." Philosophische Rundschau* 25 (1978): 264-77.

McKenzie, David. *Wolfhart Pannenberg and Religious Philosophy.* Washington: University Press of America, 1980.

Mühlenberg, Ekkehard. "Gott in der Geschichte: Erwägung zur Geschichtstheologie von W. Pannenberg." *Kerygma und Dogma* 24 (October-December 1978): 244-61.

Mikelic, Peter. "Universal History Within the Christologies of Hegel and Pannenberg." Th.D., Union Theological Seminary in Virginia, 1981.

216 *Nature and History in Pannenberg's Theology*

O'Donnell, John. "Exploring the Human: Theology in Dialogue." *Gregorianum* 67/1 (1986): 125-32.

_____. "Pannenberg's Doctrine of God." *Gregorianum* 72, 1 (1991): 84-90.

Olive, Don H. *Wolfhart Pannenberg*. Waco, Texas: Word Books, 1973.

Olson, Roger. "Trinity and Eschatology: The Historical Being of God in Jürgen Moltmann and Wolfhart Pannenberg." *Scottish Journal of Theology* 36/2 (1983): 213-27.

Nowell, David Zedic. "Futurity and Contingency: An Alternative Paradigm." Ph.D., Baylor University, 1991.

Pasquariello, Ronald D. "Pannenberg's Philosophical Foundations." *The Journal of Religion* 56 (1976): 338-47.

Peacocke, Arthur R., ed. *The Sciences and Theology in the Twentieth Century.* Papers from the Oxford International Symposium, Christ Church College, 1979. Notre Dame: University of Notre Dame, 1981.

Peters, Karl E., ed. "Nature, Mind, and Method." *Zygon: Journal of Science and Religion* 16 (March 1981): 3-94.

Peters, Ted. "Truth in History: Gadamer's Hermeneutics and Pannenberg's Apologetic Method." *The Journal of Religion* 55 (January 1975): 36-56.

Peters, Ted, ed. *Cosmos as Creation: Theology and Science in Consonance.* Nashville: Abingdon, 1989.

Placher, William C. "The Present Absence of Christ: Some Thoughts on Pannenberg and Moltmann." *Encounter* 40 (Spring 1979): 169-79.

Polk, David. P. *On the Way to God: An Exploration into the Theology of Wolfhart Pannenberg*. Lanham: University Press of America, 1989.

Robinson, James M. and John B. Cobb, Jr., eds. *Theology as History. New Frontiers in Theology*. New York: Harper & Row, 1967.

Rohls, Jan, Gunther Wenz, eds. *Vernunft des Glaubens: Wissenschaftliche Theologie und kirchliche Lehre: Festschrift zum 60. Geburtstag von Wolfhart Pannenberg*. Göttingen: Vandenhoeck & Ruprecht, 1988.

Russell, Robert John. "Contingency in Physics and Cosmology: A Critique of the Theology of Wolfhart Pannenberg." *Zygon* 23, 1 (1988): 23-43.

Schmalenberg, Erich. "Zum Verhältnis von Theologie und Wissenschaft." *Kerygma und Dogma* 24 (1978): 194-203.

Schott, Faye. "Comparing Eberhard Jüngel and Wolfhart Pannenberg on Theological Method and Religious Pluralism." *Dialog* 31 (1992): 129-35.

Schulz, Michael. "Zur Hegelkritik Wolfhart Pannenbergs und zur Kritik am 'Antizipationsgedanken' Pannenbergs im Sinne Hegels." *Münchener Theologische Zeitschrift* 43, 2 (1992): 197-227.

Stock, Konrad. "Creatio nova—creatio ex nihilo: Bemerkungen zum Problem einer eschatologischen Schöpfungslehre." *Evangelische Theologie* 36 (1976): 202-16.

Tupper, E. Frank. *The Theology of Wolfhart Pannenberg*. Philadelphia: Westminster, 1972.

Villa-Vicencio, Charles. "History in the Thought of Reinhold Niebuhr and Wolfhart Pannenberg." Ph.D., Drew, 1975.

Wagner, Falk. "Vernünftige Theologie und Theologie der Vernunft." *Kerygma und Dogma* 24 (October-December 1978): 262-84.

Welker, Michael. "Das theologische Prinzip des Verhaltens zu Zeiterscheinungen: Erörterung eines Problems im Blick auf die theologische Hegelrezeption, Gen 3,22." *Evangelische Theologie* 36 (1976): 225-53.

Wicken, Jeffrey S. "Theology and Science in the Evolving Cosmos: A Need for Dialogue." *Zygon* 23, 1 (1988): 45-55.

Selected General Works

Birch, Charles, William Eakin, and Jay B. McDaniel, eds. *Liberating Life: Contemporary Approaches to Ecological Theology.* New York: Orbis, 1990.

Blumenberg, Hans. *The Legitimacy of the Modern Age.* Trans. Robert M. Wallace. Cambridge: MIT, 1985.

Buber, Martin. *I and Thou.* Trans. Walter Kaufmann. New York: Charles Scribner's Sons, 1970.

Cobb, John B., Jr. "In Defense of Realism." In *Theology at the End of Modernity: Essays in Honor of Gordon D. Kaufman,* ed. Sheila Greeve Davaney. Philadelphia: Trinity Press International, 1991.

Daecke, Sigurd Martin. "Das 'Interdisziplinäre Geschpräch' von 1972 bis 1978: Eine Zusammenfassung." In *Gott—Geist—Materie: Theologie und Naturwissenschaft in Geschpräch,* ed. Hermann Dietzfelbinger und Lutz Mohaupt. Hamburg: Lutherisches Verlagshaus, 1980.

Engel, Mary Potter. *John Calvin's Perspectival Anthropology.* Atlanta: Scholars, 1988.

Gadamer, Hans-Georg. "Hans Blumenberg: *Die Legitimität der Neuzeit.*" *Philosophische Rundschau* 15, 3 (1968): 201-9.

Gustafson, James. *Ethics from a Theocentric Perspective.* Vol. 1, *Theology and Ethics.* Chicago: University of Chicago, 1981.

Hawking, Stephen. *A Brief History of Time: From the Big Bang to Black Holes.* New York: Bantam, 1988.

Heschel, Abraham J. *Who is Man?* Stanford: Stanford University, 1965.

Kohak, Erazim. *The Embers and the Stars: A Philosophical Inquiry into the Moral Sense of Nature.* Chicago: University of Chicago, 1984.

Küng, Hans. *Global Responsibility: In Search of a New World Ethic.* Trans. John Bowden. London: SCM, 1991.

———. "Science and the Problem of God." *Journal of the Interdenominational Theological Center* (1982): 95-107.

Leiss, William. *The Domination of Nature*. New York: George Braziller, 1972.

Lewis, C. S. *Studies in Words*. 2d ed. Cambridge: Cambridge University, 1960, 1967.

_____. *The Abolition of Man*. London: Harper Collins, 1943, 1946, 1978.

Likens, Gene E. "Toxic Winds: Whose Responsibility?" In *Ecology, Economics, Ethics: The Broken Circle*, ed. F. Herbert Bormann and Stephen R. Kellert. New Haven: Yale University, 1991.

Löwith, Karl. "Hans Blumenberg: *Die Legitimität der Neuzeit*," *Philosophische Rundschau* 15, 3 (1968): 195-201.

_____. *Meaning in History*. Chicago: University of Chicago, 1949.

Moltmann, Jürgen. *God in Creation: A New Theology of Creation and the Spirit of God*. Trans. Margaret Kohl. London: SCM, 1985.

Musfeldt, Klaus. "Wird der Löwe Stroh fressen?" *Neue Zeitschrift für Systematische Theologie und Religionsphilosophie* 33, 3 (1991): 300-15.

Niebuhr, H. Richard. *The Meaning of Revelation*. New York: Macmillan, 1941.

O'Donavan, Oliver. *Resurrection and Moral Order: An Outline for Evangelical Ethics*, 2d ed. Leicester: Apollos, Grand Rapids: Eerdmans, 1994.

Rolston III, Holmes. "Environmental Ethics: Values in and Duties to the Natural World." In *Ecology, Economics, Ethics: The Broken Circle*, ed. F. Herbert Bormann and Stephen R. Kellert. New Haven: Yale University, 1991.

Santmire, H. Paul. "St. Augustine's Theology of the Biophysical World." *Dialog* 19, 3 (1980): 174-85.

_____. *The Travail of Nature*. Philadelphia: Fortress, 1985.

Szerszynski, Bronislaw. "The Metaphysics of Environmental Concern—A Critique of Ecotheological Antidualism." *Studies in Christian Ethics* 6,2 (1993): 67-70.

Troeltsch, Ernst. *Historismus und Seine Probleme*. Vol. 3, *Gesammelte Schriften*. Tübingen: Mohr, 1922.

_____. *Historismus und seine Überwindung*. Berlin: Pan Verlag Rolf Heise, 1924.

Volf, Miroslav. *Zukunft der Arbeit, Arbeit der Zukunft: Der Arbeitsbegriff bei Karl Marx und seine theologische Wertung*. Grünwald: Kaiser, 1988.

von Rad, Gerhard. *Old Testament Theology*. Vol. 1. Trans. D. M. G. Stalker. London: SCM, 1975.

Wilson, Edward O. "Biodiversity, Prosperity, and Value." In *Ecology, Economics, Ethics: The Broken Circle*, ed. F. Herbert Bormann and Stephen R. Kellert. New Haven: Yale University, 1991.

INDEX

VOCABULAIRE
DES CONVENTIONS
COLLECTIVES

BIBLIOTHÈQUE ADMINISTRATIVE
Ministère des Communications
Éléments de catalogage avant publication

Pétrin, Hélène.

 Vocabulaire des conventions collectives: vocabulaire français-
anglais/Hélène Pétrin; [collaboration, Robert Auclair... et al, [pour]
l'Office de la langue française]. — Québec: Publications du Québec, [1991?].

 (Cahiers de l'Office de la langue française)
 (Terminologie de la gestion)

 ISBN 2-551-14810-3

1. Conventions collectives — Dictionnaires   2. Conventions collectives
— Dictionnaires anglais   3. Français (Langue) — Dictionnaires
anglais   4. Anglais (Langue) — Dictionnaires français I. Auclair, Robert.
II. Québec (Province). Office de la langue française. III. Titre. IV. Collection.

A11L3/C33

Cahiers de l'Office
de la langue française

V O C A B U L A I R E
DES CONVENTIONS
COLLECTIVES

Terminologie de la gestion

Vocabulaire français-anglais

Hélène Pétrin

Québec ⬧⬧

Ce vocabulaire a été préparé
sous la direction de Jean-Marie Fortin,
directeur des services linguistiques.

Cette édition a été produite par
Les Publications du Québec
1279, boul. Charest Ouest
Québec (Québec)
G1N 4K7

Révision : Denis Juneau

Traitement de texte : Ginette Paquet

Collaboration technique : Joss-Linn Gagné

Conception graphique de la couverture :
Delisle, Caron, Thivierge et Associés

Avec la collaboration de

Robert Auclair
Juge
Tribunal du travail

Claude D'Aoust
Avocat
Professeur
École de relations industrielles
Université de Montréal

Gilles Giguère
Avocat
Permanent syndical
Syndicat canadien de la fonction publique

Gilles Lavallée
Avocat
Consultant principal en relations du travail
Société d'électrolyse et de chimie Alcan

*Le contenu de cette publication est également diffusé,
sous diverses formes, par le réseau public
de la Banque de terminologie du Québec.*

Remerciements

En premier lieu, je tiens à remercier chaleureusement MM. Robert Auclair, Claude D'Aoust, Gilles Giguère et Gilles Lavallée, membres du comité de référence, ainsi que M. François Grou, aujourd'hui conseiller en francisation à l'Office de la langue française qui a fait partie de l'équipe dans les premières années, de m'avoir prêté leur concours maintes et maintes fois depuis le début de la conception du vocabulaire.

Bien des gens ont eu à intervenir dans l'élaboration de cet ouvrage et je veux sincèrement leur exprimer toute ma gratitude, que leur contribution se soit située sur le plan du choix des entrées ou de leur équivalent, de la révision notionnelle ou technique, ou de la présentation matérielle et du secrétariat. Quels que soient leur profession et leur milieu de travail, qu'ils habitent le Québec, la France ou la Suisse, j'ai grandement apprécié leur collaboration.

En dernier lieu, j'aimerais particulièrement souligner la participation extraordinaire des personnes qui ont pris le temps de me rencontrer ou de me faire part de leurs commentaires, que ce soit par téléphone ou par écrit, à la suite de la parution de l'édition provisoire du vocabulaire. À mes interlocutrices et interlocuteurs occasionnels et permanents, encore une fois, un gros merci.

Préfaces

Un praticien des relations de travail éprouvera sans doute bien des remords en lisant cette seconde édition du *Vocabulaire des conventions collectives,* rédigée par Mme Hélène Pétrin. La précision des définitions, comme l'exactitude des traductions du français à l'anglais et la pertinence des commentaires, lui rappelleront parfois cruellement, les impropriétés de langage, les approximations, les barbarismes ou les anglicismes dont il aura parfois, dans la lassitude du moment, parsemé les conventions, les opinions ou les jugements qu'il rédigeait.

Dans le domaine des relations de travail, le maintien ou l'implantation d'une langue conforme aux usages et aux règles du français et, en même temps, capable d'évolution et d'adaptation au milieu, demeure un problème délicat. L'environnement nord-américain a fortement influencé la langue de la pratique des relations de travail, comme celui du droit. Les pratiques syndicales et la législation se sont inspirées largement des expériences américaines. Cette situation a multiplié les difficultés linguistiques.

Le travail effectué par Mme Pétrin permet de mieux comprendre et utiliser le langage des relations de travail au Québec et spécialement celui des conventions collectives. Il inclut l'ensemble des termes généralement utilisés dans la rédaction de ces conventions. Recherchant une terminologie conforme aux usages courants, l'auteure a découvert ou proposé des équivalents adaptés à la pratique québécoise ou justifiés par le développement de celle-ci, mais conformes aux règles et aux structures de la langue. Fort utilement, elle a aussi préparé un vocabulaire français-anglais assez étendu. En même temps, l'œuvre signale les mauvaises habitudes ou les erreurs courantes dans la terminologie québécoise des relations de travail et propose des solutions de rechange.

Les linguistes et les juristes discuteront longtemps de telle ou telle suggestion. Leurs opinions s'affronteront mais le travail de Mme Pétrin demeurera une étape importante dans l'évolution d'un français clair, conforme aux normes internationales et en même temps, respectueux de certains particularismes de la langue des relations de travail au Québec.

Louis LeBel
Juge à la Cour d'appel

Tous les efforts faits pour améliorer l'usage de la langue française au Québec n'auraient pas beaucoup de sens si le milieu du travail était ignoré. Il est bien connu que franciser le milieu du travail n'est pas une mince tâche. Pendant si longtemps, nous avons toléré l'utilisation de termes anglais à tel point que souvent le mot français était inconnu. Les communications verbales et écrites dans les usines, surtout les plus grandes, se faisaient en anglais. On sait qu'il y a amélioration mais il y a encore place pour aller beaucoup plus loin.

Cet ouvrage se veut un outil utile et je dirais même indispensable pour franciser les rapports du travail. Mme Hélène Pétrin, conseillère en francisation, qui a réalisé cette œuvre, mérite nos remerciements pour le service qu'elle rend à tous les Québécois et Québécoises.

Que tous les intéressés dans le milieu du travail se servent de ce vocabulaire et ainsi la cause du français, chez nous, progressera. C'est le vœu que je formule.

Marcel Pepin
Professeur
École de relations industrielles
Université de Montréal

Introduction

Des millions de gens travaillent. Ces gens discutent de leurs conditions de travail, partie intégrante de leur vie quotidienne. Les médias d'information traitent des questions professionnelles des secteurs privé et public. D'innombrables expressions sont véhiculées sans que l'on s'interroge sur le bien-fondé de leur utilisation. La réalité québécoise se confond en majeure partie avec la réalité nord-américaine, celle-ci n'étant parfois dénommée qu'en anglais. Il n'y a pas si longtemps, la plupart des documents étaient traduits sans qu'il y ait eu au préalable une recherche terminologique approfondie, ce qui donnait lieu à l'implantation d'expressions souvent non justifiables. Le galimatias dans les différents textes juridiques n'apporte que de la confusion puisque chacun reprend, pour son compte, les mots avec un sens qu'il décide de leur attribuer. En outre, bon nombre d'expressions ne sont compréhensibles qu'en territoire québécois. Leur ratification est-elle souhaitable?

C'est dans un souci d'uniformiser la terminologie des conventions collectives que ce vocabulaire a été élaboré. Il était d'ailleurs pertinent que ce travail soit accompli puisque, dans la Charte de la langue française, il est mentionné que les conventions collectives et leurs annexes doivent être rédigées en français.

De la conception à la publication du vocabulaire, nous avons consulté les membres du comité de référence formé de personnes provenant des milieux patronal, syndical, universitaire et du ministère du Travail. Leur rôle consistait principalement à désigner le terme approprié correspondant à un concept et à circonscrire la réalité sous-jacente à ce terme. Il est indispensable de consulter des experts afin de s'assurer de l'aspect fonctionnel des termes à l'intérieur d'un milieu déterminé. Le vocabulaire peut alors être investi d'une crédibilité d'autant plus grande.

Nous avons effectué deux missions : l'une documentaire, l'autre terminologique. La première, en France, visait à dresser la liste de tout document pouvant être utile à l'élaboration du vocabulaire et à établir des contacts avec des personnes-ressources avec lesquelles nous avons communiqué à quelques reprises pour connaître leurs positions face à différents problèmes terminologiques. La seconde, en France et en Suisse (Bureau international du travail), a permis de confronter l'avis d'experts québécois avec celui de spécialistes francophones qui ont une connaissance approfondie du domaine du travail — droit du travail français, droit comparé du travail, relations professionnelles, conventions collectives, gestion du personnel, etc. — que ce soit par le biais de l'enseignement, de l'écriture, de la terminologie, de la traduction, de l'élaboration d'un thésaurus, de l'expérience pertinente dans le secteur privé ou public. Il est essentiel de consulter un certain nombre de spécialistes parce qu'ils n'appartiennent pas tous à la même école et que, par conséquent, les terminologies peuvent différer. De retour au Québec, le comité de référence s'est réuni de nouveau quelques fois afin de revoir certains problèmes particulièrement difficiles à résoudre et d'étudier les solutions ou amorces suggérées par nos collègues d'outre-mer.

Quelques mois plus tard, paraissait l'édition provisoire du vocabulaire. Nous avons par la suite reçu des commentaires. Pour tenir compte de ces derniers, le comité de référence a siégé de nouveau afin d'apporter les corrections jugées nécessaires et d'enrichir la publication par l'ajout de termes nouveaux (une cinquantaine de notions additionnelles) soit parce que leur implantation est particulièrement difficile, soit parce qu'ils expriment des idées innovatrices.

Au cours de notre travail, nous avons parfois rencontré des termes qui se faisaient concurrence. L'un, issu de la francophonie internationale; l'autre, de la francophonie québécoise. Quand la réalité identifiée par ces termes était la même d'un continent à l'autre, il nous a semblé préférable de privilégier l'expression à vocation internationale quitte à indiquer en synonymie ou en note celle du Québec, par exemple : *congé annuel payé* que l'on retrouve partout. *Vacances* est tout à fait correct; aussi est-il un synonyme parfaitement recommandable. Il y a, cependant, quelques exceptions à cette règle comme la notion de congédiement. Dans les ouvrages généraux, on retrouve la même signification que nous lui avons prêtée. Toutefois, dans les textes spécialisés, *licenciement, congédiement* et *renvoi* sont de parfaits synonymes. Dans ce cas, nous avons cru bon de maintenir la distinction. Par contre, quand pour exprimer une réalité nord-américaine les termes québécois utilisés étaient bien formés, nous les avons retenus, par exemple : *accréditation*. Cette notion n'existe dans aucun autre pays francophone; il n'a donc pas été possible d'établir une comparaison pertinente. Nous croyons que ce terme peut subir l'extension de sens que nous proposons et qui est acceptée au Québec depuis fort longtemps. Pour certains concepts américains qui n'avaient pas d'équivalents, il nous est arrivé de créer des néologismes.

Le vocabulaire comprend bon nombre de notes explicatives. Des notes d'ordre linguistique, cela va de soi. Cependant, tant de notes d'ordre technique peuvent surprendre. Mais, en raison de la complexité des termes à traiter et de la nature juridique des conventions collectives, il nous a paru indispensable de compléter les définitions par des observations qui mettent plus clairement en contexte ces termes. En effet, il nous a fallu tenir compte notamment de l'existence simultanée du *Code canadien du travail* et du *Code du travail* du Québec dans lesquels les mêmes expressions n'ont pas nécessairement une aire sémantique identique. Nous avons donc tâché de n'omettre aucune indication afin qu'il n'y ait pas d'incompréhension au sujet des termes dont nous souhaitons l'intégration dans la langue du travail contrairement à ceux qui en font actuellement partie à mauvais escient.

Et maintenant, nous vous présentons ce document dont nous avons élargi le cadre afin d'y inclure certaines expressions d'intérêt linguistique. Ainsi, nous espérons faciliter la tâche de celles et ceux qui ont recours à cette terminologie mouvante des conventions collectives.

Hélène Pétrin

Abréviations et remarques liminaires

abrév.	abréviation
adj.	adjectif
FR	France
loc. adj.	locution adjectivale
loc. prép.	locution prépositive
loc. v.	locution verbale
n.	nom
n. f.	nom féminin
n. m.	nom masculin
n. m. pl.	nom masculin pluriel
n. f. pl.	nom féminin pluriel
syn.	synonyme
US	États-Unis
v.	verbe ou voir
v. a.	voir aussi
v. o.	variante orthographique
□	domaine d'emploi

1. Présentation

a) Les entrées sont en français et en caractères gras. Elles sont présentées selon l'ordre alphabétique discontinu sans que l'on ait tenu compte de la marque du pluriel.

b) Un terme français qui recouvre plus d'une notion est immédiatement suivi d'un indice numérique 1, 2, 3.

c) Les synonymes français sont séparés par un point-virgule. Ils peuvent être utilisés en remplacement de l'entrée, terme privilégié, sous réserve d'une note qui précise les possibilités de substitution. Il faut remarquer que les synonymes des entrées principales ne sont pas systématiquement repris dans les syntagmes.

Les termes à éviter sont mentionnés avant les équivalents anglais. Les termes peuvent être à éviter pour plusieurs raisons : anglicismes, barbarismes, etc. Il faut distinguer le terme à éviter dans un contexte bien défini du même terme correct dans un autre contexte. Par exemple, *éligible,* lorsqu'il signifie «qui peut être nommé à une fonction par voie de suffrage» est tout à fait approprié, mais il ne faut pas le confondre avec *admissible.* On retrouve aussi les termes à éviter dans l'ordre alphabétique des entrées.

d) Les équivalents anglais sont en italique. Ils ne sont mentionnés qu'à titre indicatif et ils sont séparés par un point-virgule, quel que soit le genre de relation qui existe entre eux (synonymie ou quasi-synonymie).

e) Les définitions sont d'ordre juridique plutôt que sociologique.

f) Les notes précisent différents points de nature juridique, terminologique, etc. Lorsqu'on écrit *on rencontre aussi,* cela veut dire que les termes sont acceptables, mais n'ont pas été privilégiés parce que leur usage est moins courant.

g) La mention **v.** (voir) indique qu'il faut retourner au terme principal pour savoir de quoi il s'agit.

h) La mention **v. a.** (voir aussi) suggère d'aller lire un article qui contient une notion connexe.

2. Bibliographie

Le vocabulaire est suivi d'une bibliographie qui comprend les documents utilisés lors du traitement terminologique des données, classés par ordre alphabétique d'auteurs ou d'organismes.

3. Index

À la fin de l'ouvrage, après la bibliographie, un index des termes anglais permet de trouver le numéro de l'article où ces termes sont traités.

Liste de primes et d'indemnités

Nous avons établi une liste de syntagmes ayant pour base les termes *prime* ou *indemnité* suivis d'un déterminant. Ce sont des termes que nous avons relevés au cours de nos lectures et dépouillements et qui n'ont pas besoin d'être définis parce qu'ils sont plutôt explicites. Cependant, il nous paraît utile de les mentionner puisque parfois l'on s'interroge sur la façon de rendre telle ou telle réalité.

PRIME	INDEMNITÉ
prime d'altitude	indemnité d'éloignement
prime d'amplitude	indemnité d'intempéries
prime d'assiduité	indemnité d'isolement
prime d'habillement	indemnité de chaussures
prime d'insalubrité	indemnité de clientèle
prime d'outillage	indemnité de départ à la retraite
prime de bicyclette	indemnité de dérangement
prime de bleus	indemnité de grève
prime de chaleur	indemnité de lait
prime de danger	indemnité de non-concurrence
prime de froid	indemnité de résidence
prime de hauteur	indemnité de route
prime de langue	indemnité de transfert
prime de pénibilité	indemnité de transport
prime de salissure	indemnité différentielle de maladie
prime de suggestion	indemnité pour frais de
prime de transfert	représentation
prime du dimanche	indemnité pour recherche d'emploi
prime vestimentaire	indemnité vestimentaire

Arbre du domaine du travail

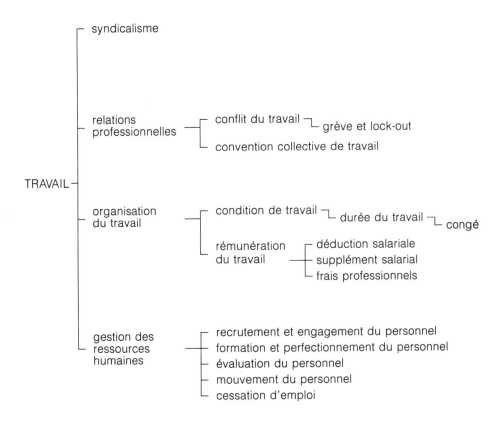

TRAVAIL
- syndicalisme
- relations professionnelles
  - conflit du travail
    - grève et lock-out
  - convention collective de travail
- organisation du travail
  - condition de travail
    - durée du travail
      - congé
  - rémunération du travail
    - déduction salariale
    - supplément salarial
    - frais professionnels
- gestion des ressources humaines
  - recrutement et engagement du personnel
  - formation et perfectionnement du personnel
  - évaluation du personnel
  - mouvement du personnel
  - cessation d'emploi

Vocabulaire

1. absence autorisée
Syn. de **congé 2**

2. accident de trajet n. m.;
accident du trajet n. m.
travelling accident;
commuting accident
Accident survenu au cours du trajet normal accompli habituellement par le salarié pour se rendre de son domicile à son lieu de travail et en revenir.
☐ condition de travail

3. accident du trajet
Syn. de **accident de trajet**

4. accident du travail n. m.
occupational accident;
industrial accident;
work accident
Accident qui survient par le fait ou à l'occasion du travail.
☐ condition de travail

5. accréditation
Syn. de **accréditation syndicale**

6. accréditation patronale n. f.
employer's certification;
accreditation
Acte par lequel l'organisme gouvernemental compétent désigne officiellement une association d'employeurs comme représentante exclusive des entreprises qui en font partie aux fins de la négociation et de l'application des conventions collectives.
☐ syndicalisme

7. accréditation syndicale n. f.;
accréditation n. f.
Terme à éviter : certification
certification;
union certification
Acte par lequel l'organisme gouvernemental compétent désigne officiellement comme agent négociateur un syndicat qui a obtenu l'adhésion de la majorité des salariés d'une unité de négociation.
☐ syndicalisme

8. acompte sur salaire n. m.
advance on salary;
advance on wages;
advance
Paiement avant terme d'une partie du salaire.
V. a. **avance sur salaire**
☐ rémunération du travail

9. action positive
Terme à éviter
V. **mesure de rattrapage**

10. action positive
Terme à éviter
V. **plan d'égalité professionnelle**

11. admissible adj.
Terme à éviter : éligible
eligible
Se dit d'une personne dont la demande est recevable.
☐ travail

12. affectation n. f.
Terme à éviter : assignation
assignment
Désignation de quelqu'un à un poste ou à un emploi.
☐ mouvement du personnel

13. **agent d'affaires**
Terme à éviter
V. **agent syndical**

14. **agent de maîtrise** n. m.
agente de maîtrise n. f.
first-line supervisor
Cadre hiérarchique de premier niveau.
□ travail

15. **agent de négociation**
Syn. de **agent négociateur**

16. **agent négociateur** n. m. ;
agent de négociation n. m.
bargaining agent
Syndicat qui représente exclusivement les salariés de l'unité de négociation et dont le but principal est la négociation et l'application de la convention collective.
Note. — Le *Code canadien du travail* désigne comme agent négociateur le syndicat qui a été accrédité ou reconnu volontairement par l'employeur. Quant au *Code du travail* du Québec, il n'utilise, depuis 1969, que le terme *association accréditée* pour dénommer cette réalité. Il serait toutefois préférable d'employer *syndicat accrédité*.
□ syndicalisme

17. **agent syndical** n. m.
agente syndicale n. f.
Terme à éviter : agent d'affaires
business agent;
union representative
Personne engagée par la section locale pour s'occuper des intérêts syndicaux de cette dernière.
V. a. **permanent syndical**
□ syndicalisme

18. **agent syndical en chef** n. m.
agente syndicale en chef n. f.
Terme à éviter : gérant d'affaires
business manager;
chief representative;
head representative
Responsable de plusieurs agents syndicaux.
□ syndicalisme

19. **agente de maîtrise**
V. **agent de maîtrise**

20. **agente syndicale**
V. **agent syndical**

21. **agente syndicale en chef**
V. **agent syndical en chef**

22. **aide** n.
helper
Travailleur qui assiste un ouvrier dans l'exécution de son travail.
Note. — Ne pas confondre avec *apprenti.*
□ travail

23. **alliance**
V. **syndicat**

24. **allocation**
Syn. de **prestation**

25. **allocation de vacances**
Terme à éviter
V. **indemnité de congé payé**

26. **ancienneté** n. f.
Termes à éviter : séniorité; ancienneté absolue; ancienneté complexe; ancienneté mixte; ancienneté pure; ancienneté relative; ancienneté simple; ancienneté stricte
seniority
Durée de service reconnu au salarié pour l'exercice de certains droits ou l'obtention de certains avantages.
Note. — Lorsqu'on veut rendre les termes anglais *straight seniority* et *qualified seniority*, il faut, en français, avoir recours à une périphrase. En effet, l'ancienneté n'est pas modifiée mais on tient compte, dans le premier cas, uniquement de l'ancienneté comme critère et dans le second cas, de l'ancienneté parmi d'autres critères, par exemple, une promotion est accordée en fonction de l'ancienneté seulement ou en fonction de la compétence et de l'ancienneté. Les termes *ancienneté pure, simple, absolue* et *stricte* ainsi que *ancienneté mixte, complexe* et *relative* sont donc inexacts.
V. a. **service continu**
□ durée du travail

27. **ancienneté absolue**
Terme à éviter
V. **ancienneté**

28. **ancienneté complexe**
Terme à éviter
V. **ancienneté**

29. ancienneté d'emploi n. f.;
ancienneté professionnelle n. f.
Termes à éviter : ancienneté d'occupation; ancienneté occupationnelle
occupational seniority;
job seniority;
classification seniority
Ancienneté d'un salarié dans un emploi.
☐ durée du travail

30. ancienneté d'entreprise n. f.
companywide seniority
V. o. *company-wide seniority;*
employerwide seniority
Ancienneté d'un salarié dans une entreprise.
☐ durée du travail

31. ancienneté d'établissement n. f.
plant seniority
Ancienneté d'un salarié dans un établissement.
☐ durée du travail

32. ancienneté d'occupation
Terme à éviter
V. **ancienneté d'emploi**

33. ancienneté d'usine n. f.
plant seniority
Ancienneté d'un salarié dans une usine.
☐ durée du travail

34. ancienneté de département
Terme à éviter
V. **ancienneté de service**

35. ancienneté de service n. f.
Termes à éviter : ancienneté de département; ancienneté départementale
departmental seniority;
department seniority
Ancienneté d'un salarié dans un service.
☐ durée du travail

36. ancienneté départementale
Terme à éviter
V. **ancienneté de service**

37. ancienneté majorée n. f.;
ancienneté privilégiée n. f.
Terme à éviter : ancienneté préférentielle
superseniority;
preferential seniority;
top seniority

Ancienneté particulière et artificielle supé-
rieure à l'ancienneté réelle d'un salarié.
Note. — Les représentants syndicaux sont
très souvent les bénéficiaires de l'ancienneté majorée. Celle-ci ne leur est cependant
pas exclusive.
☐ durée du travail

38. ancienneté mixte
Terme à éviter
V. **ancienneté**

39. ancienneté occupationnelle
Terme à éviter
V. **ancienneté d'emploi**

40. ancienneté préférentielle
Terme à éviter
V. **ancienneté majorée**

41. ancienneté privilégiée
Syn. de **ancienneté majorée**

42. ancienneté professionnelle
Syn. de **ancienneté d'emploi**

43. ancienneté pure
Terme à éviter
V. **ancienneté**

44. ancienneté relative
Terme à éviter
V. **ancienneté**

45. ancienneté simple
Terme à éviter
V. **ancienneté**

46. ancienneté stricte
Terme à éviter
V. **ancienneté**

47. annexe n. f.
Terme à éviter : appendice
appendix
Texte portant sur un sujet particulier et
regroupant des clauses applicables soit à
une catégorie particulière de salariés, soit
à tous les salariés.
☐ convention collective de travail

48. annuel
Syn. de **salarié annuel**

49. annuelle
V. **salarié annuel**

50. appellation d'emploi n. f.
Terme à éviter : titre d'emploi
job title

Dénomination attachée à un emploi pour l'identifier et le distinguer des autres.
☐ organisation du travail

51. appendice
Terme à éviter
V. **annexe**

52. appointé
Syn. de **salarié appointé**

53. appointée
V. **salarié appointé**

54. appointements n. m. pl.
salary
Rémunération du salarié appointé.
V. a. **salarié appointé**
☐ rémunération du travail

55. appréciation du personnel n. f.;
notation du personnel n. f.;
évaluation du personnel n. f.
merit rating;
rating;
merit appraisal
Jugement porté par la direction d'une entreprise sur chacun des salariés en fonction des exigences de son emploi, et basé sur certains critères.
☐ évaluation du personnel

56. apprenti n. m.
apprentie n. f.
apprentice
Personne en apprentissage.
Note. — Ne pas confondre avec *aide.*
☐ formation et perfectionnement du personnel

57. apprentie
V. **apprenti**

58. apprentissage
Syn. de **formation professionnelle**

59. apprêts
Syn. de **travail d'apprêts**

60. arbitrage n. m.
arbitration

Mode de règlement d'une mésentente par un conseil d'arbitrage ou un tribunal d'arbitrage.
☐ conflit du travail

61. arbitre n.
arbitrator;
umpire
Personne faisant partie d'un conseil d'arbitrage ou d'un tribunal d'arbitrage ou constituant à elle seule un tribunal d'arbitrage.
☐ conflit du travail

62. arrêt de travail
Syn. de **grève**

63. assesseur n. m.
assesseure n. f.
assessor
Personne nommée par chacune des parties pour assister le tribunal d'arbitrage.
☐ conflit du travail

64. assesseure
V. **assesseur**

65. assignation
Terme à éviter
V. **affectation**

66. assimilé n. m.
assimilée n. f.
related worker
Personne qui a le statut d'une certaine catégorie de personnel à laquelle elle n'appartient pas en propre.
☐ gestion des ressources humaines

67. assimilée
V. **assimilé**

68. association accréditée
V. **agent négociateur**

69. association d'employeurs n. f.
employers' association
Groupement d'employeurs ayant pour but l'étude de la sauvegarde des intérêts de ses membres et l'assistance dans la négociation et l'application des conventions collectives.
☐ relations professionnelles

70. assurance juridique n. f.
prepaid legal services

Ensemble des dispositions qui permettent au salarié de faire appel gratuitement en tout ou en partie aux services d'un avocat, d'un notaire pour certaines situations prédéterminées.

Note. — Actuellement, au Québec, l'entreprise General Motors du Canada offre cette assurance qu'elle désigne par *régime de services juridiques.*

☐ supplément salarial

71. astreinte n. f.
stand-by
V. o. *stand by;*
on-call
V. o. *on call*

Période pendant laquelle le salarié doit être prêt à répondre aux appels de l'employeur.

Note. — Par exemple, *être d'astreinte, heure d'astreinte.*

V. a. **disponibilité**
☐ durée du travail

72. atelier de misère n. m.;
      sale boîte n. f. (FR)
sweatshop

Établissement où les taux de salaire, les normes de sécurité et les conditions de travail sont inférieurs à ce qui est généralement en vigueur dans le métier, l'industrie, la région.

☐ condition de travail

73. atelier fermé n. m.
closed shop

Forme de sécurité syndicale en vertu de laquelle le syndicat obtient le monopole de recrutement des salariés d'un employeur et, parfois, s'engage à lui fournir, parmi ses membres, par l'intermédiaire d'un bureau de placement syndical, les salariés dont il a besoin, ces derniers devant maintenir leur appartenance syndicale pendant toute la durée de leur emploi.

☐ syndicalisme

74. atelier modifié
      V. atelier syndical

75. atelier ouvert n. m.
open shop

Forme périmée de sécurité syndicale minimale en vertu de laquelle l'adhésion au syndicat est tolérée, mais le syndicat lui-même ne bénéficie d'aucune reconnaissance et n'est partie à aucune convention.

Note. — De nos jours, le terme *atelier ouvert* ne peut désigner qu'une entreprise où il n'y a pas de syndicat accrédité ; il est peu usité en ce sens.

☐ syndicalisme

76. atelier préférentiel n. m.
preferential shop

Forme de sécurité syndicale par laquelle l'employeur s'engage à accorder un traitement de faveur dans diverses circonstances particulières soit au syndicat lui-même, soit à ses membres.

☐ syndicalisme

77. atelier syndical n. m.
union shop

Forme de sécurité syndicale en vertu de laquelle tous les salariés doivent adhérer au syndicat dans un certain délai suivant l'engagement et en rester membres comme condition du maintien de leur emploi.

Note. — On utilise parfois comme synonyme *atelier syndical parfait* en opposition à *atelier syndical imparfait* (ou *atelier modifié)* qui signifie que les salariés en place qui ne sont pas membres du syndicat au moment de la signature de la convention collective ne sont pas obligés de le devenir.

☐ syndicalisme

78. atelier syndical imparfait
      V. atelier syndical

79. atelier syndical parfait
      V. atelier syndical

80. attrition n. f.
attrition

Diminution de l'effectif d'une entreprise par suite de départs.

Note. — Nous retenons *attrition* pour trois raisons : 1) il est consigné dans le *Petit Robert* depuis au moins 1977 et dans *la Clé des mots,* du Conseil international de la langue française, 1973, n° 2 ; 2) il ne crée pas de difficulté quant à son extension de sens si l'on tient compte de son étymologie ; 3) c'est un terme plutôt qu'une périphrase explicative.

V. a. **rotation du personnel**
☐ mouvement du personnel

81. augmentation statutaire
      Terme à éviter
      V. **avancement d'échelon**

82. autorisation d'absence n. f.
leave of absence
Permission accordée au salarié de s'absenter de son poste pour des raisons précises avec ou sans rémunération.
Note. — Lorsque l'autorisation est écrite, il s'agit d'un *permis d'absence*.
☐ durée du travail

83. avance n. f.
advance
Somme versée à une personne pour lui permettre d'effectuer des dépenses dont elle devra rendre compte plus tard.
☐ rémunération du travail

84. avance sur salaire n. f.
advance on wages;
pay advance
Prêt consenti par l'employeur avant que ne débute l'exécution du travail.
V. a. **acompte sur salaire**
☐ rémunération du travail

85. avancement d'échelon n. m.
Terme à éviter : augmentation statutaire
pay increment;
wage progression
Passage à un échelon supérieur de rémunération sans augmentation de responsabilités.
V. a. **promotion**
☐ évaluation du personnel

86. avantages sociaux n. m. pl.
Terme à éviter : bénéfices marginaux
fringe benefits;
employee benefits
Éléments de rémunération dont bénéficie le salarié en sus du salaire.
☐ supplément salarial

87. avertissement n. m.
Terme à éviter : avis
warning;
disciplinary warning
Sanction disciplinaire verbale ou écrite qui souligne au salarié la faute qu'il a commise dans le but de l'inciter à modifier son comportement.
Note. — L'avertissement se situe au premier niveau de gravité des sanctions disciplinaires. À ce niveau, il y a cependant un ordre croissant allant de la simple observation jusqu'au blâme sévère. L'avertissement peut également mentionner les conséquences de la récidive.
V. a. **sanction disciplinaire**
☐ gestion des ressources humaines

88. avis
Terme à éviter
V. **avertissement**

B

89. barème des salaires
Syn. de **échelle des salaires**

90. bénéfices marginaux
Terme à éviter
V. **avantages sociaux**

91. bien-fondé n. m.
merit
Conformité d'une demande aux règles de droit qui lui sont applicables.
☐ travail

92. blâme
V. **sanction disciplinaire**

93. boni
Syn. de **prime de rendement**

94. boni d'ancienneté
Terme à éviter
V. **prime d'ancienneté**

95. boni de vie chère
Terme à éviter
V. **indemnité de cherté de vie**

96. bonus
Terme à éviter
V. **prime de rendement**

97. bureau n. m.
Termes à éviter : bureau de direction ; comité exécutif
officers
Groupe constitué par des dirigeants syndicaux élus par tous les syndiqués à certains postes.
Note. — Il s'agit des postes de président, vice-président, secrétaire, trésorier, etc.
☐ syndicalisme

98. **bureau de direction**
Terme à éviter
V. **bureau**

99. **bureau de direction**
Terme à éviter
V. **conseil syndical**

C

100. **cadre** n.
management
Salarié exerçant des fonctions de direction ou de conseil dans une entreprise ou une administration.
☐ travail

101. **cadre hiérarchique** n.
line manager
Salarié qui exerce des fonctions de supervision et de direction.
Note. — Les cadres hiérarchiques, sauf exception, ne sont pas syndiqués.
☐ travail

102. **cahier des revendications syndicales**
Syn. de **projet de convention collective**

103. **calendrier de production** n. m.;
programme de production n. m.
Terme à éviter : cédule de production
production schedule
Tableau prévoyant des tâches à accomplir et le moment de leur exécution.
Note. — *Céduler la production* est aussi à remplacer par *planifier, programmer, dresser le calendrier de la production*, etc.
☐ organisation du travail

104. **carte de compétence**
Terme à éviter
V. **certificat de qualification**

105. **carte de poinçon**
Terme à éviter
V. **carte de pointage**

106. **carte de pointage** n. f.
Terme à éviter : carte de poinçon
punch card;
clock card

Carte du salarié sur laquelle sont inscrites ses heures d'entrée et de sortie au moyen de l'horodateur.
V. a. **feuille de présence**
☐ durée du travail

107. **cédule de production**
Terme à éviter
V. **calendrier de production**

108. **cédule de travail**
Terme à éviter
V. **horaire de travail**

109. **cédule des salaires**
Terme à éviter
V. **échelle des salaires**

110. **cédule des vacances**
Terme à éviter
V. **ordre des départs**

111. **céduler l'horaire de travail**
Terme à éviter
V. **horaire de travail**

112. **centrale syndicale**
Syn. de **confédération**

113. **certificat de qualification** n. m.
Terme à éviter : carte de compétence
competency card;
ticket;
certificate;
papers;
diploma
Document délivré par un organisme autorisé attestant le niveau de compétence acquise dans un métier ou une profession selon des normes préétablies.
Note. — On obtient généralement ce document à la suite d'examens théoriques ou pratiques.
☐ formation et perfectionnement du personnel

114. **certification**
Terme à éviter
V. **accréditation syndicale**

115. **cessation d'emploi** n. f.;
départ n. m.
Termes à éviter : séparation ; terminaison d'emploi
separation;
termination of employment;
termination

Rupture du contrat de travail à l'initiative de l'employeur ou du salarié.
☐ cessation d'emploi

116. champ d'application n. m. ;
domaine d'application n. m. ;
domaine n. m.
Terme à éviter : juridiction
jurisdiction;
scope;
coverage
Aire de délimitation du groupe de salariés auxquels s'applique la convention collective.
Note. — Selon le *Code du travail* du Québec, le champ d'application est déterminé par l'accréditation.
V. a. **compétence**
☐ convention collective de travail

117. charge
Syn. de **charge de travail**

118. charge de travail n. f. ;
charge n. f.
work load
Quantité de travail qu'un salarié doit accomplir.
☐ travail

119. chef d'atelier
V. **chef de service**

120. chef d'équipe n.
lead hand;
charge hand
V. o. *chargehand*
Personne qui a la responsabilité professionnelle et parfois administrative d'un groupe constitué de collègues.
Note. — La caractéristique principale du chef d'équipe c'est qu'il exerce en partie les mêmes fonctions que ses collègues.
☐ durée du travail

121. chef de chantier
V. **chef de service**

122. chef de la fabrication
V. **chef de service**

123. chef de service n.
Terme à éviter : surintendant
superintendent;
department head

Personne qui, au sein de l'entreprise, est responsable d'un service.
Note. — Selon le cas, il peut également s'agir d'un chef d'atelier, chef des travaux, chef de chantier, chef de la fabrication, etc.
☐ travail

124. chef des travaux
V. **chef de service**

125. chiffre
Terme à éviter
V. **poste 1**

126. chômage partiel
Syn. de **travail à horaire réduit**

127. clause d'échappatoire
Syn. de **clause de désistement**

128. clause d'échelle mobile
Syn. de **clause d'indexation**

129. clause d'indexation n. f. ;
clause d'échelle mobile n. f. ;
clause de sauvegarde n. f. (FR)
escalator clause
Clause contenant le rajustement des salaires en fonction des variables tel l'indice des prix à la consommation.
Notes. — 1. On rencontre aussi parfois en France *clause de sauvegarde.*
2. Il faut utiliser *indexation sur le coût de la vie* plutôt qu'*indexation au coût de la vie.*
V. a. **indemnité de cherté de vie**
☐ convention collective de travail

130. clause de désistement n. f. ;
clause d'échappatoire n. f.
escape clause;
open period
Clause permettant, dans une période déterminée, à ceux qui le désirent de démissionner du syndicat.
☐ syndicalisme

131. clause de non-concurrence n. f.
restrictive trade agreement
Clause interdisant au salarié d'ouvrir un établissement similaire ou de passer au service d'une maison concurrente à l'expiration de son contrat de travail pendant un temps et dans un espace déterminés.
☐ cessation d'emploi

132. **clause de sauvegarde**
Syn. de **clause d'indexation**

133. **clause monétaire**
Terme à éviter
V. **clause pécuniaire**

134. **clause non pécuniaire** n. f. ;
clause non salariale n. f.
Terme à éviter : clause normative
non-monetary clause
Clause relative à l'ensemble des conditions de travail du salarié à l'exclusion des éléments de rémunération.
Note. — Dans le cas du terme *clause normative*, l'emploi de l'adjectif *normatif* est nettement abusif puisque, d'une part, *norme* signifie « règle » et que, d'autre part, le salaire constitue un point majeur des conditions de travail.
☐ convention collective de travail

135. **clause non salariale**
Syn. de **clause non pécuniaire**

136. **clause normative**
Terme à éviter
V. **clause non pécuniaire**

137. **clause pécuniaire** n. f. ;
clause salariale n. f.
Terme à éviter : clause monétaire
monetary clause
Clause qui touche la rémunération directe ou indirecte du salaire.
☐ convention collective de travail

138. **clause salariale**
Syn. de **clause pécuniaire**

139. **col blanc**
Syn. de **employé**

140. **col bleu**
Syn. de **ouvrier**

141. **comité conjoint**
Terme à éviter
V. **comité mixte**

142. **comité conjoint**
Terme à éviter
V. **comité paritaire**

143. **comité des griefs** n. m. ;
comité des réclamations n. m.
grievance committee

Comité chargé de la discussion et du règlement des griefs formulés par les salariés concernant l'interprétation et l'application de la convention collective.
☐ conflit du travail

144. **comité des réclamations**
Syn. de **comité des griefs**

145. **comité exécutif**
Terme à éviter
V. **bureau**

146. **comité exécutif**
Terme à éviter
V. **conseil syndical**

147. **comité mixte** n. m.
Terme à éviter : comité conjoint
joint committee
Groupement formé de représentants provenant des parties patronale et syndicale.
☐ relations professionnelles

148. **comité paritaire** n. m.
Terme à éviter : comité conjoint
joint committee;
parity committee
Comité mixte formé d'un nombre égal des représentants de chaque partie.
☐ relations professionnelles

149. **compagne**
V. **compagnon**

150. **compagnon** n. m.
compagne n. f.
journeyman;
craftsman;
tradesman
Ouvrier qualifié qui a terminé son apprentissage et possède un certificat de qualification.
☐ formation et perfectionnement du personnel

151. **compétence 1** n. f.
Terme à éviter : qualifications
qualification
Connaissances qu'un salarié a acquises dans son champ professionnel.
☐ gestion des ressources humaines

152. **compétence 2** n. f.
Terme à éviter : juridiction
jurisdiction

Aptitude reconnue officiellement à une autorité pour se prononcer dans un domaine précis.

Note. — Dans certains organismes syndicaux, 1) la compétence peut s'exercer selon différents critères : un groupe de salariés en vertu de l'accréditation ; une catégorie professionnelle ; un territoire ; 2) l'exercice de la compétence peut se répartir à plusieurs niveaux : local, régional, etc.
Il faut également utiliser *conflit de compétence* au lieu de *conflit de juridiction*.
V. a. **champ d'application**
☐ travail

153. compte rendu n. m.
Terme à éviter : minutes
report
Exposé détaillé et circonstancié d'une situation, d'un état de travail et de recherches, de la réalisation d'un objectif.
Note. — Au pluriel : comptes rendus.
V. a. **procès-verbal**
☐ travail

154. conciliateur n. m.
conciliatrice n. f.
conciliator;
conciliation officer
Personne nommée par l'autorité publique pour la conciliation à l'occasion d'un différend.
☐ conflit du travail

155. conciliation n. f.
conciliation
Procédure d'intervention d'un conciliateur visant à susciter un accord entre les parties à l'occasion d'un différend.
☐ conflit du travail

156. conciliatrice
V. **conciliateur**

157. condition d'embauchage
Syn. de **condition d'engagement**

158. condition d'embauche
Syn. de **condition d'engagement**

159. condition d'emploi 1
Syn. de **condition d'engagement**

160. condition d'emploi 2
Syn. de **condition de travail**

161. condition d'engagement n. f. ;
condition d'emploi 1 n. f. ;
condition d'embauche n. f. ;
condition d'embauchage n. f.
condition of employment;
condition of hiring;
terms and conditions of employment
Exigence préalable à l'emploi que pose l'employeur au futur salarié.
Note. — Le salarié doit habituellement continuer de satisfaire aux conditions d'engagement pour conserver son emploi.
☐ recrutement et engagement du personnel

162. condition de travail n. f. ;
condition d'emploi 2 n. f.
working condition;
condition of employment
Tout aspect de la situation professionnelle inscrit ou non dans une convention collective ou un contrat individuel de travail.
☐ condition de travail

163. conducteur n. m.
conductrice n. f.
Terme à éviter : opérateur
operator;
driver;
tender
Salarié qui fait fonctionner un appareil, qui conduit un engin.
Note. — L'emploi d'*opérateur* est limité en français. Il est utilisé en parlant de personnes qui font fonctionner un appareil photographique, cinématographique, radiotélégraphique à bord des navires et des avions particulièrement et quelques machines électroniques.
☐ travail

164. conductrice
V. **conducteur**

165. confédération n. f. ;
centrale syndicale n. f.
confederation
Regroupement de syndicats, d'unions ou de fédérations.
Note. — La confédération constitue le sommet de l'organisation syndicale. En pratique, la confédération peut également regrouper des syndicats. Au Québec, il y a quatre confédérations ou centrales syndicales : la CEQ, la CSD, la CSN, et la FTQ.
☐ syndicalisme

166. confirmé adj.
senior;
seasoned
Se dit d'une personne dont la compétence a été reconnue avec certitude.
☐ travail

167. confirmer v.
to confirm
Transformer le statut provisoire ou d'essai en statut définitif.
☐ recrutement et engagement du personnel

168. conflit de compétence
V. **compétence**

169. conflit de juridiction
Terme à éviter
V. **compétence**

170. congé 1 n. m.
dismissal;
discharge
Acte unilatéral par lequel l'employeur fait connaître au salarié sa décision de mettre fin au contrat de travail.
☐ cessation d'emploi

171. congé 2 n. m.;
absence autorisée n. f.
Terme à éviter : congé autorisé
leave of absence;
authorized absence
Absence pour laquelle un salarié a obtenu l'autorisation de son employeur.
Note. — L'employeur peut être tenu d'accorder son autorisation en vertu de la loi ou de la convention collective.
☐ congé

172. congé à traitement différé
Terme à éviter
V. **congé autofinancé**

173. congé annuel
Syn. de **congé annuel payé**

174. congé annuel acquis n. m.
earned vacation;
earned leave
Congé annuel auquel le salarié a droit à l'expiration de l'année de référence.
V. a. **jour de congé annuel accumulé**
☐ congé

175. congé annuel payé n. m.;
congé annuel n. m.;
congé payé n. m.;
vacances n. f. pl.;
vacances payées n. f. pl.
vacation;
vacations;
holidays;
annual leave
Période de repos rémunérée à laquelle le salarié a droit annuellement.
Note. — En tête de chapitre, le terme *congé annuel payé* et ses deux premiers synonymes sont très souvent utilisés au pluriel.
☐ congé

176. congé autofinancé n. m.
Terme à éviter : congé à traitement différé
self-financed leave
Congé pour convenances personnelles de longue durée accordé au salarié et payé à même une partie de la rémunération acquise et retenue à cette fin par l'employeur.
Note. — Par exemple, un salarié travaille et touche les deux tiers de sa rémunération pendant deux ans; durant la troisième année, où il est en congé, il perçoit également les deux tiers de sa rémunération. Ce congé doit être approuvé par l'employeur qui se charge de la gestion particulière du salaire ou qui la confie à un fiduciaire.
☐ congé

177. congé autorisé
Terme à éviter
V. **congé 2**

178. congé compensateur n. m.;
congé compensatoire n. m.
compensating time off
Congé accordé au salarié en dédommagement des heures supplémentaires ou en remplacement d'un congé dont il n'a pas bénéficié.
V. a. **heure supplémentaire**
☐ congé

179. congé compensatoire
Syn. de **congé compensateur**

180. congé d'adoption n. m.
adoption leave
Congé auquel a droit la salariée ou le salarié à l'occasion de l'adoption d'un enfant.
☐ congé

181. congé d'éducation syndicale
Syn. de **congé de formation syndicale**

182. congé de décès n. m.;
congé de deuil n. m.
bereavement leave;
compassionate leave
Congé accordé au salarié à l'occasion du décès d'un membre de sa famille.
□ congé

183. congé de deuil
Syn. de **congé de décès**

184. congé de formation
Syn. de **congé de formation professionnelle**

185. congé de formation professionnelle n. m.;
congé de formation n. m.;
congé-éducation n. m.
educational leave
Congé accordé au salarié pour lui permettre de parfaire ses connaissances.
□ congé

186. congé de formation syndicale n. m.;
congé d'éducation syndicale n. m.
union training leave
Congé accordé au salarié pour lui permettre d'assister à des sessions organisées par un organisme syndical.
□ congé

187. congé de maladie n. m.
sick leave
Congé accordé au salarié en raison d'une maladie ou d'un accident.
□ congé

188. congé de mariage n. m.
wedding leave;
marriage leave;
absence on wedding day
Congé accordé au salarié à l'occasion de son mariage ou de celui d'un proche parent.
□ congé

189. congé de maternité n. m.
maternity leave

Congé auquel a droit la salariée à l'occasion d'un accouchement ou d'une interruption de grossesse naturelle ou provoquée légalement.
□ congé

190. congé de naissance
Syn. de **congé de paternité**

191. congé de paternité n. m.;
congé de naissance n. m. (FR)
paternity leave
Congé auquel a droit le salarié à l'occasion de la naissance de son enfant.
□ congé

192. congé de préretraite n. m.
preretirement leave
V. o. *pre-retirement leave;*
early retirement leave
Congé accordé pour des raisons précises par l'employeur au salarié soit avant la retraite normale, soit avant la retraite anticipée et dont la rémunération est fixée d'après des modalités préétablies.
□ congé

193. congé-éducation
Syn. de **congé de formation professionnelle**

194. congé flottant
Terme à éviter
V. **congé mobile**

195. congé mobile n. m.
Terme à éviter : congé flottant
floater;
floating holiday
Congé accordé au salarié qui peut en fixer la date à la convenance ou avec l'assentiment de l'employeur.
□ congé

196. congé non payé n. m.;
congé sans solde n. m.
leave of absence without pay;
leave without pay
Congé que prend le salarié sans recevoir de rémunération.
Note. — *Congé sans solde* est de plus en plus utilisé dans le sens de «congé non payé»; on le retrouve aussi dans certaines conventions collectives françaises.
□ congé

197. congé parental n. m.;
  congé parental d'éduca-
  tion n. m. (FR);
  congé postnatal n. m. (FR)
parental leave
Congé que peut prendre la salariée ou le salarié à la suite du congé de maternité, de paternité ou d'adoption, pour élever son enfant.
Note. — En France, le congé parental d'éducation et le congé postnatal sont tous deux régis par des règles différentes et bien déterminées.
☐ congé

198. congé parental d'éducation
  Syn. de **congé parental**

199. congé payé
  Syn. de **congé annuel payé**

200. congé payé
  Terme à éviter
  V. **jour férié payé**

201. congé postnatal
  Syn. de **congé parental**

202. congé pour activité syndicale
  V. **congé pour fonctions syndicales**

203. congé pour affaires personnelles
  V. **congé pour convenances personnelles**

204. congé pour convenances personnelles n. m.
leave of absence for personal reasons;
personal leave;
leave for personal reasons
Congé que prend le salarié pour des motifs qui lui sont propres et qu'il n'a pas habituellement à préciser.
Note. — Au Québec, on utilise dans ce sens *congé pour affaires personnelles*. Cependant, dans les pays francophones, c'est *congé pour convenances personnelles* qui prévaut. Il nous semble préférable de retenir ce dernier terme.
☐ congé

205. congé pour événements familiaux n. m.
  Terme à éviter : congé social
leave for family reasons

Congé accordé au salarié en certaines circonstances précisées dans la convention collective : naissance et adoption, mariage et décès.
☐ congé

206. congé pour fonctions judiciaires n. m.
jury-duty leave;
jury and witness duty leave
Congé accordé au salarié pour lui permettre d'être témoin ou juré dans une affaire judiciaire.
☐ congé

207. congé pour fonctions publiques n. m.
leave of absence for public office
Congé accordé au salarié pour lui permettre d'exercer des fonctions officielles.
Note. — Il peut exercer, par exemple, les fonctions de maire, de député, de commissaire d'école, etc.
☐ congé

208. congé pour fonctions syndicales n. m.;
  libération syndicale n. f.;
  décharge de service n. f. (FR)
union leave;
leave of absence for union business;
leave for union business
Congé accordé au salarié pour l'exercice de fonctions syndicales.
Note. — En France, on dit que le salarié est en *délégation*, qu'il bénéficie d'une *décharge de service* ou encore qu'il utilise son *crédit d'heures*, ses *heures de délégation*. Au Québec, on rencontre *congé pour activité syndicale*. On utilise également *libération syndicale*. De même, on désigne par *libéré* ou *libérée* la personne qui exerce cette fonction.
☐ congé

209. congé sabbatique n. m.
sabbatical leave
Congé accordé au salarié pour lui permettre d'étudier, de faire des travaux de recherche ou de se reposer.
Note. — Pour s'en prévaloir, le salarié doit avoir un certain nombre d'années d'ancienneté. Quant aux conditions touchant au congé sabbatique, notamment la durée,

la fréquence, les exigences, elles varient sensiblement d'un organisme à un autre.
☐ congé

210. congé sans solde
Syn. de **congé non payé**

211. congé social
Terme à éviter
V. **congé pour événements familiaux**

212. congé social
Terme à éviter
V. **congé spécial**

213. congé spécial n. m.
Terme à éviter : congé social
special leave;
special leave of absence

Tout congé autre que le congé annuel payé.
☐ congé

214. congé statutaire
Terme à éviter
V. **jour férié**

215. congédiement n. m.;
renvoi n. m.
discharge;
dismissal

Rupture unilatérale et définitive de la part de l'employeur qui met fin au contrat de travail du salarié pour des motifs imputables au salarié, motifs d'ordre disciplinaire ou non.
Note. — En France, on utilise indifféremment *licenciement* ou *congédiement*. Au Québec, l'usage n'est pas fixé. Cependant, à l'article 47.3 du *Code du travail* du Québec le mot *renvoi* est utilisé pour *licenciement* et *congédiement*.
V. a. **licenciement**
☐ cessation d'emploi

216. congédiement discriminatoire n. m.;
renvoi discriminatoire n. m.
discriminatory dismissal

Congédiement fondé sur des motifs interdits par la législation québécoise ou sur le traitement différent de salariés dans des situations équivalentes.
☐ cessation d'emploi

217. congédiement justifié n. m.;
renvoi justifié n. m.;

congédiement pour cause juste et suffisante n. m.;
renvoi pour cause juste et suffisante n. m.
Termes à éviter : congédiement pour cause; renvoi pour cause
dismissal for just cause;
discharge for cause;
discharge for just cause

Congédiement fondé sur un motif valable et suffisant.
Note. — Devant l'arbitre de griefs, la motivation du congédiement doit être établie. À ce moment-là, le motif est clairement exprimé (le congédiement est dit *motivé*) et les règles de la procédure doivent avoir été respectées. Ensuite, si les motifs sont fondés et proportionnels à la faute reprochée, l'arbitre maintiendra le congédiement qui est alors justifié.
☐ cessation d'emploi

218. congédiement motivé
V. **congédiement justifié**

219. congédiement pour activité syndicale n. m.;
renvoi pour activité syndicale n. m.
dismissal for union activity

Congédiement fondé sur la participation du salarié à une activité syndicale reconnue par la loi.
☐ cessation d'emploi

220. congédiement pour cause
Terme à éviter
V. **congédiement justifié**

221. congédiement pour cause juste et suffisante
Syn. de **congédiement justifié**

222. conseil central
V. **union**

223. conseil d'arbitrage n. m.
arbitration board

Réunion de trois personnes chargées de régler un différend par sentence arbitrale.
Note. — Cette réunion est composée d'un arbitre patronal, d'un arbitre syndical et d'une troisième personne, le président, choisie par les deux parties ou, à défaut d'accord, par le ministre du Travail au

Québec. L'arbitre de différends, qui peut être assisté de deux assesseurs, tient lieu de conseil d'arbitrage.
□ conflit du travail

224. **conseil du travail**
V. **union**

225. **conseil syndical** n. m.
Termes à éviter : bureau de direction ; comité exécutif
executive board;
executive council
Groupe constitué du bureau et de délégués se réunissant entre les assemblées générales d'un organisme syndical.
□ syndicalisme

226. **conseiller syndical**
V. **permanent syndical**

227. **conseiller technique**
V. **permanent syndical**

228. **constitution**
Terme à éviter
V. **statuts**

229. **contrat de travail** n. m. ;
contrat individuel de travail n. m.
labour contract
V. o. *labor contract;*
contract of employment;
contract for services
Contrat par lequel une personne s'engage à travailler pour une autre personne, sous son autorité, pour une durée déterminée ou indéterminée, moyennant rémunération.
□ recrutement et engagement du personnel

230. **contrat individuel de travail**
Syn. de **contrat de travail**

231. **contribution patronale**
Syn. de **cotisation patronale**

232. **convention arbitrée** n. f.
contract settled by arbitration
Convention collective établie par un arbitre.
Note. — Cela peut se présenter soit volontairement après entente entre les parties, soit par effet de la loi.
□ convention collective de travail

233. **convention collective** n. f. ;
convention collective de travail n. f.

collective labour agreement
V. o. *collective labor agreement;*
labour agreement
V. o. *labor agreement;*
collective agreement
Entente écrite relative aux conditions de travail conclue entre une ou plusieurs associations accréditées et un ou plusieurs employeurs ou associations d'employeurs.
Note. — Cette définition est tirée du *Code du travail* du Québec.
□ convention collective de travail

234. **convention collective cadre** n. f.
Terme à éviter : convention collective maîtresse
master agreement;
framework agreement
Accord intervenu entre une ou plusieurs associations de salariés et un employeur à la tête de plusieurs établissements ou une association d'employeurs laissant place à la négociation locale ou à des aménagements locaux en certaines matières.
□ convention collective de travail

235. **convention collective de travail**
Syn. de **convention collective**

236. **convention collective maîtresse**
Terme à éviter
V. **convention collective cadre**

237. **convention collective modèle** n. f.
standard agreement;
model agreement
Projet de convention collective formant un ensemble cohérent qu'une centrale syndicale ou une fédération professionnelle propose comme objectif à ses syndicats affiliés.
□ convention collective de travail

238. **convention collective type** n. f.
pattern agreement
Convention collective intervenue entre un employeur et un syndicat et utilisée comme point d'appui par l'une des parties pour obtenir des conditions de travail similaires au cours d'une autre négociation.
□ convention collective de travail

239. **corporation professionnelle**
Terme à éviter
V. **ordre professionnel**

240. **cotisation patronale** n. f. ;
contribution patronale n. f.

employer's contribution
Quote-part que débourse l'employeur à des fins particulières et déterminées.
☐ travail

241. cotisation syndicale n. f.
union dues;
dues
Somme que doit verser périodiquement le salarié à son syndicat.
V. a. **droit d'entrée**
☐ syndicalisme

242. crédit d'heures
V. **congé pour fonctions syndicales**

D

243. date d'ancienneté
Terme à éviter
V. **point de départ de l'ancienneté**

244. débauchage
V. **licenciement**

245. débutant adj.
Terme à éviter : junior
junior
Se dit du travailleur qui fait ses premiers pas dans la profession.
V. a. **second; apprenti; stagiaire**
☐ gestion des ressources humaines

246. décharge de service
Syn. de **congé pour fonctions syndicales**

247. déclaration d'aptitudes
V. **liste d'admissibilité**

248. déclassement
Syn. de **rétrogradation**

249. délai-congé n. m.;
délai de préavis n. m.
Terme à éviter : notice
notice period;
period
Délai que doit respecter le salarié ou l'employeur qui désire mettre fin au contrat de travail à durée indéterminée.
☐ cessation d'emploi

250. délai de préavis
Syn. de **délai-congé**

251. délégation
V. **congé pour fonctions syndicales**

252. délégué d'atelier
V. **délégué syndical**

253. délégué syndical n. m.
déléguée syndicale n. f.
shop steward
Salarié élu par ses compagnons de travail pour servir d'agent de liaison avec le syndicat et pour veiller à l'application de la convention collective.
Note. — On rencontre aussi le terme *délégué d'atelier* ou *déléguée d'atelier*.
☐ syndicalisme

254. déléguée d'atelier
V. **délégué syndical**

255. déléguée syndicale
V. **délégué syndical**

256. démission n. f.
Terme à éviter : résignation
quit;
resignation
Action de signifier volontairement son intention de mettre fin à son service à partir d'une date déterminée.
Note. — Le verbe *résigner* est transitif; on ne peut donc l'employer sans objet direct. On peut dire que l'on *résigne sa charge*, *son emploi, ses fonctions*.
☐ cessation d'emploi

257. démotion
Terme à éviter
V. **rétrogradation**

258. départ
Syn. de **cessation d'emploi**

259. département
Terme à éviter
V. **service**

260. déplacement n. m.
transfer
Action d'affecter un salarié à un autre poste ou emploi contre son gré.
☐ mouvement du personnel

261. **désaccréditation**
     Syn. de **révocation d'accréditation**

262. **description d'emploi** n. f. ;
     description de poste n. f. ;
     description des tâches n. f. ;
     description des fonctions n. f.
job description
Énumération des activités, des devoirs et des responsabilités reliés à un emploi.
☐ organisation du travail

263. **description de poste**
     Syn. de **description d'emploi**

264. **description des fonctions**
     Syn. de **description d'emploi**

265. **description des tâches**
     Syn. de **description d'emploi**

266. **désistement**
     V. **clause de désistement**

267. **différend** n. m.
labour dispute
V. o. *labor dispute;*
dispute;
industrial dispute
Mésentente relative à la négociation ou au renouvellement d'une convention collective ou à sa révision par les parties en vertu d'une clause le permettant expressément.
Note. — Cette définition est tirée du *Code du travail* du Québec.
V. a. **grief**
☐ conflit du travail

268. **directeur** n. m.
     directrice n. f.
     Terme à éviter : gérant
manager
Personne qui, au sein de l'entreprise, occupe un poste de direction.
Note. — Ne pas confondre avec *gérant* qui, dans la langue commerciale, est une personne qui administre pour le compte d'autrui.
☐ organisation du travail

269. **direction**
     V. **service**

270. **directrice**
     V. **directeur**

271. **dirigeant syndical** n. m.
     dirigeante syndicale n. f.
     Termes à éviter : officier syndical ;
     officier de syndicat
union officer;
labour leader
V. o. *labor leader*
Personne exerçant des fonctions de direction au sein d'un organisme syndical.
☐ syndicalisme

272. **dirigeante syndicale**
     V. **dirigeant syndical**

273. **discipline** n. f.
discipline
Ensemble de règles régissant le comportement des salariés dans le but d'assurer la bonne exécution du travail.
☐ gestion des ressources humaines

274. **discrimination** n. f.
discrimination
Distinction qui défavorise une personne ou un groupe de personnes.
Note. — La discrimination peut être exercée en raison de la race, du sexe, de la religion, des convictions politiques, des activités syndicales, etc. *Discrimination* semble de plus en plus avoir une connotation d'injustice. Cette nuance est confirmée dans le *Petit Robert* depuis au moins 1977 et dans certains documents touchant le domaine du travail. Cependant, au Québec, cette acception est fort courante depuis longtemps.
☐ travail

275. **disponibilité** n. f.
availability
Situation d'un salarié qui est déchargé de l'exercice de ses fonctions mais qui continue, pour un certain temps, à recevoir sa rémunération.
Note. — On dit que l'employeur *met* le salarié *en disponibilité*. La mise en disponibilité peut être causée par la suppression d'un poste, par le manque de travail ou par l'incapacité du salarié.
☐ cessation d'emploi

276. **division**
     V. **service**

277. **domaine**
     Syn. de **champ d'application**

278. **domaine d'application**
Syn. de **champ d'application**

279. **double emploi**
Syn. de **emploi secondaire**

280. **droit d'ancienneté** n. m.
seniority rights

Droit que peut exercer un salarié en raison de son ancienneté.

Note. — Un salarié peut exercer son droit d'ancienneté mais non son ancienneté.
□ durée du travail

281. **droit d'association**
V. **droit syndical**

282. **droit d'entrée** n. m.
Terme à éviter : frais d'initiation
initiation fee

Montant exigé par les statuts du syndicat comme une des conditions essentielles pour en devenir membre.

V. a. **cotisation syndicale**
□ syndicalisme

283. **droit syndical** n. m.
right to unionization;
trade union legislation;
union legislation

Faculté des salariés de se grouper dans le cadre professionnel pour la défense de leurs intérêts communs et la promotion de leurs droits par l'action collective.

Note. — Dans le *Code du travail* du Québec, on utilise *droit d'association* qui est plus vaste que *droit syndical.*
□ syndicalisme

284. **droits de gérance**
Terme à éviter
V. **droits de la direction**

285. **droits de l'employeur**
Syn. de **droits de la direction**

286. **droits de la direction** n. m. pl. ;
droits de l'employeur n. m. pl.
Terme à éviter : droits de gérance
management rights

Prérogatives dont dispose l'employeur pour la conduite de l'entreprise.
□ travail

287. **droits parentaux** n. m. pl.
parental rights

Dispositions qui régissent le congé de maternité, de paternité, d'adoption et le congé parental.
□ congé

288. **durée du travail** n. f.
hours of work

Nombre d'heures de travail calculé sur une base journalière, hebdomadaire, mensuelle ou annuelle.

E

289. **échappatoire**
V. **clause de désistement**

290. **échelle de rémunération**
Syn. de **échelle des salaires**

291. **échelle des salaires** n. f. ;
échelle de rémunération n. f. ;
grille de rémunération n. f. ;
tarif de rémunération n. m. ;
barème des salaires n. m. ;
échelle salariale n. f.
Terme à éviter : cédule des salaires
wage scale;
wage schedule;
wage structure;
salary schedule;
salary scale

Tableau indiquant les taux de salaire en ordre croissant.
□ rémunération du travail

292. **échelle mobile**
V. **clause d'indexation**

293. **échelle salariale**
Syn. de **échelle des salaires**

294. **échelon** n. m.
grade;
level;
step;
increment

Niveau de rémunération à l'intérieur d'une échelle des salaires.
□ rémunération du travail

295. **égalité professionnelle**
V. **plan d'égalité professionnelle**

296. **éligible**
Terme à éviter
V. **admissible**

297. **embauchage**
Syn. de **engagement**

298. **embauche**
Syn. de **engagement**

299. **emploi** n. m.;
travail 1 n. m.
Termes à éviter : occupation; position
job;
occupation;
employment
Activité professionnelle rémunérée.
☐ travail

300. **emploi à plein temps**
Syn. de **travail à temps plein**

301. **emploi à temps partiel**
Syn. de **travail à temps partiel**

302. **emploi à temps plein**
Syn. de **travail à temps plein**

303. **emploi clé**
Syn. de **poste clé**

304. **emploi de, à l'**
Terme à éviter
V. **service de, au**

305. **emploi occasionnel** n. m.;
travail occasionnel n. m.
casual job
Emploi qui requiert les services d'un salarié engagé temporairement lorsqu'il y a un surcroît de travail ou pour un projet spécial.
☐ durée du travail

306. **emploi partagé** n. m.
job sharing
Emploi occupé par plus d'un salarié.
Note. — Cet emploi qui correspondait à un poste à temps plein correspond maintenant à plusieurs postes à temps partiel.
V. a. **partage du travail**
☐ gestion des ressources humaines

307. **emploi permanent** n. m.;
travail permanent n. m.
Terme à éviter : emploi régulier
permanent job
Emploi qui est susceptible de retenir, en vue de l'exécution de certaines tâches, les services d'une personne pour une durée indéterminée, à moins de la cessation des activités de l'entreprise ou de causes économiques entraînant une réduction du personnel.
☐ gestion des ressources humaines

308. **emploi protégé**
Syn. de **emploi réservé**

309. **emploi régulier**
Terme à éviter
V. **emploi permanent**

310. **emploi repère** n. m.
bench-mark job
V. o. *benchmark job*
Emploi que l'on choisit comme base de comparaison en vue d'une classification des emplois.
☐ organisation du travail

311. **emploi réservé** n. m.;
emploi protégé n. m.;
travail réservé n. m.;
travail protégé n. m.
restricted job;
sheltered job
Emploi dont l'accessibilité est limitée à certaines catégories de personnes selon des critères déterminés.
☐ organisation du travail

312. **emploi saisonnier** n. m.;
travail saisonnier n. m.
seasonal employment
Emploi accompli durant une période de l'année seulement en raison de la nature de l'activité exercée.
☐ organisation du travail

313. **emploi secondaire** n. m.;
travail secondaire n. m.;
double emploi n. m.
moonlighting;
sideline;
second job
Emploi occupé par un salarié en plus de celui qu'il exerce chez son employeur principal.
☐ organisation du travail

314. **emploi temporaire** n. m.;
travail temporaire n. m.
temporary employment
Emploi qui requiert les services d'une personne pour une courte durée.
☐ organisation du travail

315. emploi vacant
Syn. de **poste vacant**

316. employé n. m.
employée n. f.;
col blanc n.
employee;
white-collar worker
Salarié travaillant dans un bureau, un magasin ou un autre service.
Note. — *Employé*, en ce sens, est plus usité en France qu'au Québec. Il correspond à la notion sociologique américaine de *col blanc*. Il s'oppose à *ouvrier*. Le Logos-Bordas donne d'*employé* comme première définition ce qui suit : «Personne rémunérée (généralement salariée) considérée dans ses relations juridiques ou professionnelles avec son patron, son employeur; droits et obligations réciproques des employés et des employeurs; contrat de travail liant un employé à son employeur. N.B. : Dans ce sens, tous les salariés, qu'ils soient cadres, employés de bureau (sens 2) ou bien ouvriers sont, du point de vue de la loi, des employés». Ce sens est fortement répandu au Québec. Toutefois, comme *employé* a un autre sens plus restreint qui le distingue de *cadre* ou *ouvrier*, il serait préférable d'utiliser *salarié* comme générique et *employé* comme spécifique.
V. a. **salarié**
☐ travail

317. employé clérical
Terme à éviter
V. **employé de bureau**

318. employé de bureau n. m.
employée de bureau n. f.
Terme à éviter : employé clérical
clerical employee;
office employee;
white-collar worker;
office worker
Salarié effectuant un travail d'ordre plutôt intellectuel.
☐ travail

319. employé régulier
Terme à éviter
V. **permanent**

320. employée
V. **employé**

321. employée de bureau
V. **employé de bureau**

322. employées et assimilées
V. **employés et assimilés**

323. employés et assimilés n. m. pl.
employées et assimilées n. f. pl.
Terme à éviter : fonctionnaires
office employees and equivalents
Catégorie de personnel regroupant les employés de bureau, les agents administratifs, techniques et autres qui occupent un emploi dans les cadres d'une administration publique.
Notes. — 1. Dans la fonction publique, le terme *employé* est utilisé au sens de «salarié travaillant dans un bureau».
2. Le terme *fonctionnaires* est couramment employé à tort dans la fonction publique québécoise pour ne désigner qu'une catégorie déterminée de salariés comme il est mentionné à l'article 65 de la *Loi sur la fonction publique*.
☐ travail

324. employeur n. m.
employeuse n. f.
employer
Personne physique ou morale qui fait exécuter, contre rémunération, un travail par une ou plusieurs personnes pour son compte et sous sa subordination.
Note. — S'il s'agit d'une personne morale, *employeur* ne prend pas la forme du féminin.
☐ travail

325. employeuse
V. **employeur**

326. engagement n. m.;
embauchage n. m.;
embauche n. f.
hiring;
employment
Acte par lequel un employeur convient avec une personne qu'elle entrera à son service.
Notes. — 1. Plusieurs dictionnaires généraux mentionnent qu'*embauchage* s'applique davantage aux ouvriers. Cependant, nous avons constaté que, dans les documents français, l'hésitation entre *embauchage* et *engagement* est fréquente à quelque niveau hiérarchique que ce soit. Nous

croyons donc que la précision que pourrait apporter *embauchage* n'est pas des plus pertinentes.
2. Des dictionnaires généraux et quelques ouvrages spécialisés enregistrent *embauche* dans le sens d'«embauchage», d'«engagement». D'autres le qualifient de familier.
3. L'employeur peut agir par l'entremise d'un mandataire, par exemple, le bureau de placement syndical.
☐ recrutement et engagement du personnel

327. entente de principe
Syn. de **protocole d'accord**

328. entraînement
Terme à éviter
V. **formation**

329. entrée en fonction n. f.
V. o. **entrée en fonctions** n. f.
effective date of employment;
starting date
Moment où le salarié occupe un poste.
Note. — Au moment de l'entrée en service du salarié, il y a évidemment coïncidence avec son entrée en fonction.
☐ recrutement et engagement du personnel

330. entrée en fonctions
V. o. de **entrée en fonction**

331. entrée en service n. f.
date of hiring;
starting date;
hiring date;
date of hire
Moment où le salarié commence à travailler à la suite de son engagement.
Note. — Au moment de l'entrée en service du salarié, il y a évidemment coïncidence avec son entrée en fonction.
☐ recrutement et engagement du personnel

332. équipe 1 n. f.;
quart 1 n. m.
Terme à éviter : shift
shift
Groupe de salariés qui effectue son travail durant une période déterminée dans la journée.

Notes. — 1. *Quart* est un terme tiré du vocabulaire de la marine que le *Grand Robert* définit comme suit : «Période de quatre heures (primitivement six heures, quart de la journée) pendant laquelle une partie de l'équipage, à tour de rôle, est de service. (...) Par métonymie. *Les hommes de quart. Relever le quart.*» Au Québec, *quart* est fortement répandu dans le sens d'«équipe». Par extension, il peut être utilisé.
2. *Travailler sur le shift de* ou *être sur le shift de* est à remplacer par *être affecté à l'équipe de.*
V. a. **poste 1**
☐ organisation du travail

333. équipe 2 n. f.
crew;
gang;
team
Groupe de salariés qui exécutent un travail en commun.
☐ organisation du travail

334. équipe alternante n. f.;
équipe rotative n. f.;
équipe tournante n. f.
rotating shift
Équipe affectée aux divers postes de l'horaire de fonctionnement de l'entreprise selon le mode de rotation prévu.
V. a. **rotation des postes**
☐ durée du travail

335. équipe chevauchante n. f.
overlapping shift
Équipe dont l'horaire coïncide en partie avec celui d'une autre équipe.
☐ durée du travail

336. équipe d'après-midi n. f.;
quart d'après-midi 1 n. m.
afternoon shift;
second shift
Équipe affectée au poste d'après-midi.
Note. — *Quart d'après-midi* est d'usage québécois.
☐ durée du travail

337. équipe de jour n. f.;
équipe du matin n. f.;
quart de jour 1 n. m.;
quart du matin 1 n. m.
day shift;
first shift

Équipe affectée au poste de jour.
Note. — *Quart de jour* est d'usage québécois.
□ durée du travail

338. équipe de nuit n. f.;
quart de nuit 1 n. m.
night shift;
third shift
Équipe affectée au poste de nuit.
Note. — *Quart de nuit* est d'usage québécois.
□ durée du travail

339. équipe de relève n. f.;
quart de relève n. m.
relief shift;
swing shift
Équipe supplémentaire nécessaire à l'établissement du travail continu.
Note. — *Quart de relève* est d'usage québécois.
□ durée du travail

340. équipe du matin
Syn. de **équipe de jour**

341. équipe fixe n. f.
fixed shift
Équipe toujours affectée au même poste.
□ durée du travail

342. équipe rotative
Syn. de **équipe alternante**

343. équipe tournante
Syn. de **équipe alternante**

344. équipe volante n. f.
spares
Équipe dont les salariés polyvalents sont affectés individuellement ou collectivement à différents postes pour combler les besoins particuliers de l'entreprise au fur et à mesure qu'ils se présentent.
V. a. **ouvrier de renfort**
□ durée du travail

345. essai professionnel n. m.
Terme à éviter : test
trade test;
test

Épreuve pratique qui permet à l'employeur de se rendre compte de la qualification et des possibilités d'utilisation de l'intéressé.
□ recrutement et engagement du personnel

346. établir l'horaire de travail
V. **horaire de travail**

347. établissement n. m.
Terme à éviter : place d'affaires
place of business;
business place;
plant;
works
Unité technique de production pouvant coïncider avec l'entreprise ou au contraire n'en constituer qu'une fraction.
Note. — Lorsque l'unité technique de production dépend d'une entreprise : a) elle ne jouit pas de l'autonomie juridique; b) elle possède le pouvoir de décision pour les actes de gestion correspondant à la nature de ses activités; c) elle tend à accomplir l'objectif social qui lui a été confié selon les ordres, les directives et les instructions de la direction en fonction de la politique générale de l'entreprise.
□ travail

348. étape
Syn. de **stade**

349. étiquette syndicale n. f.;
label n. m.
Terme à éviter : marque d'union
union label
Marque apposée sur un produit fabriqué par des travailleurs syndiqués.
□ syndicalisme

350. être affecté au poste de
V. **poste 1**

351. être de
V. **poste 1**

352. évaluation des emplois n. f.;
évaluation des postes n. f.;
évaluation des tâches n. f.;
évaluation des fonctions n. f.;
qualification du travail n. f.
job evaluation
Hiérarchisation des emplois à partir d'une étude détaillée des fonctions.
□ organisation du travail

353. évaluation des fonctions
Syn. de **évaluation des emplois**

354. évaluation des postes
Syn. de **évaluation des emplois**

355. évaluation des tâches
Syn. de **évaluation des emplois**

356. évaluation du personnel
Syn. de **appréciation du personnel**

F

357. faction
Syn. de **poste**

358. factionnaire
Syn. de **travailleur par équipes**

359. faire du piquet
Syn. de **piqueter**

360. faute disciplinaire n. f. ;
manquement disciplinaire n. m. ;
infraction disciplinaire n. f.
offense
disciplinary infraction
Violation de la discipline.
☐ gestion des ressources humaines

361. faute lourde n. f.
serious offense;
gross negligence;
gross misconduct
Faute qui démontre chez son auteur une insouciance, une témérité, une incurie hors de l'ordinaire.
☐ gestion des ressources humaines

362. fédération n. f.
federation
Regroupement de syndicats sur le plan professionnel.
Note. — En pratique, certains grands syndicats jouent le rôle de fédération. Cette définition est d'ordre strictement terminologique. Elle ne correspond pas nécessairement ni à la désignation ni à l'importance des diverses organisations syndicales québécoises.
☐ syndicalisme

363. femme à tout faire
V. **travailleur toutes mains**

364. femme à toutes mains
V. **travailleur toutes mains**

365. femme de métier
V. **ouvrier qualifié**

366. femme toutes mains
V. **travailleur toutes mains**

367. fête légale
V. **jour férié**

368. feuille de présence n. f.
time card;
time sheet
Feuille individuelle ou collective où l'on consigne la présence du ou des salariés au travail.
V. a. **carte de pointage**
☐ durée du travail

369. fonction n. f.
position;
job
Emploi pour lequel on sous-entend les tâches à accomplir.
☐ travail

370. fonctionnaire n.
civil servant
Personne qui occupe un emploi dans les cadres d'une administration publique.
☐ travail

371. fonctionnaires
Terme à éviter
V. **employés et assimilés**

372. fonctionnement continu
Syn. de **marche continue**

373. fonctions
Syn. de **tâches**

374. fond n. m.
Terme à éviter : mérite
merit
Ce qui appartient au contenu essentiel du litige.
☐ conflit du travail

375. forfait quotidien
Syn. de **indemnité forfaitaire quotidienne**

376. formation n. f.
Terme à éviter : entraînement
training
Acquisition de connaissances pour l'exercice d'une activité.
☐ formation et perfectionnement du personnel

377. formation continue n. f.
continuing education;
recurrent education;
further training
Formation professionnelle ultérieure à la formation initiale et poursuivie par des personnes ayant déjà exercé une profession.
☐ formation et perfectionnement du personnel

378. formation en cours d'emploi
Syn. de **formation sur le tas**

379. formation professionnelle n. f.;
apprentissage n. m.
vocational training
Acquisition des connaissances théoriques et pratiques pour l'exercice d'une profession.
Note. — On réserve l'utilisation du terme *apprentissage* pour des métiers dans certains domaines par exemple, le bâtiment et l'imprimerie.
☐ formation et perfectionnement du personnel

380. formation sur le tas n. f.;
formation en cours d'emploi n. f.
on-the-job training;
in-plant training
Formation donnée sur les lieux de travail.
☐ formation et perfectionnement du personnel

381. formule Rand n. f.
Rand formula;
agency shop (US)
Forme de sécurité syndicale en vertu de laquelle l'employeur convient de prélever sur la paie de chaque salarié, qu'il soit ou non membre du syndicat, un montant égal à la cotisation syndicale, pour le verser au syndicat.

Notes. — 1. Sens usuel.
2. En vertu du *Code du travail* du Québec, la formule Rand est le régime légal depuis 1977. Elle s'applique dès l'accréditation du syndicat.
V. a. **retenue de la cotisation syndicale**
☐ syndicalisme

382. fractionnement des congés n. m.
split vacation;
split leave
Division du congé annuel payé en deux ou plusieurs périodes.
☐ congé

383. frais d'initiation
Terme à éviter
V. **droit d'entrée**

384. frais de déplacement
V. **indemnité de déplacement**

385. frais de voyage n. m. pl.
travelling expenses
Coût du transport du salarié et de ses bagages à l'occasion de son déplacement.
V. a. **indemnité de déplacement**
☐ frais professionnels

386. fraternité
V. **syndicat**

G

387. gains n. m. pl.
earnings
Somme d'argent effectivement gagnée par le salarié après une période de temps.
V. a. **salaire**
☐ rémunération du travail

388. garantie d'emploi
Syn. de **sécurité d'emploi**

389. garantie de travail n. f.
guaranteed hours of work;
guarantee of employment
Assurance donnée au salarié d'avoir du travail pendant un certain nombre d'heures, de jours ou de semaines au cours d'une période déterminée.
☐ organisation du travail

390. gérant
Terme à éviter
V. **directeur**

391. gérant d'affaires
Terme à éviter
V. **agent syndical en chef**

392. gratification n. f.
bonus;
premium
Récompense, périodique ou occasionnelle, attribuée par l'employeur pour marquer sa satisfaction en fonction du travail accompli.
□ supplément salarial

393. grève n. f.;
arrêt de travail n. m.
strike;
work stoppage
Cessation concertée du travail par un groupe de salariés en vue d'appuyer leurs revendications.
Notes. — 1. Il est à noter que la définition du *Code du travail* du Québec est la suivante : «Cessation concertée du travail par un groupe de salariés».
2. Le terme *arrêt de travail* peut être un synonyme de grève. Il a parfois un sens plus large.
□ conflit du travail

394. gréviste n.
striker
Salarié en grève.
□ conflit du travail

395. grief n. m.;
réclamation n. f.
grievance
Plainte officiellement formulée par un salarié, un groupe de salariés, le syndicat ou l'employeur, pour faire reconnaître l'existence d'un droit en vertu d'une convention collective et obtenir réparation s'il y a lieu.
Note. — Nous retenons le terme *grief* parce que l'extension de sens de *grief* de «motif de plainte» à «plainte officiellement formulée» évite de faire de *grief* un anglicisme mais plutôt un québécisme qui désigne un aspect spécifique de la culture nord-américaine pour les relations professionnelles. Toutefois, l'extension du sens de *grief* à «mésentente» comme il est défini par le *Code du travail* du Québec est abusive et

il nous semble préférable d'utiliser *litige.* Le litige correspond à ce que certains auteurs nomment *conflit de droit*; il se distingue donc du différend qui est un conflit d'intérêt. Dans le *Code du travail* du Québec, le terme *recours* est utilisé à quelques reprises (art. 69 - 70 - 71). Le terme *réclamation* que l'on retrouve en France ne recouvre pas exactement la même notion et il est rarement employé au Québec. Cependant, l'utilisation de *réclamation*, dans la langue française, est justifiée.
V. a. **différend**
□ conflit du travail

396. grille de rémunération
Syn. de **échelle des salaires**

H

397. handicapé
Syn. de **personne handicapée**

398. handicapée
Syn. de **personne handicapée**

399. harcèlement sexuel n. m.
sexual harassment
Pression indue exercée sur une personne soit pour obtenir des faveurs sexuelles soit pour ridiculiser ses caractéristiques sexuelles, ce qui a pour effet de compromettre son droit à l'égalité professionnelle.
□ gestion des ressources humaines

400. hebdomadaire
Syn. de **salarié hebdomadaire**

401. heure compensée
V. **heure supplémentaire**

402. heure de délégation
V. **congé pour fonctions syndicales**

403. heure effectuée
Syn. de **heure travaillée**

404. heure indemnisée
V. **heure supplémentaire**

405. heure majorée
V. **heure supplémentaire**

406. heure-prime n. f.
premium hour;
hour allowed

Heure pour laquelle le salarié est indemnisé bien qu'il n'ait pas effectivement travaillé durant ce temps.

Note. — Ce terme est utilisé dans le contexte des heures supplémentaires.
□ durée du travail

407. heure supplémentaire n. f.
Termes à éviter : surtemps; temps supplémentaire
overtime

Heure de travail effectuée en sus ou en dehors des heures normales.

Notes. — 1. Le terme *heure supplémentaire* est très souvent utilisé au pluriel.
2. Les heures supplémentaires peuvent comporter des majorations de salaire ou d'autres avantages compensatoires. Ainsi, lorsque les heures supplémentaires sont rémunérées, elles sont dites *indemnisées*, quel que soit le taux horaire. Cependant, elles sont dites *majorées* si le taux horaire est supérieur au taux horaire de base. Finalement, lorsque les heures supplémentaires donnent lieu à un congé compensateur, elles sont dites *compensées*.
V. a. **congé compensateur**
□ durée du travail

408. heure travaillée n. f. ;
heure effectuée n. f.
hour worked

Heure pendant laquelle le salarié a été effectivement au travail.
□ durée du travail

409. homme à tout faire
Syn. de **travailleur toutes mains**

410. homme à toutes mains
Syn. de **travailleur toutes mains**

411. homme de métier
Syn. de **ouvrier qualifié**

412. homme toutes mains
Syn. de **travailleur toutes mains**

413. honoraires n. m. pl.
fee

Rétribution accordée en échange de leurs services aux personnes exerçant une profession libérale.
□ rémunération du travail

414. horaire
Syn. de **salarié horaire**

415. horaire au choix n. m.
preferred shift;
preferred schedule;
free choice of scheduling

Horaire fixe que choisit le salarié pour une période déterminée assez longue.
□ durée du travail

416. horaire comprimé n. m.
compressed work schedule;
compressed schedule

Horaire de travail permettant de réduire le nombre de jours ouvrables dans une semaine en augmentant la durée quotidienne des heures de travail.
□ durée du travail

417. horaire de travail n. m.
Terme à éviter : cédule de travail
work schedule;
time schedule

Répartition des heures de travail.

Note. — *Céduler l'horaire de travail* est à remplacer par *établir l'horaire de travail*.
□ durée du travail

418. horaire décalé n. m.
staggered working hours

Horaire fixe imposé par l'employeur dont le début et la fin sont soit avancés, soit retardés comparativement à l'horaire normal précédent.
□ durée du travail

419. horaire fixe n. m. ;
horaire uniforme n. m.
fixed work schedule;
fixed schedule

Horaire de travail où le début et la fin de chaque période de travail sont déterminés et stables.
□ durée du travail

420. horaire flexible
Syn. de **horaire variable**

421. horaire fractionné n. m.
split work schedule;
split schedule
Horaire de travail comprenant des périodes de travail alternant avec des interruptions assez longues.
☐ durée du travail

422. horaire libre n. m.
flexible hours
Horaire de travail selon lequel le salarié effectue, quand bon lui semble, un nombre déterminé d'heures de travail dans le cadre d'une semaine.
☐ durée du travail

423. horaire uniforme
Syn. de **horaire fixe**

424. horaire variable n. m.;
horaire flexible n. m.
flexible hours of work;
flexible work schedule;
flexible schedule;
flextime
Horaire de travail permettant au salarié de choisir le début et la fin de sa journée tout en ayant une période de présence prédéterminée et obligatoire.
Note. — De l'horaire fixe à l'horaire libre, il y a l'horaire variable qui peut prendre différentes formes.
☐ durée du travail

425. horloge de pointage
Syn. de **horodateur**

426. horloge pointeuse
Syn. de **horodateur**

427. horodateur n. m.;
horloge de pointage n. f.;
horloge pointeuse n. f.;
pointeuse 1 n. f.
time clock;
punch clock
Horloge munie d'un mécanisme permettant d'imprimer la date et l'heure, qui est utilisée pour enregistrer l'heure d'entrée et de sortie du salarié d'un établissement ou l'heure du début et de la fin d'un travail.
V. a. **totalisateur**
☐ durée du travail

I

428. indemnité n. f.
compensation;
allowance
Somme d'argent versée au salarié pour compenser certaines pertes ou pour rembourser certains frais.
V. a. **prime**
☐ supplément salarial

429. indemnité compensatrice de congé payé n. f.
vacation pay on termination;
pay in lieu of vacation
Indemnité versée par l'employeur au salarié qui quitte l'entreprise avant d'avoir pris son congé annuel, en tout ou en partie.
☐ supplément salarial

430. indemnité compensatrice de délai-congé
Syn. de **indemnité compensatrice de préavis**

431. indemnité compensatrice de préavis n. f.;
indemnité compensatrice de délai-congé n. f.;
indemnité de préavis n. f.;
indemnité de délai-congé n. f.
compensation in lieu of notice;
pay in lieu of notice
Indemnité versée au salarié en compensation du salaire qu'il aurait touché pendant le préavis si l'employeur ne l'avait dispensé de travailler durant cette période.
☐ supplément salarial

432. indemnité de cessation d'emploi n. f.;
indemnité de départ n. f.
Terme à éviter : prime de séparation
severance pay;
termination pay;
separation pay;
termination allowance
Indemnité versée au salarié à l'occasion de son départ.
Note. — Cette indemnité est généralement calculée en fonction de son ancienneté.
☐ supplément salarial

433. indemnité de changement de résidence
Syn. de **indemnité de déménagement**

434. indemnité de cherté de vie n. f.;
indemnité de vie chère n. f.
Terme à éviter : boni de vie chère
cost-of-living allowance
Abrév. *COLA*
V. o. *cost of living allowance;*
cost-of-living bonus
V. o. *cost of living bonus*
Indemnité versée au salarié en raison de l'augmentation du coût de la vie.
V. a. **clause d'indexation**
☐ supplément salarial

435. indemnité de congé
Syn. de **indemnité de congé payé**

436. indemnité de congé payé n. f.;
indemnité de congé n. f.
Termes à éviter : paie de vacances;
allocation de vacances
vacation pay
Indemnité équivalant au substitut du salaire touché par le salarié pendant son congé annuel.
☐ supplément salarial

437. indemnité de délai-congé
Syn. de **indemnité compensatrice de préavis**

438. indemnité de déménagement n. f.;
indemnité de changement de résidence n. f.
relocation allowance;
moving allowance
Indemnité versée par l'employeur en remboursement des frais occasionnés par un changement du lieu de travail nécessitant un changement de résidence.
☐ supplément salarial

439. indemnité de départ
Syn. de **indemnité de cessation d'emploi**

440. indemnité de déplacement n. f.
travel allowance
Indemnité versée par l'employeur en remboursement des frais de voyage et de séjour du salarié dans des lieux extérieurs à l'entreprise et pour les besoins de celle-ci.

Note. — Quand le salarié doit se déplacer pour les besoins de l'entreprise tout en pouvant regagner son domicile le jour même, on pourra tenir compte d'indemnités pour défrayer les repas et le transport. On pourra utiliser alors *indemnité de petit déplacement.*
V. a. **frais de voyage**
☐ supplément salarial

441. indemnité de licenciement n. f.
severance pay;
dismissal compensation;
dismissal pay;
lay-off pay
V. o. *layoff pay*
Indemnité versée au salarié pour le dédommager du préjudice que lui cause son licenciement.

Note. — Cette indemnité est généralement calculée en fonction de son ancienneté.
☐ supplément salarial

442. indemnité de panier
Syn. de **indemnité de repas**

443. indemnité de petit déplacement
V. **indemnité de déplacement**

444. indemnité de préavis
Syn. de **indemnité compensatrice de préavis**

445. indemnité de précarité d'emploi n. f.
instability of work bonus;
instability bonus
Indemnité à laquelle a droit le salarié d'une entreprise de travail temporaire pour chaque mission effectivement accomplie.

Note. — Cette notion existe dans le *Code du travail* français.
☐ supplément salarial

446. indemnité de présence n. f.
reporting pay;
call-in pay
Indemnité versée au salarié qui, s'étant présenté au travail à l'heure convenue, n'est affecté à aucune tâche par l'employeur.
☐ supplément salarial

447. indemnité de repas n. f.;
indemnité de panier n. f. (FR);
prime de panier n. f. (FR)
meal allowance

Indemnité versée au salarié contraint de prendre une collation ou un repas en raison des conditions particulières de travail ou de son horaire.
☐ supplément salarial

448. indemnité de séjour n. f.
living allowance
Indemnité versée par l'employeur au salarié en remboursement des frais de repas et de logement du salarié en déplacement.
☐ supplément salarial

449. indemnité de vie chère
Syn. de **indemnité de cherté de vie**

450. indemnité forfaitaire quotidienne
n. f.;
forfait quotidien n. m.;
prix de journée n. m. (FR)
Terme à éviter : per diem
per diem allowance
Indemnité fixe accordée chaque jour à un salarié en déplacement pour tenir lieu du remboursement de certains frais.
☐ supplément salarial

451. indemnité kilométrique n. f.
mileage allowance
Indemnité calculée au kilomètre parcouru et versée au salarié qui se sert de son véhicule personnel pour les besoins du service.
V. a. **indemnité pour usage de véhicule personnel**
☐ supplément salarial

452. indemnité pour fonctions judiciaires
n. f.
jury and witness duty allowance
Indemnité accordée par l'employeur au salarié appelé à agir à titre de juré ou à comparaître comme témoin.
☐ supplément salarial

453. indemnité pour usage de véhicule personnel n. f.
mileage allowance
Indemnité forfaitaire versée au salarié qui se sert de son véhicule personnel pour les besoins du service.
V. a. **indemnité kilométrique**
☐ supplément salarial

454. indexation
V. **clause d'indexation**

455. infraction disciplinaire
Syn. de **faute disciplinaire**

456. intérimaire n.
temporary employee
Salarié qui remplace temporairement un membre du personnel de l'entreprise.
☐ gestion des ressources humaines

J

457. jour chômé n. m.
non-working day;
day off
Jour où il y a cessation de travail.
☐ durée du travail

458. jour civil n. m.
Terme à éviter : jour de calendrier
calendar day
Jour allant de 0 à 24 heures.
☐ durée du travail

459. jour de calendrier
Terme à éviter
V. **jour civil**

460. jour de congé annuel accumulé
n. m.
accrued leave;
accrued vacation
Jour de congé annuel que le salarié accumule chaque mois et qu'il ne pourra habituellement prendre qu'à l'expiration de la période de référence.
V. a. **congé annuel acquis**
☐ congé

461. jour de repos n. m.
day off
Jour pendant lequel le salarié ne travaille pas.
☐ durée du travail

462. jour férié n. m.
Termes à éviter : congé statutaire;
jour non juridique
holiday;
statutory holiday;
legal holiday;
public holiday;
non-juridical day

Jour où il y a cessation de travail pour la célébration d'une fête religieuse ou civile soit en vertu d'une loi (fête légale) ou en vertu d'une entente entre la direction et le syndicat.
☐ durée du travail

463. jour férié payé n. m.
Terme à éviter : congé payé
paid holiday;
paid statutory holiday;
paid legal holiday;
paid public holiday
Jour férié pour lequel le salarié est rémunéré.
☐ travail

464. jour juridique
Terme à éviter
V. **jour ouvrable**

465. jour non juridique
Terme à éviter
V. **jour férié**

466. jour ouvrable n. m.
Terme à éviter : jour juridique
working day;
juridical day
Jour normalement consacré au travail.
☐ durée du travail

467. journalier
Syn. de **manœuvre**

468. journalière
V. **manœuvre**

469. junior
Terme à éviter
V. **débutant**

470. junior
Terme à éviter
V. **second**

471. juridiction
Terme à éviter
V. **champ d'application**

472. juridiction
Terme à éviter
V. **compétence**

L

473. label
Syn. de **étiquette syndicale**

474. libération syndicale
Syn. de congé pour fonctions syndicales

475. libéré
V. **congé pour fonctions syndicales**

476. libérée
V. **congé pour fonctions syndicales**

477. licenciement n. m.
lay-off
V. o. *layoff;*
dismissal;
discharge
Rupture unilatérale et définitive de la part de l'employeur qui met fin au contrat de travail du salarié pour des motifs non imputables au salarié, motifs d'ordre économique ou technique.
Notes. — 1. En France, on utilise indifféremment *licenciement* ou *congédiement*. Au Québec, l'usage n'est pas fixé.
2. On rencontre *débauchage* comme synonyme de *licenciement*. Il ne nous semble pas utile de le retenir.
V. a. **congédiement**
☐ cessation d'emploi

478. lieu de travail n. m.
work place;
work area;
work space;
place of work;
place of employment;
working point
Endroit où le salarié effectue son travail.
Note. — On rencontre aussi *point d'attache* dans les dictionnaires généraux et *port d'attache*, notamment dans la fonction publique québécoise. *Port d'attache* aurait subi un glissement de sens. Sans rejeter ces termes, nous privilégions *lieu de travail*.
☐ condition de travail

479. ligne de piquetage
Syn. de **piquet de grève**

480. liste d'admissibilité n. f.
Terme à éviter : liste d'éligibilité
eligibility list

Liste des noms des personnes jugées aptes à exercer un emploi ou à subir les épreuves de sélection en vue de l'obtenir.

Note. — Dans la fonction publique québécoise, on utilise *déclaration d'aptitudes*.

☐ recrutement et engagement du personnel

481. liste d'éligibilité
Terme à éviter
V. **liste d'admissibilité**

482. litige
V. **grief**

483. local
Terme à éviter
V. **section locale**

484. lock-out n. m.
lockout
V. o. *lock-out*

Refus par un employeur de fournir du travail à ses salariés en vue de les contraindre à accepter certaines conditions de travail ou de contraindre pareillement des salariés d'un autre employeur.

Note. — La définition est fondée sur celle du *Code du travail* du Québec.

☐ grève et lock-out

M

485. maintien d'affiliation n. m.
maintenance of membership

Forme de sécurité syndicale en vertu de laquelle les salariés qui sont déjà membres d'un syndicat au moment de la conclusion d'une convention collective ou qui le deviennent par la suite sont obligés de le demeurer pendant toute sa durée comme condition de la conservation de leur emploi.

☐ syndicalisme

486. maintien d'emplois fictifs n. m.
featherbedding

Pratique syndicale visant à protéger les emplois devenus inutiles.

☐ syndicalisme

487. maître n.
master;
journeyman

Dans certains métiers, ouvrier qualifié ayant acquis un haut niveau de compétence par sa formation et son expérience professionnelles.

Note. — Les maîtres électriciens et les maîtres tuyauteurs (dénommés *maîtres mécaniciens en tuyauterie*) sont autorisés par la loi à travailler à leur compte.

☐ formation et perfectionnement du personnel

488. maladie industrielle
Terme à éviter
V. **maladie professionnelle**

489. maladie occupationnelle
Terme à éviter
V. **maladie professionnelle**

490. maladie professionnelle n. f.
Termes à éviter : maladie industrielle ; maladie occupationnelle
occupational illness;
industry-related illness;
industrial disease;
occupational disease

Altération de la santé du salarié survenant par le fait ou à l'occasion du travail.

☐ condition de travail

491. manoeuvre n.;
journalier n. m.
journalière n. f.
labourer
V. o. *laborer;*
unskilled worker

Ouvrier affecté à des tâches n'exigeant qu'une mise au courant sommaire.

Note. — *Journalier* est d'usage québécois.

☐ gestion des ressources humaines

492. manquement disciplinaire
Syn. de **faute disciplinaire**

493. maraudage n. m.
raiding

Tentative de la part d'un syndicat de convaincre des salariés d'y adhérer en quittant celui auquel ils appartiennent.

☐ syndicalisme

494. **marche continue** n. f.;
fonctionnement continu n. m.
Terme à éviter : opération continue
continuous operation
Suite ininterrompue de travaux, en raison
même de la nature du travail, devant être
nécessairement assurée à tout moment du
jour, de la nuit et de la semaine.
☐ durée du travail

495. **marque d'union**
Terme à éviter
V. **étiquette syndicale**

496. **médiateur** n. m.
médiatrice n. f.
mediator
Personne chargée de la médiation.
☐ conflit du travail

497. **médiation** n. f.
mediation
Procédure exceptionnelle d'intervention
dans un conflit de travail non prévue par
le *Code du travail* du Québec qui survient
habituellement lorsque la conciliation a
échoué.
☐ conflit du travail

498. **médiatrice**
V. **médiateur**

499. **membre d'un ordre professionnel** n.
member of a professional corporation
Personne qui effectue un travail à caractère
intellectuel ou technique sous le contrôle
d'un ordre professionnel pour son propre
compte ou pour le compte d'autrui.
Note. — Ce terme a fait l'objet d'un avis de
recommandation de l'Office de la langue
française, paru à la *Gazette officielle* du
28 avril 1990.
☐ travail

500. **membre d'une profession libérale**
Syn. de **professionnel libéral**

501. **membre du bureau** n.
Terme à éviter : officier
officer
Dirigeant syndical élu au bureau d'un organisme syndical.
☐ syndicalisme

502. **mémoire d'entente**
Syn. de **protocole d'accord**

503. **mensuel**
Syn. de **salarié mensuel**

504. **mensuelle**
Syn. de **salarié mensuel**

505. **mérite**
Terme à éviter
V. **fond**

506. **mésentente**
V. **différend**

507. **mesure de rattrapage** n. f.;
mesure de redressement n. f.
Terme à éviter : action positive
affirmative action
Mesure qui vise à éliminer la discrimination
passée ou actuelle subie par un groupe de
personnes en leur accordant temporairement certains avantages préférentiels.
☐ gestion des ressources humaines

508. **mesure de redressement**
Syn. de **mesure de rattrapage**

509. **mesure disciplinaire**
Syn. de **sanction disciplinaire**

510. **métier** n. m.;
profession 1 n. f.
Terme à éviter : occupation
craft;
trade;
occupation;
profession
Activité pour laquelle une personne a été
formée et dont elle tire ses moyens
d'existence.
Note. — Ce terme a fait l'objet d'un avis de
recommandation de l'Office de la langue
française, paru à la *Gazette officielle* du
28 avril 1990.
☐ travail

511. **mettre en disponibilité**
V. **disponibilité**

512. **minutes**
Terme à éviter
V. **compte rendu**

513. **minutes**
Terme à éviter
V. **procès-verbal**

514. mise à jour n. f.
refresher course;
updating
Formation professionnelle permettant de tenir au courant les salariés des plus récentes innovations intervenues dans leur secteur d'activité.
☐ formation et perfectionnement du personnel

515. mise à pied conservatoire n. f.
suspension pending investigation
Mesure provisoire prise par l'employeur qui entraîne la cessation du travail du salarié jusqu'à la conclusion d'une enquête sur les agissements de ce dernier.
Note. — Nous avons opté pour l'adjectif *conservatoire* parce que : 1) il est utilisé en France ; 2) le terme *mise à pied administrative* n'est pas vraiment implanté ici ; 3) il est facile de faire un lien avec cet adjectif pour les personnes ayant des notions de droit.
V. a. **mise à pied disciplinaire ; mise à pied économique**
☐ cessation d'emploi

516. mise à pied disciplinaire n. f.
lay-off
V. o. *layoff;*
suspension;
disciplinary lay-off
V. o. *disciplinary layoff*
Décision de l'employeur de suspendre de façon temporaire ou indéterminée l'exécution du contrat de travail du salarié pour des motifs d'ordre disciplinaire.
Note. — En France, le terme *mise à pied* utilisé sans qualificatif a le sens de « mise à pied disciplinaire » ; au Québec, il est utilisé au sens de « mise à pied économique ». Dans les documents lexicographiques français, on utilise *suspension* surtout pour les fonctionnaires publics. Cependant, contrairement au Québec, leur rémunération est maintenue à moins d'avis contraire. Dans le droit du travail français, on trouve fréquemment *suspension du contrat de travail*. Le contrat est effectivement suspendu lorsque les parties sont temporairement dans l'impossibilité d'exécuter leurs obligations. Les causes peuvent être le fait du salarié, de l'employeur ou étrangères à la volonté de l'une ou l'autre partie. Voici quelques cas de suspension : maladie, grève, mise à pied disciplinaire, force majeure, etc.

V. a. **mise à pied économique ; mise à pied conservatoire**
☐ cessation d'emploi

517. mise à pied économique n. f. ;
mise en chômage technique n. f.
(FR)
lay-off
V. o. *layoff*
Décision de l'employeur de suspendre de façon temporaire ou indéterminée l'exécution du contrat de travail du salarié pour des motifs non imputables au salarié, motifs d'ordre économique ou technique.
Note. — En France, on utilise souvent *mise en chômage technique*.
V. a. **mise à pied disciplinaire ; mise à pied conservatoire**
☐ cessation d'emploi

518. mise en chômage technique
Syn. de **mise à pied économique**

519. mise en disponibilité
V. **disponibilité**

520. monétaire
Terme à éviter
V. **pécuniaire**

521. monopole syndical n. m.
exclusive representation
Droit exclusif d'un syndicat d'organiser ou de représenter un groupe de travailleurs donné.
☐ syndicalisme

522. motivation du congédiement
V. **congédiement justifié**

523. mutation n. f.
transfer
Changement de poste ou d'emploi pouvant entraîner un changement du lieu de résidence.
Note. — Le terme *mutation* est utilisé lorsque : 1) la rémunération est identique ; 2) les responsabilités sont du même niveau ; 3) le changement est effectué à la demande ou avec le consentement du salarié.
V. a. **transfert**
☐ mouvement du personnel

N

524. négociateur n. m.
négociatrice n. f.
negotiator

Personne mandatée par une partie pour discuter en vue d'en arriver à un accord avec une autre.
☐ conflit du travail

525. négociation collective n. f.
collective bargaining

Ensemble des discussions entre la partie patronale et la partie syndicale en vue d'en arriver à un accord qui se concrétisera sous la forme d'une convention collective.
☐ conflit du travail

526. négociation de branche n. f.
Terme à éviter : négociation sectorielle
industry-wide bargaining

Négociation collective qui a lieu pour une industrie ou un service donné dans les limites d'un territoire plus ou moins vaste où les représentants de tous les syndicats et de tous les employeurs se réunissent à une même table de négociation.
☐ conflit du travail

527. négociation sectorielle
Terme à éviter
V. **négociation de branche**

528. négociatrice
Syn. de **négociateur**

529. non-concurrence
V. **clause de non-concurrence**

530. notation du personnel
Syn. de **appréciation du personnel**

531. notice
Terme à éviter
V. **délai-congé**

O

532. observation
V. **avertissement**

533. occasionnel n. m.
occasionnelle n. f.
casual employee

Salarié engagé temporairement en raison d'un surcroît de travail ou pour un projet spécial.
☐ gestion des ressources humaines

534. occasionnel
Terme à éviter
V. **temporaire**

535. occasionnelle
V. **occasionnel**

536. occupation
Terme à éviter
V. **emploi**

537. occupation
Terme à éviter
V. **métier**

538. officier
Terme à éviter
V. **membre du bureau**

539. officier de syndicat
Terme à éviter
V. **dirigeant syndical**

540. officier syndical
Terme à éviter
V. **dirigeant syndical**

541. opérateur
Terme à éviter
V. **conducteur**

542. opération continue
Terme à éviter
V. **marche continue**

543. opération continue
Terme à éviter
V. **travail continu**

544. ordonnance des vacances
Terme à éviter
V. **ordre des départs**

545. ordre des départs n. m.
Termes à éviter : cédule des vacances; ordonnance des vacances
vacation schedule

Ordre dans lequel les salariés vont partir en congé.
□ congé

546. ordre professionnel n. m.
Terme à éviter : corporation professionnelle
professional corporation

Groupement professionnel, ayant une personnalité juridique, auquel sont affiliés les membres de la profession et bénéficiant de prérogatives étatiques telles que le pouvoir réglementaire et le pouvoir disciplinaire.

Note. — Ce terme a fait l'objet d'un avis de recommandation de l'Office de la langue française, paru à la *Gazette officielle* du 28 avril 1990.

V. a. **profession**
□ travail

547. organisateur
V. **permanent syndical**

548. ouvrier n. m.
ouvrière n. f.;
col bleu n.;
travailleur manuel n. m.
travailleuse manuelle n. f.
labourer
V. o. *laborer;*
manual worker;
blue-collar worker

Salarié effectuant un travail manuel dans une usine, un atelier ou sur un chantier.

Note. — Ce sens se rapproche de la notion sociologique américaine de *col bleu*. Il s'oppose à *employé.*
□ travail

549. ouvrier de relève n. m.
ouvrière de relève n. f.
relief worker

Ouvrier supplémentaire nécessaire à l'établissement du travail continu.
□ durée du travail

550. ouvrier de renfort n. m.
ouvrière de renfort n. f.
spare

Salarié polyvalent affecté à un poste ou à un autre pour combler un besoin particulier de l'entreprise.

V. a. **équipe volante**
□ durée du travail

551. ouvrier général
Terme à éviter
V. **travailleur toutes mains**

552. ouvrier professionnel
Syn. de **ouvrier qualifié**

553. ouvrier qualifié n. m.
ouvrière qualifiée n. f.;
ouvrier professionnel n. m. (FR)
ouvrière professionnelle n. f. (FR);
homme de métier n. m.;
femme de métier n. f.
skilled worker;
tradesman

Ouvrier exécutant des travaux qualifiés courants exigeant des connaissances qui ne peuvent être acquises que par une formation professionnelle d'une certaine durée ou la pratique suffisante d'un métier.

Note. — Les hommes de métier sont des ouvriers qualifiés qui travaillent dans l'industrie de la construction, par exemple, les électriciens, soudeurs, menuisiers, peintres, etc. Au Québec, le terme *homme de métier* est d'usage courant. Il est réservé aux métiers dits traditionnels.
□ formation et perfectionnement du personnel

554. ouvrier spécialisé n. m.
ouvrière spécialisée n. f.
semi-skilled worker

Ouvrier qui, sans avoir fait un véritable apprentissage ou avoir reçu un enseignement professionnel particulier, exécute des travaux nécessitant une certaine formation préalable ou une certaine expérience.
□ formation et perfectionnement du personnel

555. ouvrière
V. **ouvrier**

556. ouvrière de relève
V. **ouvrier de relève**

557. ouvrière de renfort
V. **ouvrier de renfort**

558. ouvrière professionnelle
V. **ouvrier qualifié**

559. ouvrière qualifiée
V. **ouvrier qualifié**

560. ouvrière spécialisée
V. **ouvrier spécialisé**

561. paie n. f.
V. o. **paye** n. f.
pay

Somme d'argent que touche périodiquement le salarié en contrepartie de son travail.
☐ rémunération du travail

562. paie de vacances
Terme à éviter
V. **indemnité de congé payé**

563. paiemaître
Terme à éviter
V. **payeur**

564. paiement en espèces n. m.
payment in cash;
cash payment

Versement du salaire en argent comptant.
☐ rémunération du travail

565. paiement par chèque n. m.
payment by cheque

Versement du salaire par chèque.

Note. — Au point de vue strictement juridique, le chèque est tiré sur une banque. Dans l'usage, il est tiré sur toute institution financière.
☐ rémunération du travail

566. paiement par dépôt direct
Terme à éviter
V. **paiement par virement automatique**

567. paiement par virement automatique n. m.
Terme à éviter : paiement par dépôt direct
payment by direct deposit

Versement du salaire par le transfert de fonds du compte de l'employeur à celui du salarié.
☐ rémunération du travail

568. partage du travail n. m.
work sharing

Politique qui consiste soit à maintenir ou à accroître le nombre d'emplois disponibles, évitant ainsi la mise à pied ou le licenciement des travailleurs dans une entreprise.

Note. — Pour atteindre cet objectif, diverses mesures peuvent être prises : l'augmentation des postes à temps partiel, la réduction de la durée du travail, l'allongement des congés payés, etc.
V. a. **emploi partagé**
☐ gestion des ressources humaines

569. paye
V. o. de **paie**

570. payeur n. m.
payeuse n. f.
Terme à éviter : paiemaître
paymaster

Salarié chargé de payer le personnel dans une entreprise, une administration ou un bureau.
☐ rémunération du travail

571. payeuse
V. **payeur**

572. pécule de vacances
Syn. de **prime de vacances**

573. pécuniaire adj.
Terme à éviter : monétaire
monetary

Qui a rapport à l'argent.

Note. — Dans le contexte de la négociation, il peut s'agir, par exemple, d'offres pécuniaires ou plus précisément salariales faites par l'employeur.
☐ rémunération du travail

574. per diem
Terme à éviter
V. **indemnité forfaitaire quotidienne**

575. perfectionnement n. m.
professional development;
additional training;
further training

Formation ayant pour but d'augmenter la compétence et l'efficacité du salarié.
☐ formation et perfectionnement du personnel

576. période d'adaptation n. f.;
période de familiarisation n. f.
familiarization period;
orientation period;
trial period

Période pendant laquelle le salarié s'initie à de nouvelles fonctions puisqu'il occupe un nouveau poste.

Note. — On ne rencontre le terme *période de familiarisation* que dans certaines conventions collectives québécoises.
□ mouvement du personnel

577. période d'éligibilité
Terme à éviter
V. **période de référence 2**

578. période d'essai n. f.
Terme à éviter : période de probation
probationary period;
trial period;
probation;
probation period
Période suivant l'entrée en service du salarié pendant laquelle l'employeur porte un jugement sur ce dernier.
Note. — Si le jugement de l'employeur est positif, l'engagement est confirmé.
□ recrutement et engagement du personnel

579. période de familiarisation
Syn. de **période d'adaptation**

580. période de probation
Terme à éviter
V. **période d'essai**

581. période de qualification
Terme à éviter
V. **période de référence 2**

582. période de référence 1 n. f.
accounting period
Période sur laquelle est calculée la durée normale du travail dans le cadre de l'horaire variable.
□ durée du travail

583. période de référence 2 n. f.
Termes à éviter : période de qualification ; période d'éligibilité
eligibility period;
qualifying period
Période pendant laquelle le salarié acquiert certains droits.
Note. — Il y a une période de référence pour le congé annuel, l'assurance-chômage, etc.
□ congé

584. période des congés
Syn. de **période des congés annuels**

585. période des congés annuels n. f.;
période des congés n. f.;
période des vacances n. f.
vacation period
Période de l'année au cours de laquelle le salarié doit prendre ses vacances.
□ durée du travail

586. période des vacances
Syn. de **période des congés annuels**

587. permanent n. m.
permanente n. f.;
travailleur permanent n. m.
travailleuse permanente n. f.;
salarié permanent n. m.
salariée permanente n. f.
Termes à éviter : régulier ; salarié régulier ; travailleur régulier ; employé régulier
permanent employee;
regular employee
Salarié dont l'engagement devient définitif après avoir réussi sa période d'essai.
□ gestion des ressources humaines

588. permanent syndical n. m.
permanente syndicale n. f.
union staff;
union representative;
union staff member
Personne engagée à long terme par un organisme syndical pour y exercer des fonctions de nature syndicale.
Note. — Ce terme est générique et englobe les notions de *représentant syndical*, de *conseiller syndical* ou *technique*, d'*organisateur*, etc.
V. a. **agent syndical**
□ syndicalisme

589. permanente
V. **permanent**

590. permanente syndicale
V. **permanent syndical**

591. permis d'absence
V. **autorisation d'absence**

592. permutation n. f.
permutation;
exchange of duties
Action qui consiste pour deux salariés à échanger leur poste ou leur emploi qui sont équivalents.

Note. — La permutation s'effectue sur la demande des salariés ; elle est autorisée par l'employeur. Elle implique généralement un changement de lieu.
☐ mouvement du personnel

593. personne handicapée n. f. ;
handicapé n. m.
handicapée n. f.
handicapped person ;
disabled person

Personne dont les possibilités d'acquérir ou de conserver un emploi sont effectivement réduites par suite d'une insuffisance ou d'une diminution de ses capacités physiques ou mentales.

Note. — D'un point de vue strictement terminologique, il est possible d'utiliser le terme *handicapé*. Cependant, pour des raisons sociologiques, nous privilégions *personne handicapée*.
☐ condition de travail

594. personnel appointé
V. **salarié appointé**

595. personnel horaire
V. **salarié horaire**

596. phase
Syn. de **stade**

597. piquet de grève n. m. ;
ligne de piquetage n. f.
picket line

Regroupement de piqueteurs.

Note. — *Ligne de piquetage* est d'usage québécois.
☐ grève et lock-out

598. piquetage n. m.
picketing

Manifestation collective de salariés aux abords d'un lieu de travail à l'occasion d'une mésentente.

Notes. — 1. Il peut y avoir piquetage sans qu'il y ait conflit du travail.
2. *Piquetage* est d'usage québécois.
☐ conflit du travail

599. piqueter v. ;
faire du piquet loc. v.
picket, to

Faire du piquetage.

Note. — *Piqueter* est d'usage québécois.
☐ conflit du travail

600. piqueteur n. m.
piqueteuse n. f.
picket ;
picketer

Personne participant à un piquetage.

Note. — *Piqueteur* est d'usage québécois.
☐ conflit du travail

601. piqueteuse
V. **piqueteur**

602. place d'affaires
Terme à éviter
V. **établissement**

603. plage fixe n. f.
core time ;
core hours

Période de la journée, dans le cadre de l'horaire variable, pendant laquelle tout le personnel doit être présent.
☐ durée du travail

604. plage mobile n. f.
flexible band ;
flexible core

Période de la journée, dans le cadre de l'horaire variable, pendant laquelle le personnel peut choisir ses temps de présence ou d'absence.
☐ durée du travail

605. plan d'égalité professionnelle n. m. ;
programme d'accès à l'égalité n. m.
Terme à éviter : action positive
affirmative action program ;
affirmative action plan

Programme ayant pour objectif d'éliminer la discrimination subie par un groupe de personnes en favorisant leur accès à l'emploi et en leur obtenant un traitement équitable dans le parcours professionnel.

Note. — Dans la législation fédérale, on utilise *programme d'équité en matière d'emploi*.
☐ gestion des ressources humaines

606. planifier le calendrier de la production
V. **calendrier de production**

607. poinçonnage
Terme à éviter
V. **pointage**

608. point d'attache
V. **lieu de travail**

609. point de départ de l'ancienneté n. m.
Terme à éviter : date d'ancienneté
date of seniority;
seniority date

Moment à partir duquel l'ancienneté s'accumule.
☐ durée du travail

610. pointage n. m.
Terme à éviter : poinçonnage
punch

Enregistrement, au moyen d'un appareil, du temps de présence du salarié.
V. a. **horodateur**; **totalisateur**
☐ durée du travail

611. pointeau
Syn. de **pointeur**

612. pointeur n. m.
pointeuse 2 n. f.;
pointeau n. m.
Terme à éviter : preneur de temps
time keeper

Salarié chargé de la gestion du temps du personnel.
☐ durée du travail

613. pointeuse 1
Syn. de **horodateur**

614. pointeuse 2
V. **pointeur**

615. port d'attache
V. **lieu de travail**

616. position
Terme à éviter
V. **emploi**

617. position
Terme à éviter
V. **poste de travail 3**

618. poste 1 n. m.;
poste de travail 1 n. m.;
quart 2 n. m.;
faction n. f.
Termes à éviter : chiffre; shift
shift

Période comprenant un certain nombre d'heures dans une journée durant lesquelles le salarié effectue son travail.

Notes. — 1. *Quart* est un terme tiré du vocabulaire de la marine que le *Grand Robert* définit comme suit : «Période de quatre heures (primitivement six heures, quart de la journée) pendant laquelle une partie de l'équipage, à tour de rôle, est de service.» Au Québec, *quart* est fortement répandu dans le sens de «poste» qui peut être utilisé par extension.
2. *Travailler sur le shift de* ou *être sur le shift de* est à remplacer par *être affecté au poste de* ou *être de.*
V. a. **équipe**
☐ durée du travail

619. poste 2
Syn. de **poste de travail 2**

620. poste 3
Syn. de **poste de travail 3**

621. poste clé n. m.;
emploi clé n. m.
key job

Poste d'importance considéré comme essentiel au fonctionnement d'une organisation.
☐ organisation du travail

622. poste d'après-midi
Syn. de **poste du soir**

623. poste de jour n. m.;
poste du matin n. m.;
quart de jour 2 n. m.;
quart du matin 2 n. m.
day shift;
first shift

Période de travail qui débute le matin et se termine durant l'après-midi.

Notes. — 1. Si l'on désire mettre l'accent sur le début de la période de travail plutôt que sur la période elle-même, on utilisera *poste du matin.*
2. *Quart de jour* est d'usage québécois.
☐ durée du travail

624. poste de nuit n. m.;
quart de nuit 2 n. m.
night shift;
third shift;
graveyard shift

Période de travail qui débute généralement à minuit et se termine durant la matinée.

Note. — *Quart de nuit* est d'usage québécois.
☐ durée du travail

625. poste de travail 1
Syn. de **poste 1**

626. poste de travail 2 n. m. ;
poste 2 n. m.
work station;
work area;
work location

Lieu où une personne effectue son travail.
□ condition de travail

627. poste de travail 3 n. m. ;
poste 3 n. m.
Terme à éviter : position
job

Emploi déterminé dans une entreprise dont une personne est titulaire.
□ organisation du travail

628. poste du matin
Syn. de **poste de jour**

629. poste du soir n. m. ;
poste d'après-midi n. m. ;
quart du soir n. m. ;
quart d'après-midi 2 n. m.
evening shift;
second shift

Période de travail qui débute l'après-midi et se termine durant la soirée.
Notes. — 1. Si l'on désire mettre l'accent sur le début de la période de travail plutôt que sur la période elle-même, on utilisera *poste d'après-midi*.
2. *Quart du soir* est d'usage québécois.
□ durée du travail

630. poste fractionné n. m.
split shift

Poste dont la durée est répartie en au moins deux tranches.
□ durée du travail

631. poste vacant n. m. ;
emploi vacant n. m. ;
vacance n. f.
job vacancy;
job opening;
vacancy;
opening

Poste sans titulaire.
□ organisation du travail

632. préavis n. m.
notice

Avis que la partie qui prend l'initiative de la rupture d'un contrat de travail est tenue de remettre à l'autre partie dans un délai et des conditions déterminées.
□ cessation d'emploi

633. précompte de la cotisation syndicale
Syn. de **retenue de la cotisation syndicale**

634. précompte syndical
Syn. de **retenue de la cotisation syndicale**

635. premier
Syn. de **principal**

636. preneur de temps
Terme à éviter
V. **pointeur**

637. prestation n. f. ;
allocation n. f.
allowance;
benefit;
compensation

Somme d'argent versée par l'État que reçoit une personne dans des situations particulières.
Note. — Dans certains cas, il peut s'agir d'une somme versée par un employeur, un assureur, etc.
□ supplément salarial

638. prestation complémentaire de chômage n. f.
Terme à éviter : prestation supplémentaire de chômage
supplementary unemployment benefit
Abrév. *SUB*

Prestation versée en vertu d'une clause de convention collective, à même une caisse d'indemnités complémentaires de chômage afin de combler, en tout ou en partie, lorsque des salariés sont mis à pied, la différence entre le salaire normal et les prestations du régime public d'assurance-chômage.
Note. — Il s'agit bien d'un complément et non d'un supplément.
□ supplément salarial

639. prestation supplémentaire de chômage
Terme à éviter
V. **prestation complémentaire de chômage**

640. prime n. f.
premium;
bonus

Somme d'argent versée au salarié en compensation de certains inconvénients ou risques ou encore à titre de récompense ou d'encouragement.
V. a. **indemnité**
☐ supplément salarial

641. **prime d'ancienneté** n. f.
Termes à éviter : prime de service ; boni d'ancienneté
seniority bonus ;
long service pay
Prime accordée au salarié en raison de son ancienneté.
☐ supplément salarial

642. **prime d'après-midi**
Syn. de **prime du soir**

643. **prime d'équipe 1**
Syn. de **prime de poste**

644. **prime d'équipe 2**
Syn. de **prime de rendement collectif**

645. **prime de nuit** n. f.
night shift premium ;
night shift differential
Prime accordée au salarié affecté au poste de nuit.
☐ supplément salarial

646. **prime de panier**
Syn. de **indemnité de repas**

647. **prime de poste** n. f. ;
prime d'équipe 1 n. f. ;
prime de quart n. f.
shift premium ;
shift differential
Prime accordée au salarié pour compenser les inconvénients du travail par équipes.
Note. — *Prime de quart* est d'usage québécois.
☐ supplément salarial

648. **prime de quart**
Syn. de **prime de poste**

649. **prime de rendement** n. f. ;
boni n. m.
Terme à éviter : bonus
incentive pay ;
production bonus
Prime versée au salarié qui atteint ou dépasse un certain niveau de rendement.

Notes. — 1. *Travailler au bonus* est à remplacer par *travailler au rendement.*
2. Le synonyme *boni* est peu usité.
☐ supplément salarial

650. **prime de rendement collectif** n. f. ;
prime d'équipe 2 n. f.
group bonus
Prime accordée à un groupe de salariés en raison de la qualité de leur production et de l'amplitude de leur performance collective.
☐ supplément salarial

651. **prime de séparation**
Terme à éviter
V. **indemnité de cessation d'emploi**

652. **prime de service**
Terme à éviter
V. **prime d'ancienneté**

653. **prime de vacances** n. f. ;
pécule de vacances n. m.
vacation pay ;
vacation bonus ;
holiday allowance
Somme versée au salarié en sus de l'indemnité de congé payé à l'occasion de ses vacances.
☐ supplément salarial

654. **prime du soir** n. f. ;
prime d'après-midi n. f.
evening shift premium ;
evening shift differential ;
afternoon shift premium ;
afternoon shift differential
Somme accordée au salarié affecté au poste du soir.
☐ supplément salarial

655. **principal** adj. ;
premier adj.
Terme à éviter : sénior
senior
Se dit du travailleur qui a atteint le grade supérieur dans une catégorie.
☐ gestion des ressources humaines

656. **prix de journée**
Syn. de **indemnité forfaitaire quotidienne**

657. **procédure de grief**
Syn. de **procédure de règlement des griefs**

658. procédure de réclamation
Syn. de **procédure de règlement des griefs**

659. procédure de règlement des griefs n. f. ;
procédure de grief n. f. ;
procédure de réclamation n. f.
grievance procedure
Ensemble des formalités qui doivent être observées pour parvenir au règlement des griefs.
V. a. **grief**
☐ conflit du travail

660. procès-verbal n. m.
Terme à éviter : minutes
minutes
Compte rendu officiel rédigé à la suite de ce qui a été dit, fait ou décidé au cours d'une réunion ou d'une assemblée délibérante.
V. a. **compte rendu**
☐ travail

661. profession 1
Syn. de **métier**

662. profession 2 n. f.
profession ;
occupation
Métier à caractère intellectuel ou artistique, qui confère un certain prestige à ceux qui l'exercent.
Notes. — 1. Le terme anglais *profession* a un sens plus restreint que son équivalent français. Il est limité aux métiers auxquels on accède par des études supérieures, principalement les professions libérales (médecine, droit, architecture, enseignement).
2. Plusieurs de ces professions sont régies par le *Code des professions*, dont l'application relève de l'Office des professions. Le terme *Code des professions* devrait être remplacé par *Code des ordres professionnels* et l'appellation *Office des professions*, par *Office des ordres professionnels*.
☐ travail

663. professionnel
Terme à éviter
V. **spécialiste**

664. professionnel libéral n. m.
professionnelle libérale n. f. ;
membre d'une profession libérale n.

professional
Personne qui effectue un travail à caractère intellectuel sans qu'un lien de subordination soit relevé entre celui qui l'effectue et celui pour le compte duquel il est effectué, et dont la rémunération ne revêt en principe aucun caractère commercial ou spéculatif.
Note. — Le terme *professionnel libéral* est attesté dans le *Trésor de la langue française*, dans *le Point* et dans l'*Argus*, revue française et dans *Terminologie comptable* de l'Ordre des comptables agréés du Québec.
☐ travail

665. professionnelle libérale
V. **professionnel libéral**

666. programme d'accès à l'égalité
Syn. de **plan d'égalité professionnelle**

667. programme d'équité en matière d'emploi
V. **plan d'égalité professionnelle**

668. programme de production
Syn. de **calendrier de production**

669. programmer le calendrier de la production
V. **calendrier de production**

670. projet de convention collective n. m. ;
cahier des revendications syndicales n. m.
union demands ;
union requests ;
union proposals
Document contenant les demandes de la partie syndicale relatives à la prochaine convention collective.
☐ convention collective de travail

671. projet de règlement n. m.
proposed settlement ;
tentative agreement ;
draft agreement
Document contenant les propositions définitives relatives à la future convention collective devant être soumises à l'approbation des intéressés.
☐ convention collective de travail

672. promotion n. f.
promotion;
advancement

Accès à un poste comportant plus de responsabilités et d'avantages.

Note. — Les avantages prennent généralement la forme d'une hausse de rémunération obtenue à plus ou moins longue échéance.

V. a. **avancement d'échelon**
☐ mouvement du personnel

673. protocole d'accord n. m.;
mémoire d'entente n. m.;
entente de principe n. f.
memorandum of agreement;
memorandum of settlement

Document schématique ou détaillé résultant d'une entente de principe intervenue entre les représentants des parties et contenant les sujets sur lesquels celles-ci se sont mises d'accord au cours de la négociation.
☐ convention collective de travail

674. protocole de retour au travail n. m.
return-to-work agreement;
back-to-work agreement

Entente écrite contenant les conditions du règlement d'une grève ou d'un lock-out et les modalités de la reprise du travail.
☐ convention collective de travail

Q

675. qualification du travail
Syn. de **évaluation des emplois**

676. qualification professionnelle n. f.
occupational qualification;
vocational qualification;
qualifications;
skill

Valeur d'un salarié déterminée par sa formation et son expérience et correspondant à un niveau précis de la classification des emplois.
☐ gestion des ressources humaines

677. qualifications
Terme à éviter
V. **compétence**

678. quart 1
Syn. de **équipe 1**

679. quart 2
Syn. de **poste 1**

680. quart d'après-midi 1
Syn. de **équipe d'après-midi**

681. quart d'après-midi 2
Syn. de **poste du soir**

682. quart de jour 1
Syn. de **équipe de jour**

683. quart de jour 2
Syn. de **poste de jour**

684. quart de nuit 1
Syn. de **équipe de nuit**

685. quart de nuit 2
Syn. de **poste de nuit**

686. quart de relève
Syn. de **équipe de relève**

687. quart du matin 1
Syn. de **équipe de jour**

688. quart du matin 2
Syn. de **poste de jour**

689. quart du soir
Syn. de **poste du soir**

R

690. rappel au travail 1 n. m.
recall

Acte par lequel un employeur demande au salarié de revenir au travail après une grève, un lock-out ou une mise à pied.

V. a. **réintégration; rengagement**
☐ cessation d'emploi

691. rappel au travail 2 n. m.
call back;
call-in

Acte par lequel un employeur demande à un salarié de revenir au travail en dehors des heures normales.
☐ durée du travail

692. rappel de salaire n. m.
back pay;
retroactive pay

Arriéré de salaire dû par l'employeur au salarié.

Notes. — 1. Par exemple, le salarié recevra un rappel de salaire à la suite d'une augmentation de salaire.
2. Ne pas confondre avec *rétroactivité*.
V. a. **rétroactivité**
☐ supplément salarial

693. réadaptation professionnelle n. f.;
rééducation professionnelle n. f.
vocational rehabilitation;
rehabilitation

Action qui consiste pour un salarié diminué physiquement à la suite d'un accident ou d'une maladie à acquérir de nouveau une capacité professionnelle qui lui permettra de fonctionner normalement dans son milieu de travail.
☐ condition de travail

694. réclamant n. m.
réclamante n. f.
grievant

Salarié qui présente un grief.
☐ conflit du travail

695. réclamante
V. **réclamant**

696. réclamation
Syn. de **grief**

697. reclassement n. m.
Terme à éviter : relocalisation
reclassification;
relocation

Réaffectation d'un salarié dont l'emploi a été supprimé, modifié en profondeur ou reclassifié ou, parfois, qui n'est plus apte à exercer son activité antérieure.

Note. — On rencontre aussi *replacement* qui désigne plus précisément la réaffectation collective des salariés touchés par la fermeture totale ou partielle d'une entreprise. *Reclassement* est utilisé dans la *Loi sur la formation et la qualification professionnelles de la main-d'œuvre.*
☐ mouvement du personnel

698. reconnaissance syndicale n. f.
union recognition;
trade union recognition

Acte par lequel un employeur reconnaît officiellement un syndicat comme agent négociateur.

Note. — Cette notion est disparue du *Code du travail* du Québec en 1969, mais elle existe encore dans le *Code canadien du travail.*
☐ syndicalisme

699. recours
V. **grief**

700. recyclage n. m.
retraining

Formation professionnelle qui permet au salarié de s'adapter aux nouvelles techniques dues à l'essor technologique.
☐ formation et perfectionnement du personnel

701. rééducation professionnelle
Syn. de **réadaptation professionnelle**

702. réembauchage
Syn. de **rengagement**

703. réembauche
Syn. de **rengagement**

704. réengagement
Syn. de **rengagement**

705. régime de services juridiques
V. **assurance juridique**

706. régulier
Terme à éviter
V. **permanent**

707. réintégration n. f.
reinstatement

Rétablissement d'un salarié dans son emploi ou dans son poste.

Note. — La réintégration s'accompagne du maintien, en tout ou en partie, des avantages acquis.
V. a. **rengagement; rappel au travail**
☐ cessation d'emploi

708. relation de travail n. f.
work relation;
employment relationship

Tout rapport entre personnes occasionné par une activité professionnelle quelconque au sein d'une entreprise.
☐ travail

709. **relations du travail**
Syn. de **relations professionnelles**

710. **relations industrielles**
V. **relations professionnelles**

711. **relations professionnelles** n. f. pl.;
relations du travail n. f. pl.
labour relations
V. o. *labor relations;*
industrial relations
Rapports qui s'établissent entre l'employeur et ses salariés.
Notes. — 1. Trois groupes peuvent entrer en jeu dans les relations professionnelles : les salariés et leurs syndicats, l'employeur et les associations patronales, ainsi que l'État. Une place particulière est accordée aux conflits du travail et à leur réglementation par l'élaboration de règles ou de conventions collectives.
2. Malgré l'usage répandu de *relations industrielles*, nous privilégions le terme retenu par le Bureau international du travail : *relations professionnelles.*
☐ relations professionnelles

712. **relocalisation**
Terme à éviter
V. **reclassement**

713. **relocalisation**
Terme à éviter
V. **transfert**

714. **rembauchage**
Syn. de **rengagement**

715. **remède**
Terme à éviter
V. **réparation**

716. **rémunération**
Syn. de **salaire**

717. **rémunération en espèces** n. f.
cash payment;
payment in cash
Somme d'argent versée à une personne en contrepartie de son travail.
☐ rémunération du travail

718. **rémunération en nature** n. f.
payment in kind
Rétribution sous forme de biens matériels ou autres avantages non pécuniaires.
☐ rémunération du travail

719. **rémunération forfaitaire** n. f.
lump sum payment
Rétribution fixée à l'avance pour un travail déterminé.
☐ rémunération du travail

720. **rengagement** n. m.;
réengagement n. m.;
rembauchage n. m.;
réembauchage n. m.;
réembauche n. f.
rehiring;
reemployment
Fait d'engager de nouveau un salarié qui bénéficie ou non de certains avantages.
V. a. **réintégration; rappel au travail**
☐ cessation d'emploi

721. **renvoi**
Syn. de **congédiement**

722. **renvoi discriminatoire**
Syn. de **congédiement discriminatoire**

723. **renvoi justifié**
Syn. de **congédiement justifié**

724. **renvoi pour activité syndicale**
Syn. de **congédiement pour activité syndicale**

725. **renvoi pour cause**
Terme à éviter
V. **congédiement justifié**

726. **renvoi pour cause juste et suffisante**
Syn. de **congédiement justifié**

727. **réparation** n. f.
Terme à éviter : remède
remedy
Correctif demandé en raison d'un litige ayant donné lieu à un grief.
☐ conflit du travail

728. **replacement**
V. **reclassement**

729. **repos hebdomadaire** n. m.
weekly rest
Jour de congé qui doit obligatoirement être accordé au salarié au cours de chaque semaine de travail.
☐ durée du travail

730. représentant syndical
V. **permanent syndical**

731. réprimande
V. **sanction disciplinaire**

732. résignation
Terme à éviter
V. **démission**

733. retenue de la cotisation syndicale n. f.;
retenue syndicale n. f.;
précompte de la cotisation syndicale n. m.;
précompte syndical n. m.
check-off of union dues;
check-off

Prélèvement qu'effectue l'employeur sur la rémunération du salarié d'un montant correspondant à la cotisation syndicale et qu'il verse au syndicat visé.
V. a. **formule Rand**
☐ déduction salariale

734. retenue syndicale
Syn. de **retenue de la cotisation syndicale**

735. rétroactivité n. f.
retroactive application
Report dans le passé des effets d'une loi, d'un jugement, d'un acte juridique.
Note. — *Rétroactivité* peut s'utiliser comme titre d'une clause, par exemple, ayant pour objet d'expliquer le fonctionnement concret de son application.
Le terme *rétroactivité* signifiant «caractère rétroactif» ne peut donc s'employer pour désigner la somme d'argent que touche le salarié. Il faut alors utiliser *rappel de salaire.*
V. a. **rappel de salaire**
☐ supplément salarial

736. rétrogradation n. f.;
déclassement n. m.
Terme à éviter : démotion
demotion;
downgrading
Fait pour un salarié d'être désigné à un poste de classification inférieure.
Note. — La rétrogration implique généralement une diminution de rémunération et ce, à plus ou moins longue échéance. La notion de *rétrogradation* a une connotation plutôt disciplinaire alors que celle de *déclassement* a une connotation plutôt administrative.
☐ mouvement du personnel

737. révocation d'accréditation n. f.;
désaccréditation n. f.
cancellation of certification;
decertification
Annulation de l'accréditation d'un syndicat.
Note. — *Désaccréditation* est un néologisme québécois.
☐ syndicalisme

738. rotation des équipes
Syn. de **rotation des postes 2**

739. rotation des postes 1 n. f.
job rotation
Méthode consistant à affecter de façon systématique le salarié à différents postes lui permettant ainsi de devenir polyvalent.
☐ organisation du travail

740. rotation des postes 2 n. f.;
rotation des équipes n. f.;
rotation des quarts n. f.
rotating shift
Mode d'organisation du travail par équipes alternantes.
Notes. — 1. *Travailler sur les shifts* ou *être sur les shifts* est à remplacer par *faire la rotation des postes, faire les trois-huit* ou *travailler par roulement.*
2. *Rotation des quarts* est d'usage québécois.
V. a. **travail par équipes; équipe alternante**
☐ durée du travail

741. rotation des quarts
Syn. de **rotation des postes 2**

742. rotation du personnel n. f.;
roulement de la main-d'œuvre n. m.
labour turnover
V. o. *labor turnover*
Cadence à laquelle se renouvelle le personnel d'une entreprise.
V. a. **attrition**
☐ mouvement du personnel

743. roulement de la main-d'œuvre
Syn. de **rotation du personnel**

S

744. salaire n. m.;
rémunération n. f.
wage;
salary
Somme convenue à l'avance payée par l'employeur en contrepartie du travail du salarié.
Note. — *Salaire* prend de plus en plus une valeur générique.
□ rémunération du travail

745. salaire au mérite n. m.
merit wage;
merit pay
Salaire établi après appréciation de l'ensemble des qualités professionnelles, intellectuelles et morales ainsi que du rendement et de l'efficacité de la personne qui remplit la fonction.
□ rémunération du travail

746. salaire au rendement n. m.
incentive wage;
pay for performance
Salaire calculé en fonction d'une relation entre le temps et la production, quelle qu'en soit la formule.
□ rémunération du travail

747. salaire au temps n. m.
time wage;
hourly wage
Salaire calculé uniquement en fonction de la durée passée par le salarié au travail.
□ rémunération du travail

748. salaire brut n. m.
gross earnings;
gross wage
Salaire avant déduction des différentes retenues.
□ rémunération du travail

749. salaire de base n. m.
base rate
Salaire payé par une entreprise ou une industrie pour une catégorie représentative de salariés placés à l'échelon inférieur de la hiérarchie des emplois.
□ rémunération du travail

750. salaire de base
Syn. de **salaire normal**

751. salaire étoilé
V. **salaire hors échelle**

752. salaire hors échelle n. m.;
salaire hors grille n. m.
red circle rate
Salaire qui dépasse le maximum fixé pour le poste.
Note. — Il est préférable d'utiliser ces termes plutôt que *salaire étoilé.*
□ rémunération du travail

753. salaire hors grille
Syn. de **salaire hors échelle**

754. salaire majoré de 100% n. m.
Terme à éviter : temps double
doubletime
V. o. *double time*
Salaire normal qui subit une augmentation de 100% dans certaines circonstances.
Note. — Le terme *salaire majoré de 100%* est surtout utilisé dans le contexte des heures supplémentaires.
□ supplément salarial

755. salaire majoré de 50% n. m.
Terme à éviter : temps et demi
time and a half
Salaire normal qui subit une augmentation de 50% dans certaines circonstances.
Note. — Le terme *salaire majoré de 50%* est surtout utilisé dans le contexte des heures supplémentaires.
□ supplément salarial

756. salaire net n. m.
take-home pay;
disposable earnings
Salaire que touche le salarié après déduction des différentes retenues.
□ rémunération du travail

757. salaire normal n. m.;
salaire de base n. m.
Termes à éviter : salaire régulier; temps simple
regular straight-time rate;
straight-time pay;
basic wage rate
Salaire élémentaire horaire, hebdomadaire, mensuel ou à la pièce auquel peuvent s'ajouter des majorations.

Note. — Ces majorations peuvent prendre la forme de primes, d'indemnités, de commissions, etc.
□ rémunération du travail

758. salaire régulier
Terme à éviter
V. **salaire normal**

759. salarial
V. **pécuniaire**

760. salarié n. m.
salariée n. f.
employee;
worker

Toute personne qui, contre rémunération, effectue un travail pour le compte d'autrui en étant sous sa subordination.
Note. — La définition de *salarié* du *Code du travail* du Québec est plus restrictive; elle exclut les cadres.
V. a. **employé**
□ gestion des ressources humaines

761. salarié à l'essai n. m.
salariée à l'essai n. f.;
travailleur à l'essai n. m.
travailleuse à l'essai n. f.;
stagiaire 1 n. (FR)
Terme à éviter : temporaire
probationary employee
Salarié effectuant une période d'essai.
Notes. — 1. En France, on appelle *stagiaire* la personne qui effectue la période d'essai dans la fonction publique.
2. Le terme *temporaire* est couramment employé à tort dans la fonction publique québécoise.
□ gestion des ressources humaines

762. salarié annuel n. m.
salariée annuelle n. f.;
annuel n. m.
annuelle n. f.
yearly paid employee
Salarié dont la rémunération est calculée sur une base annuelle.
Note. — Il est préférable d'utiliser *salarié annuel* plutôt que la périphrase *salarié payé à l'année.*
□ gestion des ressources humaines

763. salarié appointé n. m.
salariée appointée n. f.;
appointé n. m.
appointée n. f.
salaried employee
Salarié dont la base de la rémunération est la semaine, le mois ou l'année plutôt que le nombre des heures travaillées ou le rendement.
Note. — Le *personnel appointé* s'oppose au *personnel horaire.*
□ gestion des ressources humaines

764. salarié en équipes
Syn. de **travailleur par équipes**

765. salarié hebdomadaire n. m.
salariée hebdomadaire n. f.;
hebdomadaire n.
weekly paid employee
Salarié dont la rémunération est calculée sur une base hebdomadaire.
Note. — Il est préférable d'utiliser *salarié hebdomadaire* plutôt que la périphrase *salarié payé à la semaine.*
□ gestion des ressources humaines

766. salarié horaire n. m.
salariée horaire n. f.;
horaire n.
hourly paid employee
Salarié dont la rémunération est calculée sur une base horaire.
Notes. — 1. Il est préférable d'utiliser *salarié horaire* plutôt que la périphrase *salarié payé à l'heure.*
2. Le *personnel horaire* s'oppose au *personnel appointé.*
□ gestion des ressources humaines

767. salarié mensuel n. m.
salariée mensuelle n. f.;
mensuel n. m.
mensuelle n. f.
monthly paid employee
Salarié dont la rémunération est calculée sur une base mensuelle.
Note. — Il est préférable d'utiliser *salarié mensuel* plutôt que la périphrase *salarié payé au mois.*
□ gestion des ressources humaines

768. salarié par équipes
Syn. de travailleur par équipes

769. salarié payé à l'année
V. salarié annuel

770. salarié payé à l'heure
V. salarié horaire

771. salarié payé à la semaine
V. salarié hebdomadaire

772. salarié payé au mois
V. salarié mensuel

773. salarié permanent
Syn. de permanent

774. salarié posté
Syn. de travailleur par équipes

775. salarié régulier
Terme à éviter
V. permanent

776. salariée
V. salarié

777. salariée à l'essai
V. salarié à l'essai

778. salariée annuelle
V. salarié annuel

779. salariée appointée
V. salarié appointé

780. salariée en équipes
V. travailleur par équipes

781. salariée hebdomadaire
V. salarié hebdomadaire

782. salariée horaire
V. salarié horaire

783. salariée mensuelle
V. salarié mensuel

784. salariée par équipes
V. travailleur par équipes

785. salariée permanente
V. permanent

786. salariée postée
V. travailleur par équipes

787. sale boîte
Syn. de atelier de misère

788. sanction disciplinaire n. f.;
mesure disciplinaire n. f.
discipline;
disciplinary measure;
disciplinary penalty;
sanction
Disposition prise par l'employeur à la suite d'un manquement disciplinaire du salarié dans le but d'assurer le respect de la discipline.
Note. — Habituellement, on distingue trois niveaux de gravité de sanctions disciplinaires : 1) avertissement, blâme, réprimande, etc.; 2) mise à pied disciplinaire; 3) congédiement. Il existe également d'autres formes de sanctions disciplinaires, par exemple, le déplacement, le blocage de l'avancement, la rétrogradation.
V. a. avertissement
☐ gestion des ressources humaines

789. sauvegarde
V. clause d'indexation

790. second adj.
Terme à éviter : junior
junior
Se dit du travailleur qui vient immédiatement après celui qu'on qualifie de principal.
V. a. débutant
☐ gestion des ressources humaines

791. section
V. service

792. section locale n. f.;
syndicat local n. m.
Terme à éviter : local
local union;
local
Partie constitutive du syndicat, ayant toutefois une autonomie de fonctionnement.
Note. — Dans les dénominations de section locale on trouve : *loge, guilde,* etc.
☐ syndicalisme

793. section locale composée
Syn. de section locale fusionnée

794. section locale fusionnée n. f.;
section locale composée n. f.
amalgamated local union

Section locale qui regroupe plusieurs branches ou qui s'adjoint d'autres sections.

Note. — Le terme privilégié ou son synonyme doivent être utilisés d'après le sens du qualificatif.

☐ syndicalisme

795. sécurité d'emploi n. f.;
garantie d'emploi n. f.
job security;
employment security

Garantie pour un salarié de conserver son emploi au sein d'une organisation, lorsque sont remplies certaines conditions.

☐ condition de travail

796. sécurité syndicale n. f.
union security

Ensemble de dispositions destinées à assurer au syndicat le maintien ou l'accroissement de ses effectifs et la continuité de ses revenus.

☐ syndicalisme

797. sénior
Terme à éviter
V. **principal**

798. séniorité
Terme à éviter
V. **ancienneté**

799. sentence arbitrale n. f.
arbitration award;
adjudication

Décision sans appel rendue par un conseil d'arbitrage ou un tribunal d'arbitrage, et liant les parties en litige.

☐ conflit du travail

800. séparation
Terme à éviter
V. **cessation d'emploi**

801. service n. m.
Terme à éviter : département
department

Unité hiérarchique constituée par un ensemble de personnes travaillant sous l'autorité d'un même chef.

Note. — Bien que *département* soit quelque peu implanté au sens de service ou subdivision administrative ou encore branche d'activité d'une entreprise, nous privilégions l'utilisation de *service* ou encore *division*, *section* ou *direction*.

☐ travail

802. service continu n. m.
length of continuous service;
continuous service

Temps écoulé depuis l'entrée en service d'un salarié n'incluant pas les interruptions de travail.

Note. — Dans la pratique, le service continu peut inclure parfois certaines interruptions de travail. Dans certains cas, *ancienneté* et *service continu* sont de parfaits synonymes.

V. a. **ancienneté**

☐ durée du travail

803. service de, au loc. prép.
Terme à éviter : emploi de, à l'
employ of, in the

Expression qui indique le fait pour un salarié de travailler pour un employeur.

☐ travail

804. shift
Terme à éviter
V. **équipe**

805. shift
Terme à éviter
V. **poste**

806. sous-traitance n. f.
sub-contracting
V. o. *subcontracting;*
contracting out

Pratique par laquelle une organisation confie l'exécution de certains travaux à un entrepreneur autonome.

Note. — Cette définition correspond à l'un des sens de *sous-traitance* utilisés au Québec, car il s'agit, ici, d'entrepreneurs qui ne sont pas en sous-ordre.

☐ organisation du travail

807. spécialiste n.
Terme à éviter : professionnel
professional;
professional employee

Personne dont les études supérieures lui permettent d'exercer, pour son propre compte ou pour le compte d'autrui, une activité à caractère intellectuel ou technique.

Note. — Un *professionnel* est une personne qui exerce régulièrement une profession, un métier, par opposition à *amateur*.

☐ travail

808. stade n. m.;
étape n. f.;
phase n. f.
Terme à éviter : stage
stage
Chacun des degrés nettement distincts d'une procédure.
☐ travail

809. stage
Terme à éviter
V. **stade**

810. stage n. m.
traineeship;
training period
Période pendant laquelle une personne exerce une activité temporaire dans un ou plusieurs services d'une entreprise, en vue de sa formation ou de son perfectionnement professionnels.
☐ formation et perfectionnement du personnel

811. stagiaire 1
Syn. de **salarié à l'essai**

812. stagiaire 2 n.
trainee
Personne effectuant un stage.
☐ formation et perfectionnement du personnel

813. statut 1 n. m.
statutes;
policy
Ensemble des dispositions législatives au règlement qui fixent la situation des travailleurs de l'État, des collectivités publiques et de certaines grandes entreprises nationalisées en ce qui concerne le début et la fin du service, l'avancement, les devoirs, les avantages et les garanties de la fonction.
Note. — Par exemple, le statut des fonctionnaires.
☐ travail

814. statut 2 n. m.
status
Situation professionnelle d'un salarié sur un plan quelconque.
Note. — Il peut s'agir du lien contractuel du salarié avec l'entreprise, de la rémunération du salarié, etc. Exemples : le statut de permanent, le statut de temps partiel.
☐ gestion des ressources humaines

815. statuts n. m. pl.
Terme à éviter : constitution
constitution
Texte réglementaire qui définit une association, un syndicat, et en règle le fonctionnement.
☐ syndicalisme

816. supplantation n. f.
bumping
Action d'un salarié qui, en vertu de son ancienneté, évince de son poste un autre salarié.
☐ syndicalisme

817. supplantation ascendante n. f.
bumping up
Supplantation ainsi qualifiée quand un salarié en évince un autre qui occupe un poste hiérarchiquement plus élevé que le sien.
☐ syndicalisme

818. supplantation descendante n. f.
bumping down
Supplantation ainsi qualifiée quand un salarié en évince un autre qui occupe un poste hiérarchiquement moins élevé que le sien.
☐ syndicalisme

819. supplantation horizontale n. f.
lateral bumping
Supplantation ainsi qualifiée lorsque les postes des deux salariés sont du même niveau.
☐ syndicalisme

820. supplantation verticale n. f.
vertical bumping
Supplantation ainsi qualifiée lorsque les postes de deux salariés sont de niveaux différents.
☐ syndicalisme

821. surintendant
Terme à éviter
V. **chef de service**

822. surnuméraire n.
supernumerary
Salarié temporaire en sus du personnel de l'entreprise.
☐ gestion des ressources humaines

823. surtemps
Terme à éviter
V. **heure supplémentaire**

824. **suspension**
V. **mise à pied disciplinaire**

825. **syndicat** n. m.
Terme à éviter : union
union;
trade union
Association de salariés ayant pour objet la défense de leurs intérêts professionnels, sociaux et économiques.
Note. — En pratique, certains grands syndicats qui regroupent des sections locales jouent le rôle de fédération. Dans les dénominations de syndicat, on trouve *fraternité*, *alliance*, etc.
☐ syndicalisme

826. **syndicat accrédité**
V. **agent négociateur**

827. **syndicat local**
Syn. de **section locale**

828. **syndicat reconnu**
V. **agent négociateur**

T

829. **tablette** n. f.
shelf
Situation d'un salarié qui est officieusement mis à l'écart et qui continue à recevoir son traitement.
Note. — *Tablette* est un terme familier d'usage québécois.
Le *Grand Robert*, dans son édition de 1985, mentionne : «Loc. fig. (franç. du Canada). *Être sur les tablettes*, mis à l'écart, dans une position sans grandes responsabilités».
☐ travail

830. **tâches** n. f. pl.;
fonctions n. f. pl.
job content
Éléments constitutifs (activités, devoirs, responsabilités) reliés à un emploi.
☐ travail

831. **tarif de rémunération**
Syn. de **échelle des salaires**

832. **taux de salaire** n. m.
wage rate;
rate of pay;
job rate

Prix fixé pour une unité de production ou une période de temps déterminée.
☐ rémunération du travail

833. **temporaire**
Terme à éviter
V. **salarié à l'essai**

834. **temporaire** n.;
vacataire n. (FR)
Terme à éviter : occasionnel
temporary employee;
temporary worker
Salarié engagé par une entreprise pour une courte durée.
Notes. — 1. En France, on rend cette notion par *vacataire*, principalement dans la fonction publique.
2. Le terme *occasionnel* est couramment employé à tort dans la fonction publique québécoise.
☐ gestion des ressources humaines

835. **temps double**
Terme à éviter
V. **salaire majoré de 100 %**

836. **temps et demi**
Terme à éviter
V. **salaire majoré de 50 %**

837. **temps simple**
Terme à éviter
V. **salaire normal**

838. **temps supplémentaire**
Terme à éviter
V. **heure supplémentaire**

839. **terminaison d'emploi**
Terme à éviter
V. **cessation d'emploi**

840. **test**
Terme à éviter
V. **essai professionnel**

841. **titre d'emploi**
Terme à éviter
V. **appellation d'emploi**

842. **titulaire** n.
incumbent
Personne qui occupe un poste auquel elle a été nommée personnellement.
☐ recrutement et engagement du personnel

843. titularisation n. f.
incumbency
Action qui rend une personne titulaire d'un poste qu'elle occupe.
☐ recrutement et engagement du personnel

844. totalisateur n. m.
cumulative clock
Appareil qui mémorise et cumule le nombre d'heures et de minutes travaillées durant la période de référence.
☐ durée du travail

845. traitement n. m.
salary
Salaire attaché à un emploi d'une certaine importance sociale.
Note. — Extension de sens.
☐ rémunération du travail

846. transfert n. m.
    Terme à éviter : relocalisation
transfer;
relocation
Mutation survenant à la suite de l'arrivée d'un nouvel employeur ou de la transplantation d'un service dans un autre secteur géographique.
V. a. **mutation; reclassement**
☐ mouvement du personnel

847. travail 1
    Syn. de **emploi**

848. travail 2 n. m.
work
Exercice effectif d'une activité professionnelle rémunérée.
☐ travail

849. travail à forfait n. m.
jobbing
Travail dont la nature, la quantité et la rémunération sont déterminées à l'avance par contrat.
☐ organisation du travail

850. travail à horaire réduit n. m. ;
    chômage partiel n. m. (FR)
reduced workweek;
job sharing;
work sharing;
work sharing employment

Travail dont la durée est inférieure à la durée habituelle en raison de circonstances particulières.
Note. — Ne pas confondre avec *travail à temps partiel.*
☐ durée du travail

851. travail à la chaîne n. m.
assembly-line work
Travail répétitif et parcellaire où le produit en cours de fabrication se déplace le long d'une chaîne à une cadence déterminée, s'arrêtant successivement devant chaque ouvrier.
☐ durée du travail

852. travail à la pièce
    Syn. de **travail aux pièces**

853. travail à pied d'œuvre n. m.
on-site work
Travail exécuté à proximité de l'ouvrage que l'on construit.
☐ organisation du travail

854. travail à plein temps
    Syn. de **travail à temps plein**

855. travail à temps partiel n. m. ;
    emploi à temps partiel n. m.
part-time employment
Travail accompli de façon régulière pendant une durée plus courte que la durée normale des heures de travail.
Note. — Ne pas confondre avec *travail à horaire réduit.*
☐ durée du travail

856. travail à temps plein n. m. ;
    travail à plein temps n. m. ;
    emploi à plein temps n. m. ;
    emploi à temps plein n. m.
full-time employment
Travail dont la durée correspond à l'horaire normal de l'entreprise.
☐ durée du travail

857. travail au noir
    Syn. de **travail noir**

858. travail aux pièces n. m. ;
    travail à la pièce n. m.
piecework
Travail dont la rémunération est basée sur le nombre de pièces produites ou d'opérations effectuées.
☐ durée du travail

859. travail clandestin
Syn. de **travail noir**

860. travail continu n. m.;
travail en continu n. m.
Terme à éviter : opération continue
continuous operation
Travail exécuté vingt-quatre heures sur vingt-quatre, tous les jours de la semaine, dimanche et jours fériés compris.
Note. — Pour indiquer que le travail n'est pas continu, mais qu'il s'interrompt et reprend, on utilise *travail discontinu* ou *en discontinu*.
□ durée du travail

861. travail d'apprêts n. m.;
apprêts n. m. pl.
make-ready activities;
preparatory work
Activités préliminaires et souvent essentielles que doit effectuer le salarié avant de commencer à produire véritablement.
□ durée du travail

862. travail discontinu
V. **travail continu**

863. travail effectif n. m.
work actually performed
Travail réellement accompli par le salarié pendant les heures travaillées.
□ durée du travail

864. travail en continu
Syn. de **travail continu**

865. travail en discontinu
V. **travail continu**

866. travail en équipes
Syn. de **travail par équipes**

867. travail en équipes successives
Syn. de **travail par équipes**

868. travail noir n. m.;
travail au noir n. m.;
travail clandestin n. m.
moonlighting
Travail accompli en infraction à la réglementation du travail ou échappant par sa clandestinité au paiement des charges sociales et fiscales.
□ travail

869. travail occasionnel
Syn. de **emploi occasionnel**

870. travail par équipes n. m.;
travail par postes n. m.;
travail posté n. m.;
trois-huit n. m. (FR);
travail en équipes successives n. m. (FR);
travail en équipes n. m.;
travail par équipes successives n. m. (FR);
travail par roulement n. m.;
travail par quarts n. m.
shift work
Mode d'organisation du travail qui est exécuté par des salariés formant des équipes distinctes qui se succèdent les unes aux autres sur un même ouvrage.
Notes. — 1. Le terme *trois-huit* précise qu'il y a trois équipes travaillant chacune huit heures.
2. Le travail par roulement peut aussi comprendre la rotation des postes.
3. *Travail par quarts* est d'usage québécois.
V. a. **rotation des postes**
□ durée du travail

871. travail par équipes successives
Syn. de **travail par équipes**

872. travail par postes
Syn. de **travail par équipes**

873. travail par quarts
Syn. de **travail par équipes**

874. travail par roulement
Syn. de **travail par équipes**

875. travail permanent
Syn. de **emploi permanent**

876. travail posté
Syn. de **travail par équipes**

877. travail précaire n. m.
instable work;
instable job;
marginal job
Travail qui ne bénéficie pas de certaines garanties de stabilité, de régularité.
□ travail

878. travail protégé
    Syn. de emploi réservé

879. travail réservé
    Syn. de emploi réservé

880. travail saisonnier
    Syn. de emploi saisonnier

881. travail secondaire
    Syn. de emploi secondaire

882. travail semi-continu n. m.
semi-continuous operation

Travail exécuté vingt-quatre heures sur vingt-quatre mais non les fins de semaine.
□ durée du travail

883. travail supplémentaire n. m.
overtime work

Travail effectué pendant les heures supplémentaires.
Note. — On rencontre parfois *travail supplémentaire* en tête de chapitre dans les conventions collectives.
□ durée du travail

884. travail temporaire
    Syn. de emploi temporaire

885. travailler au bonus
    V. prime de rendement

886. travailler au rendement
    V. prime de rendement

887. travailleur n. m.
    travailleuse n. f.
worker

Toute personne qui exerce une activité contre rémunération.
□ travail

888. travailleur à l'essai
    Syn. de salarié à l'essai

889. travailleur autonome
    Syn. de travailleur indépendant

890. travailleur de quart
    Syn. de travailleur par équipes

891. travailleur en équipes
    Syn. de travailleur par équipes

892. travailleur indépendant n. m.
    travailleuse indépendante n. f.;
    travailleur autonome n. m.
    travailleuse autonome n. f.
self-employed worker

Travailleur qui exerce une activité professionnelle pour son propre compte et sous sa propre responsabilité.
□ travail

893. travailleur intermittent n. m.
    travailleuse intermittente n. f.
intermittent worker

Salarié dont l'activité professionnelle, en raison de sa nature, s'exerce nécessairement de façon discontinue.
□ durée du travail

894. travailleur manuel
    Syn. de ouvrier

895. travailleur par équipes n. m.
    travailleuse par équipes n. f.;
    travailleur en équipes n. m.
    travailleuse en équipes n. f.;
    travailleur posté n. m.
    travailleuse postée n. f.;
    salarié en équipes n. m.
    salariée en équipes n. f.;
    salarié par équipes n. m.
    salariée par équipes n. f.;
    salarié posté n. m.
    salariée postée n. f.;
    travailleur de quart n. m.
    travailleuse de quart n. f.;
    factionnaire n. (FR)
shift worker

Salarié effectuant un travail par équipes.
□ durée du travail

896. travailleur permanent
    Syn. de permanent

897. travailleur posté
    Syn. de travailleur par équipes

898. travailleur régulier
    Terme à éviter
    V. permanent

899. travailleur toutes mains n. m.
    travailleuse toutes mains n. f.;
    homme à tout faire n. m.;
    femme à tout faire n. f.;
    homme à toutes mains n. m.;

femme à toutes mains n. f.;
homme toutes mains n. m.;
femme toutes mains n. f.
Terme à éviter : ouvrier général
general hand;
general worker;
general helper;
handyman

Ouvrier sans spécialité pouvant être chargé de toutes sortes de travaux.
☐ travail

900. **travailleuse**
V. **travailleur**

901. **travailleuse à l'essai**
V. **salarié à l'essai**

902. **travailleuse autonome**
V. **travailleur indépendant**

903. **travailleuse de quart**
V. **travailleur par équipes**

904. **travailleuse en équipes**
V. **travailleur par équipes**

905. **travailleuse indépendante**
V. **travailleur indépendant**

906. **travailleuse intermittente**
V. **travailleur intermittent**

907. **travailleuse manuelle**
V. **ouvrier**

908. **travailleuse par équipes**
V. **travailleur par équipes**

909. **travailleuse permanente**
V. **permanent**

910. **travailleuse postée**
V. **travailleur par équipes**

911. **travailleuse toutes mains**
V. **travailleur toutes mains**

912. **tribunal d'arbitrage** n. m.
arbitration board

Arbitre unique ou formation tripartite qui, après audition des parties, est chargée de régler un grief par sentence arbitrale.

Note. — Au Québec, l'arbitre de griefs, qui peut être assisté de deux assesseurs, tient lieu de tribunal d'arbitrage.
☐ conflit du travail

913. **trois-huit**
Syn. de **travail par équipes**

914. **union**
Terme à éviter
V. **syndicat**

915. **union** n. f.
union

Regroupement de syndicats.

Note. — En France, il est souvent précisé que ce regroupement est effectué sur le plan géographique. Au Québec, pour désigner ce regroupement, la CSN utilise *conseil central* et la FTQ, *conseil du travail.* En pratique, l'union peut également regrouper des sections locales. Cette définition est d'ordre strictement terminologique. Elle ne correspond pas nécessairement ni à la désignation, ni à l'importance des diverses organisations syndicales québécoises.
☐ syndicalisme

916. **unité de négociation** n. f.
bargaining unit

Groupe de salariés représentés par un agent négociateur et constituant un groupement approprié aux fins de la négociation collective.
☐ syndicalisme

917. **vacance**
Syn. de **poste vacant**

918. vacances
Syn. de **congé annuel payé**

919. vacances payées
Syn. de **congé annuel payé**

920. vacataire
Syn. de **temporaire**

921. voiture de fonction n. f.
company car

Véhicule alloué gratuitement par l'employeur à une personne qui occupe un poste.

Note. — Cette voiture peut être utilisée à des fins personnelles ou non.
□ supplément salarial

Bibliographie

1. OUVRAGES GÉNÉRAUX

BÉNAC, Henri. *Dictionnaire des synonymes*, Paris, Hachette, 1987, 1026 p.

CENTRE NATIONAL DE LA RECHERCHE SCIENTIFIQUE. CENTRE DE RECHERCHE POUR UN TRÉSOR DE LA LANGUE FRANÇAISE, NANCY. *Trésor de la langue française : dictionnaire de la langue du XIXᵉ et du XXᵉ siècle (1789-1960)*, Paris, CNRS, 1971.

COLPRON, Gilles. *Dictionnaire des anglicismes*, Montréal, Éditions Beauchemin, 1982, 199 p.

The Compact Edition of the Oxford English Dictionary, New York, Oxford University Press, 1971, 2 vol.

DAGENAIS, Gérard. *Dictionnaire des difficultés de la langue française au Canada*, Québec, Éditions Pedagogia, 1967, 679 p.

DAVIAULT, Pierre. *Langage et traduction*, Ottawa, Secrétariat d'État, Bureau fédéral de la traduction, 1972, 397 p.

Encyclopaedia Britannica, Chicago, Encyclopaedia Britannica, 1970, 23 vol.

Encyclopaedia Universalis, Paris, Encyclopaedia Universalis, 1968, 20 vol.

GILBERT, Pierre. *Dictionnaire des mots nouveaux*, Paris, Hachette-Tchou, 1971, 572 p.

GIRAUD, Jean, et autres. *Les mots «dans le vent»*, Paris, Librairie Larousse, 1971, 251 p. (La langue vivante)

GIRAUD, Jean, et autres. *Les nouveaux mots «dans le vent»*, Paris, Librairie Larousse, 1974, 272 p. (La langue vivante)

GIRODET, Jean. *Logos : Grand dictionnaire de la langue française*, Paris, Bordas, c1976, 3 vol.

Grand dictionnaire encyclopédique Larousse, Paris, Librairie Larousse, 1982-1985, 10 vol.

The Random House Dictionary of the English Language, New York, Random House, 1971, 2059 p.

Robert Collins : dictionnaire français-anglais anglais-français, 2ᵉ éd. avec la collaboration du Comité du Robert sous la présidence de Paul Robert, Paris, Société du Nouveau Littré, 1987, 930 p.

ROBERT, Paul. *Dictionnaire alphabétique et analogique de la langue française*, 2ᵉ éd. revue et enrichie par Alain Rey, Paris, Le Robert, 1985, 9 vol.

Webster's New Twentieth Century Dictionary of the English Language Unabridged, 2nd ed., Cleveland, Collins-World, 1978.

Webster's Third New International Dictionary of the English Language Unabridged, Editor in Chief Philip Babcock Gove, Springfield, Mass., Merriam, 1976.

2. DICTIONNAIRES ET VOCABULAIRES SPÉCIALISÉS

AGENCE DE COOPÉRATION CULTURELLE ET TECHNIQUE. *Vocabulaire de l'administration*, Paris, Hachette, 1972, 187 p.

AIR CANADA/CANADIEN NATIONAL. SERVICE DE LINGUISTIQUE. SECTION DE TERMINOLOGIE. *Vocabulaire de l'administration du personnel. Personnel Administration Vocabulary*, Montréal, La Section, 1980, 59 p.

AMBASSADE DE FRANCE AUX ÉTATS-UNIS. SERVICE D'ANALYSE INDUSTRIELLE. *Glossaire syndical et terminologie des salaires : américain-français*, 3ᵉ éd. ent. ref., Washington, Ambassade de France, s. d., 154 p. (Glossaires bilingues de la terminologie américaine)

BARRAINE, Raymond. *Dictionnaire de droit*, 3ᵉ éd. ent. ref., Paris, Librairie générale de droit et de jurisprudence, 1867, 325 p.

CADIEUX, Roberte. *Glossaire anglais-français de l'arbitrage et des moyens de pression*, Montréal, Université de Montréal, 1979, 221 p.

CANADA. MINISTÈRE DU TRAVAIL. *Terminologie des relations du travail*, 3ᵉ éd., Ottawa, Approvisionnement et Services Canada, 1984, 29 p. ; 26 p.

CANADIEN NATIONAL. SERVICES LINGUISTIQUES. SECTION DE TERMINOLOGIE. *Terminologie des conventions collectives (anglais-français/français-anglais). Collective Agreement & Terminology (English-French/French-English)*, 3ᵉ éd. rev. et augm., Montréal, La Section, 1986, 195 p.

CANADIEN PACIFIQUE LIMITÉE. SERVICES ADMINISTRATIFS. CENTRE DE TRADUCTION. SECTION DE TERMINOLOGIE. *Terminologie des relations du travail (anglais-français/français-anglais). Labour Relations Terminology (English-French/French-English)*, [Montréal], La Section, 1985, 130 p.

CASSELMAN, Paul Hubert. *Labor Dictionary : a Concise Encyclopaedia of Labor Information*, New York, Philosophical Library, 1949, 554 p.

CENTRE INTERNATIONAL D'INFORMATION ET DE RECHERCHE SUR LA FORMATION PROFESSIONNELLE. *Glossaire des termes relatifs à l'éducation, à l'emploi, à l'orientation professionnelle, à l'enseignement et à la formation techniques et professionnels*, Genève, Bureau international du travail, 1971, 13 p.

COMMISSION DES COMMUNAUTÉS EUROPÉENNES. *Glossarium : glossaire du marché du travail et du mouvement syndical*, Luxembourg, Office des publications officielles des Communautés européennes, 1983, 216 p.

CORNIOT, S. *Dictionnaire de droit*, 2e éd., Paris, Librairie Dalloz, 1966, 2 t.

Dictionnaire permanent social, Paris, Éditions législatives et administratives, 1982-.

Dictionnaire social 1983, 2e éd., Paris, Éditions des Publications fiduciaires, 1983, 264 p. (Collection «Les Dictionnaires fiduciaires»)

DION, Gérard. *Dictionnaire canadien des relations du travail*, 2e éd., Québec, Les Presses de l'Université Laval, 1986, 993 p.

DOHERTY, Robert E. *Industrial and Labor Relations Terms : a Glossary for Students and Teachers*, Ithaca, The New York State School of Industrial and Labor Relations, 1962, 31 p.

DUBUC, Robert. *Vocabulaire de gestion*, Ottawa, Éditions Leméac, 1974, 135 p.

Étude gestion du personnel sur ordinateur : description des documents produits par l'ordinateur, s. l., E.D.F. — G.D.F., 1972, 172 p. (Service du traitement de l'information)

FILKINS, James H., and Donald L. CARUTH. *Lexicon of American Business Terms*, New York, Simon-Schuster, 1973, 141 p.

FRIEDRICH, Hans. *Glossaire de gestion de personnel*, Bilbao, Association européenne pour la direction du personnel, 1970, s. p.

GUILLIEN, Raymond et Jean VINCENT. *Lexique de termes juridiques*, 2e éd., Paris, Dalloz, 1972, 354 p.

ILO Thesaurus : Labour, Employment and Training Terminology. Thésaurus BIT : terminologie du travail, de l'emploi et de la formation, 3e éd., Genève, Bureau international du travail, 1985, XXVII, 463 p. (Labor Doc)

LEMEUNIER, Francis. *Dictionnaire juridique économique et financier*, Paris, Éditions J. Delmas et Cie, 1970, 366 p. (Documents actuels)

METCALFE-LAMY, Claire. *Étude d'expressions et de termes utilisés dans les conventions collectives de travail : glossaire raisonné français-anglais*, Montréal, 1968, 104 p.

MINISTÈRE DU TRAVAIL, Direction de l'économie et des recherches. *Répertoire de termes et expressions utilisés en relations industrielles et dans des domaines connexes*, Ottawa, 1967, 206 p.

PATRIS, Michel. *Flexible Working Hours : English-French. L'horaire variable : anglais-français*, Bruxelles, Institut libre Marie Haps, 1977, 145 p.

ROBERTS, Harold S. *Roberts' Dictionary of Industrial Relations*, 3rd ed., Washington, Bureau of National Affairs, 1986, 811 p.

ROMEUF, Jean. *Manuel du chef d'entreprise*, Paris, P.U.F., 1960, 1069 p.

SACQ, Jeffrey, et Ethan POSKANZER. *Labour Law Terms : a Dictionary of Canadian Labour Law*, Toronto, Lancaster House, 1984, 174 p.

SCHLIPF, Frederick A. *Collective Bargaining in Libraries*, Urbana-Champaign, University of Illinois, 1975, 179 p. (Albertan Park Institutes, 20)

SECRÉTARIAT D'ÉTAT. BUREAU DES TRADUCTIONS. DIRECTION DE LA TERMINOLOGIE. *Glossary : Labour Relations. Lexique : Relations du travail*, Ottawa, Approvisionnements et Services Canada, 1984, 32 p.

TÉZÉNAS, Jean. *Dictionnaire de l'organisation de la gestion*, Paris, Les Éditions d'organisation, 1971, 270 p.

Le travail dans l'entreprise et la société moderne, Directeur Pierre MORIN, Paris, C.E.P.L. — Retz, 1974, 512 p. (Les Dictionnaires du savoir moderne)

VAN HOOF, Henri. *Economic Terminology : English-French*, Munich, Max Hueber Verlag, 1967, 770 p.

VILLERS-SIDANI, Marie-Éva de, et Marie-Claire BOUCHER. *Les horaires de travail*, Québec, Office de la langue française, 1974, 16 p. (Terminologie de la gestion)

Vocabulaire de la gestion des ressources humaines, s. l., Hydro-Québec, 1976, 5 p.

Vocabulaire élémentaire des relations de travail, s. l. n. d.

WIRTZ, W. Willard. *Glossary of Current Industrial Relations and Wage Terms*, Washington, Government Printing Office, 1965, 103 p.

3. OUVRAGES SPÉCIALISÉS

ALLENSPACH, Heinz. *L'horaire variable*, 1re éd., Genève, B.I.T., 1975, 66 p.

BAUDRAZ, Jean-François. *L'horaire variable de travail*, Paris, Les Éditions d'organisation, 1973, 135 p.

BÉLANGER, Laurent. *Gestion des ressources humaines : approche systématique (exposés et travaux pratiques)*, 2e éd., Chicoutimi, Gaëtan Morin, 1979, 363 p.

BENAYOUN, Raphaël et Claude BOULIER. *Approches rationnelles dans la gestion du personnel : réflexions et expériences*, Paris, Dunod, 1972, 306 p.

BIGGS, M. C. *Flexible Working Hours*, Toronto, A. C. Nielsen, 1973, 10 p.

BLAISE, Jean. *Réglementation du travail et de l'emploi*, Paris, Librairie Dalloz, 1966, 439 p. (Collection Traité de droit du travail)

BROCHARD, Jean. *Manuel du contrat de travail devant le conseil de prud'hommes et la cour : les conventions collectives*, Paris, Librairie Dalloz, 1960, 475 p. (Manuels Dalloz de droit usuel)

CAMERLYNCK, G.-H. *Contrat de travail*, Paris, Librairie Dalloz, 1968, 588 p. (Collection Traité de droit du travail)

CAMERLYNCK, G.-H. *Contrat de travail*, éd. mise à jour, Paris, Librairie Dalloz, 1973, 158 p. (Collection Traité de droit du travail)

CHALENDAR, Jacques. *L'aménagement du temps*, Paris, Desclée de Brouwer, 1973, 171 p.

CHAUCHARD, Jean-Louis. *Précis de gestion du personnel et des ressources humaines*, Paris, Éditions d'organisation, 1986, 161 p.

CHAUVEAU, René. *Constitution et fonctionnement des associations et syndicats*, 5e éd., Paris, Éditions J. Delmas, 1974, pag. mult. (Ce qu'il vous faut savoir)

CHEVALIER, Jean. *Organisation du travail*, 11e éd., Paris, Dunod, 1966, t. 2.

Code du travail, Paris, Jurisprudence générale Dalloz, 1976, 1452 p. (Petits codes Dalloz)

Code du travail, Lois refondues du Québec, Québec, Assemblée nationale du Québec, 1988.

CÔTÉ, Marcel. *La gestion des ressources humaines*, Montréal, Guérin, 1975, 264 p.

COUTEAU, Raoul. *Législation sociale*, 6e éd., Paris, Bordas, 1976, 303 p. (Collection Aide-mémoire Dunod)

CUVILLIER, Rollande. *Vers la réduction du temps de travail*, 1re éd., Genève, B.I.T., 1981, 173 p.

DEBBASCH, Charles. *Science administrative : administration publique*, Paris, Éditions Dalloz, 1970, 682 p. (Précis Dalloz)

DENIS, Pierre. *Droit de la sécurité sociale*, Bruxelles, Larcier, 1973, 610 p. (Précis de la Faculté de droit de l'Université catholique de Louvain)

DESPAX, Michel. *Conventions collectives*, Paris, Librairie Dalloz, 1966, 454 p. (Collection Traité de droit du travail)

DESPAX, Michel. *Conventions collectives*, éd. mise à jour, Paris, Librairie Dalloz, 1974, 129 p. (Collection Traité de droit du travail)

DIVERREZ, Jean. *L'appréciation du personnel à partir de l'analyse du fonctionnement du groupe*, 5e éd., Paris, Entreprise moderne d'édition, 1978, 96 p. (Collection L'entreprise et les hommes)

DIVERREZ, Jean. *Politique et techniques de direction du personnel*, 8e éd., Paris, Entreprise moderne d'édition, 1983, 188 p.

DUBOIS, Laurent. *Code complet et commenté du travail : droits et obligations des salariés et des employeurs*, Paris, Éditions de Vecchi, 1976, 717 p.

DUPEYROUX, Jean-Jacques. *Droit de la sécurité sociale*, Paris, Dalloz, 1975, 125 p. (Mémentos Dalloz)

Évaluation des emplois, Neuchâtel, Éditions de la Baconnière, 1963, 110 p. (Collection Travail)

FRITZ, R. D., et A. M. STRINGARI. *Employer's Handbook for Labor Negotiations*, 3rd ed., Detroit, 1968, 423 p. (Management Labor Relations Series)

GAGNON, Robert, et autres. *Droit du travail en vigueur au Québec*, Québec, P.U.L., 1971, 441 p.

GAUTHIER, Michel et Michel-Claude LUPÉ. *Les tableaux de bord de la fonction personnel*, 2ᵉ éd., Paris, Entreprise moderne d'édition, 1978, 266 p.

GUYOT, Jean. *Le recrutement méthodique du personnel*, Paris, Entreprise moderne d'édition, 1979, 158 p.

ISSELÉ, S. *Toutes les questions pratiques sur la durée du travail : horaires — congés — absences*, 1ʳᵉ éd., Paris, Éditions J. Delmas, 1977, pag. mult. (Ce qu'il vous faut savoir)

JARDILLIER, Pierre. *L'organisation humaine des entreprises*, Paris, P.U.F., 1965, 429 p. (Collection du travail humain)

JARDILLIER, Pierre, et Michel-Claude LUPÉ. *De la qualification du travail à l'évaluation des fonctions*, Paris, Entreprise moderne d'édition, 1976, 220 p. (Collection Centor)

KAPP, Bernard et Odile PROUST. *Les horaires libres*, Paris, Chotard, 1973, 316 p.

Lamy Social, Paris, Société des services Lamy, 1984, 1645 p.

LANNÉRÉE, S., et L. ISSELÉ. *Principes et pratique du droit du travail*, 4ᵉ éd., Paris, Éditions J. Delmas, 1975, pag. mult. (Ce qu'il vous faut savoir)

LECLUSE, François. *Le contrat de travail*, Paris, Entreprise moderne d'édition, 1981, 123 p. (50 questions, 50 réponses)

LYON-CAEN, Gérard. *Les salaires*, Paris, Librairie Dalloz, 1967, 346 p. (Collection Traité de droit du travail)

LYON-CAEN, Gérard. *Les salaires*, éd. mise à jour, Paris, Librairie Dalloz, 1973, 86 p. (Collection Traité de droit du travail)

MALLETTE, Noël. *La gestion des relations du travail au Québec : du cadre juridique et institutionnel*, Montréal, McGraw-Hill, 1980, 642 p.

Mémento pratique Francis Lefebvre : social 1982 (sécurité sociale, droit du travail), Paris, Éditions Francis Lefebvre, 1982, 1056 p.

RABOURDIN, Guy. *La pratique de l'horaire variable*, Paris, CATRAL, 1973, 55 p.

REYNAUD, Jean-Daniel. *Les syndicats en France*, Paris, Éditions du Seuil, 1975, t. 1.

SEYFARTH, et autres. *Labor Relations and the Law in France and the United States*, Ann Arbor, University of Michigan, 1972, 648 p. (Michigan International Labor Studies, no. 5)

SINAY, Hélène. *La grève*, Paris, Librairie Dalloz, 1966, 522 p. (Collection Traité de droit du travail)

STRAUSS, George, et Leonard R. WAYLES. *Personnel : the Human Problems of Management*, 3rd ed., New Jersey, Prentice-Hall, 1972, 684 p.

Travail et main-d'oeuvre, 6ᵉ éd., Paris, Union des industries métallurgiques et minières, 1964, t. 1.

VALTICOS, Nicolas. *Droit international du travail*, Paris, Librairie Dalloz, 1970, 638 p. (Collection Traité de droit du travail)

VALTICOS, Nicolas. *Droit international du travail*, éd. mise à jour, Paris, Librairie Dalloz, 1973, 109 p. (Collection Traité de droit du travail)

VERDIER. J.-M. *Syndicats*, Paris, Librairie Dalloz, 1966, 504 p. (Collection Traité de droit du travail)

VITET, Claude. *Memo on Operation of Flextime Equipment*, Waterloo, Equitable Life Insurance Co of Canada, 1973, 12 p.

WEISS, Dimitri. *Les relations du travail : employeurs, personnel, syndicat, État*, 2ᵉ éd., Paris, Dunod, 1974, 160 p. (Dunod entreprise : série gestion sociale)

WEISS, Dimitri. *Relations industrielles : acteurs, auteurs, faits, tendances*, Paris, Éditions Sirey, 1973, 320 p. (Administration des entreprises)

YODER, Dale. *Personnel Management and Industrial Relations*, Englewood Cliffs, Prentice-Hall, 1970, 784 p.

4. PÉRIODIQUES

L'Actualité terminologique, Ottawa, Secrétariat d'État, Bureau des traductions, vol. 1, nº 1, 1968-.

La banque des mots, semestriel, Paris, P.U.F., vol. 1, 1971-.

C'est-à-dire, Montréal, Société Radio-Canada, Comité de linguistique, vol. 1, nº 1, 1960-.

La clé des mots, Paris, Conseil international de la langue française, vol. 1, nº 1, 1973-.

Droit social, mensuel, Paris, Éditions Jean-Jacques Dupeyroux, vol. 1, 1938-.

Fiches de Radio-Canada, Montréal, Société Radio-Canada, Service de linguistique, 1960-.

Liaisons sociales, bihebdomadaire, Paris, Bureau des liaisons sociales, vol. 1, nº 1, 1946-.

Meta, trimestriel, Montréal, P.U.M., vol. 1, nº 1, 1956-.

Québec/travail, bimensuel, Québec, ministère du Travail et de la Main-d'oeuvre, vol. 1, nº 1, 1965-.

Regards sur l'actualité, Paris, La Documentation française, nº 14, 15 octobre 1975, 64 p.

Relations industrielles. Industrial Relations, trimestriel, Québec, P.U.L., vol. 1, nᵒ 1, 1945-.

Revue internationale du travail. International Labour Review, bimensuel, Genève, B.I.T., vol. 1, nᵒ 1, 1921-.

La semaine sociale Lamy, hebdomadaire, Paris, Éditions Lamy, nᵒ 1, 1980-.

5. ARTICLES DE PÉRIODIQUES

D'AOUST, Claude, et autres. «Les causes de la cessation de l'emploi : classification et sémantique», *La Gazette du travail*, décembre 1975, p. 827-833.

«Glossaire des termes syndicaux», *Cahiers syndicaux*, Ottawa, nᵒ 5, 2 p.

«Terminologie française dans les relations du travail (Chronique)», *Québec/Travail*, Québec, ministère du Travail et de la Main-d'œuvre, vol. 1, nᵒ 1, 1965-.

Index des termes anglais

familiarization period, 576
featherbedding, 486
federation, 362
fee, 413
first-line supervisor, 14
first shift, 337, 623
fixed schedule, 419
fixed shift, 341
fixed work schedule, 419
flexible band, 604
flexible core, 604
flexible hours, 422
flexible hours of work, 424
flexible schedule, 424
flexible work schedule, 424
flextime, 424
floater, 195
floating holiday, 195
framework agreement, 234
free choice of scheduling, 415
fringe benefits, 86
full-time employment, 856
further training, 377, 575

gang, 333
general hand, 899
general helper, 899
general worker, 899
grade, 294
graveyard shift, 624
grievance, 395
grievance committee, 143
grievance procedure, 659
grievant, 694
gross earnings, 748
gross misconduct, 361
gross negligence, 361
gross wage, 748
group bonus, 650
guarantee of employment, 389
guaranteed hours of work, 389

handicapped person, 593
handyman, 899
head representative, 18
helper, 22

hiring, 326
hiring date, 331
holiday, 462
holiday allowance, 653
holidays, 175
hour allowed, 406
hour worked, 408
hourly paid employee, 766
hourly wage, 747
hours of work, 288

in-plant training, 380
incentive pay, 649
incentive wage, 746
increment, 294
incumbency, 843
incumbent, 842
industrial accident, 4
industrial disease, 490
industrial dispute, 267
industrial relations, 711
industry-related illness, 490
industry-wide bargaining, 526
initiation fee, 282
instability bonus, 445
instability of work bonus, 445
instable job, 877
instable work, 877
intermittent worker, 893

job, 299, 369, 627
job content, 830
job description, 262
job evaluation, 352
job opening, 631
job rate, 832
job rotation, 739
job security, 795
job seniority, 29
job sharing, 306, 850
job title, 50
job vacancy, 631
jobbing, 849
joint committee, 147, 148
journeyman, 150, 487
junior, 245, 790
juridical day, 466
jurisdiction, 116, 152
jury and witness duty allowance, 452

jury and witness duty leave, 206
jury-duty leave, 206

key job, 621

labor agreement, 233
labor contract, 229
labor dispute, 267
labor leader, 271
labor relations, 711
labor turnover, 742
laborer, 491, 548
labour agreement, 233
labour contract, 229
labour dispute, 267
labour leader, 271
labour relations, 711
labour turnover, 742
labourer, 491, 548
lateral bumping, 819
lay-off, 477, 516, 517
lay-off pay, 441
layoff, 477, 516, 517
layoff pay, 441
lead hand, 120
leave for family reasons, 205
leave for personal reasons, 204
leave for union business, 208
leave of absence, 82, 171
leave of absence for personal reasons, 204
leave of absence for public office, 207
leave of absence for union business, 208
leave of absence without pay, 196
leave without pay, 196
legal holiday, 462
length of continuous service, 802
level, 294
line manager, 101
living allowance, 448
local, 792
local union, 792
lock-out, 484
lockout, 484
long service pay, 641
lump sum payment, 719

maintenance of membership, 485
make-ready activities, 861
management, 100
management rights, 286
manager, 268
manual worker, 548
marginal job, 877
marriage leave, 188
master, 487
master agreement, 234
maternity leave, 189
meal allowance, 447
mediation, 497
mediator, 496
member of a professional corporation, 499
memorandum of agreement, 673
memorandum of settlement, 673
merit, 91, 374
merit appraisal, 55
merit pay, 745
merit rating, 55
merit wage, 745
mileage allowance, 451, 453
minutes, 660
model agreement, 237
monetary, 573
monetary clause, 137
monthly paid employee, 767
moonlighting, 313, 868
moving allowance, 438

negotiator, 524
night shift, 338, 624
night shift differential, 645
night shift premium, 645
non-juridical day, 462
non-monetary clause, 134
non-working day, 457
notice, 632
notice period, 249

occupation, 299, 510, 662
occupational accident, 4

S

T

Table des matières

Titre : ***Vocabulaire des conventions collectives***

Identification

Profession :   traducteur/traductrice ☐
rédacteur/rédactrice ☐
réviseur/réviseure ☐
enseignant/enseignante ☐
terminologue ☐
spécialiste du domaine traité ☐
autre ☐
précisez _____

Évaluation du contenu

En général, que pensez-vous du choix des termes ?

Très bon ☐   Bon ☐   Mauvais ☐

Les définitions sont-elles claires ?

Oui ☐   Non ☐

Trouvez-vous les termes que vous cherchez ?

Très souvent ☐   Souvent ☐   Rarement ☐   Jamais ☐

Souhaitez-vous que l'Office publie d'autres ouvrages dans le même domaine ou dans des domaines connexes ?

Oui ☐   Non ☐

Si oui, lesquels : _____

_____

_____

_____

À votre avis, existe-t-il d'autres ouvrages plus complets sur le sujet ?

Oui ☐   Non ☐

Présentation

Le format (15 cm × 21 cm) vous convient-il?

Bien ☐   Assez bien ☐   Peu ☐   Pas du tout ☐

Les pages de présentation sont-elles utiles pour la consultation?

Très ☐   Assez ☐   Peu ☐   Pas du tout ☐

Les informations sont-elles présentées clairement?

Très ☐   Assez ☐   Peu ☐   Pas du tout ☐

Mode d'acquisition

Comment avez-vous appris l'existence de cet ouvrage?

_____

_____

Où vous l'êtes-vous procuré?

_____

_____

L'avez-vous trouvé facilement?

Oui ☐   Non ☐

Retourner à: Office de la langue française
Direction des services linguistiques
Bureau du directeur
700, boulevard Saint-Cyrille Est, 2e étage
Québec (Québec)
G1R 5G7